CONTROVERSIAL

ISSUES

IN COMMUNITIES

AND ORGANIZATIONS

CONTROVERSIAL ISSUES

IN COMMUNITIES
AND ORGANIZATIONS

Edited by

Michael J. Austin
University of California, Berkeley

Jane Isaacs Lowe
University of Pennsylvania

Series Editors
Eileen Gambrill
Robert Pruger
University of California, Berkeley

ALLYN AND BACON
Boston   London   Toronto   Sydney   Tokyo   Singapore

Senior Editor: Karen Hanson
Editorial Assistant: Sarah Dunbar
Production Administrator: Susan McIntyre
Editorial-Production Service: Ruttle, Shaw & Wetherill, Inc.
Cover Administrator: Suzanne Harbison
Composition Buyer: Linda Cox
Manufacturing Buyer: Louise Richardson

Copyright © 1994 by Allyn and Bacon
A Division of Simon & Schuster, Inc.
160 Gould Street
Needham Heights, MA 02194

Library of Congress Cataloging-in-Publication Data

Austin, Michael J.
    Controversial issues in communities and organizations/Michael J.
Austin, Jane Isaacs Lowe.
        p.   cm.
    Includes bibliographical references.
    ISBN 0–205–14790–9
    1. Social work administration—United States.   2. Community
organization—United States.   I. Lowe, Jane Isaacs
II. Title
HV41.A86   1994
361.3--dc20   93–22651
                                                              CIP

Printed in the United States of America

10   9   8   7   6   5   4   3   2   98   97   96   95

Contents

II. The Dilemmas Confronting the Community Organizer

III. The Changing Nature of Human Service Organizations

IV. The Dilemmas Confronting Human Services Administrators

Foreword

by Eileen Gambrill and Robert Pruger, Series Editors

This book is part of the series *Controversial Issues in Social Work* and has four major purposes: (1) to present different perspectives on a number of current issues related to community organizing and agency administration; (2) to demonstrate the value of presenting different positions concerning an issue in a debate format; (3) to demonstrate that controversy can be carried out in a constructive manner that highlights (rather than mutes) issues involved in each topic; and (4) to offer readers some guidelines and practice opportunities to enhance their skills in identifying and countering tendencies and fallacies that result in the evasion, distortion, or confusion of issues.

Each discussant prepared a position statement arguing for or against a position and, in addition, prepared a rebuttal to the opposite side. This format allows for an engaging exchange that offers readers an opportunity to consider the relevance of rejoinder points that are made. Questions can be raised such as: Does the reply address points raised in the opposing statements? Are the replies persuasive? Is any evidence presented to support claims made? Have relevant facts been cited? Readers are encouraged to question what is widely accepted as well as what is new and innovative. There is a special need to question widely accepted views that work against the best interests of communities and organizations.

Readers will no doubt have their own views on the topics discussed in this book. Whether these are influenced by reading the debates will depend on many factors including the cogency of individual statements and rebuttals, the transparency of weak appeals that do not foster careful consideration of issues (such as use of emotional language), the reader's skill in detecting and countering fallacies in thinking, the reader's knowledge of content related to each topic, and attitudes that affect clear thinking, such as curiosity and openness to exploring opposing viewpoints.

Controversy is often downplayed and discouraged in social work. Rarely do we see a position statement followed by a number of invited responses to this position. Too rarely are panel discussions offered at conferences in which different perspectives on an issue or case are presented together with rebuttals to each view. Students seldom read or hear models of constructive controversy (Elstein et al, 1978; Nickerson et al, 1985). Reasons include a confusion between argument and debate, a reluctance to think more deeply and expose what one thinks, and an acceptance by many practitioners and authors of unsupported pronouncements rather than carefully reasoned arguments or empirical evidence (Gambrill, 1990).

A reluctance to discuss differences of opinion for fear of finding errors overlooks the advantages of discovering new ways to view events (Kottler & Blau, 1989). You cannot say you have a firm grip on your own position on an issue until you can competently state the opposite view. And you do not really understand the other side of an argument until you can state it so that those who hold that view agree you have stated it correctly. Debates that can be studied offer a route to this kind of mastery of an issue.

This book uses a debate format because it is a good way to explore issues and ideas. What matters is how the clash of ideas (rather than of persons) leads to greater clarity and understanding of an issue. A reader might conclude that one side of a debate is better argued. Nevertheless, the reader might still find issues raised in the opposing side that are useful in constructing a new view.

The discussions in this book present arguments for or against a position. *Argumentation* refers to the process of making claims, challenging them, backing them with reasons (assertions), criticizing these reasons, and responding to the criticism offered (Toulmin, Rieke, & Janik, 1979, p. 13). An argument in this sense refers to the claims and reasons offered for these; that is, "a set of assertions that is used to support a belief" (Nickerson, 1986, p. 2).

Arguments consist of parts that can be taken apart as well as put together. They may be strong (convincing) or weak (unconvincing), simple or complex. Assertions may involve statements of fact ("a belief for which there is enough evidence to justify a high degree of confidence," Nickerson, 1986, p. 36), assumptions, or hypotheses. The term *assumption* refers to "an assertion that we either believe to be true in spite of being unable to produce compelling evidence of its truth, or are willing to accept as true for purposes of debate or discussion"

(Nickerson, 1986, p. 37). A hypothesis is an assertion that we do not know to be true but that we think is testable. Assumptions, hypotheses, or statements of fact may be used as premises in an argument, or they may serve as conclusions.

An argument may be unsound for one of three reasons: (1) there may be something wrong with its logical structure; (2) it may contain false premises; or (3) it may be irrelevant or circular. Questions of concern in evaluating a logical argument include: Is it complete? Is its meaning clear? Is it valid (does the conclusion follow from the premises)? Do I believe the premises? (Nickerson, 1986, p. 88). An argument may be worthy of consideration even though it has some defects. Helpful questions when evaluating inductive arguments include the following:

- Are the facts accurate?
- Do the examples consist of isolated or universal instances?
- Do the examples cover a significant time period?
- Are the examples typical or atypical?
- Is the conclusion correctly stated?
- Is the argument really of concern—the "so what" and "what harm" questions (Huber, 1963, p. 14).

Arguments should not be dismissed simply because they are presented emotionally or because a conclusion is disliked; the emotion with which a position is presented is not necessarily related to the soundness of an argument (Scriven, 1976). Many statements, written or spoken, are opinions or points of view; "they frequently don't pass the test of providing reasons for a conclusion, reasons that can be separated from a conclusion" (Scriven, 1976, p. 67). The question is whether the premises can be established independently of the conclusion. Is the argument convincing?

Fallacies that evade the facts, such as "begging the question," appear to address them but do not. Variants of question begging include use of alleged certainty; circular reasoning; use of unfounded generalizations to support a conclusion; complex, trick, or leading questions; and ignoring the issue. Some informal fallacies overlook the facts as in the fallacy of the sweeping generalization, in which a rule or assumption that is valid in general is applied to a specific example for which it is not valid. Other informal fallacies distort facts or positions as in straw person arguments in which a position that is similar to but significantly different from the one presented is described and attacked. The informal fallacies of false cause, forcing an extension, and inappropriate use of analogues also involve the distortion of facts or positions. Diversions may be used to direct attention away from a main point of an argument. Trivial points, irrelevant objections, or emotional appeals may be made. Some fallacies work by creating confusion, such as feigned lack of understanding and excessive wordiness that obscures arguments.

Effective reasoning requires much more than logic, including skill in developing arguments and hypotheses, establishing the relevance of information to an argument, and evaluating the plausibility of assertions. That is, it requires a great deal of inventiveness. It also requires a willingness to change beliefs based on evidence gathered. The value of reasoning skills lies in the increased likelihood of deep understanding of issues so that optimal solutions or resolutions to personal and social problems can be discovered and implemented. Careful consideration of opposing viewpoints increases the likelihood of deep understanding of issues.

REFERENCES

Elstein, A. S., Shulman, L. S., Sprafka, S. A., et al. (1978). *Medical problem solving: An analysis of clinical reasoning.* Cambridge, MA: Harvard University Press.

Gambrill, E. (1990). *Critical thinking in clinical practice.* San Francisco: Jossey-Bass.

Huber, R. B. (1963). *Influencing through argument.* New York: David McKay.

Kottler, J. A., & Blau, D. S. (1989). *The imperfect therapist: Learning from failure in therapeutic practice.* San Francisco: Jossey-Bass.

Nickerson, R. S. (1986). *Reflections on reasoning.* Hillsdale, NJ: Erlbaum.

Nickerson, R. S., Perkins, D. N., & Smith, E. E. (1985). *The teaching of thinking.* Hillsdale, NJ: Erlbaum.

Scriven, M. (1976). *Reasoning.* New York: McGraw-Hill.

Toulmin, S. E., Rieke, R., & Janik, A. (1979). *An introduction to reasoning.* New York: Macmillan.

Preface

The care and feeding of partnerships is a challenge in most circumstances. Whether in a marriage, a business, intergovernmental relations, or in lay-professional relations, partnerships require special handling. This coedited book is no exception. It evolved through a network of partnerships among colleagues, strangers, practitioners, and educators. Many hours were spent in collaborative discussions which were needed to participate in an experiment. We want to take this opportunity to thank the fifty-five authors who contributed their talents to this experimental project.

This book is part of a new series designed to foster dialogue and debate in various domains of the human services. In the summer of 1991 we were asked by the series editors to design a volume that would address the controversial issues buried in the practice of organizing communities and managing organizations. As teachers of graduate social work students interested in the macro practice of community organizing and administration, we developed a list of potential controversial issues and solicited the interests of 150 faculty members in the Association of Community Organization and Administration as well as agency-based field instructors who supervise macro practice students. The deans of one hundred graduate programs were requested to send us the names of their macro practice field instructors, and we solicited the interests of 900 field instructors. Based on the response, new debate topics were added and others deleted. In some cases, authors found partners to participate in the debate, while others were assigned partners. They all met the challenge of converting their own writing style from that of a journal article or agency report to one of brief, succinct argumentation with minimal citation of relevant literature. In some cases, the authors went beyond their own personal views to frame a provocative argument. The shared goal was to develop a volume that provides students and practitioners with a forum of competing ideas for the expressed purpose of sharpening their own thinking for use in promoting community and organizational change. Rarely do students have an opportunity to see their teachers participate in a debate. Rarely do faculty members and agency practitioners have the opportunity to participate in a debate. As a result, this volume seeks to fill that void by providing this supplementary text for use with standard texts on community organizing and administration. Each debate could serve as a springboard for classroom discussion, a focal point for dialogue between students and their field instructors, a topic for further development in a term paper, the basis for a role-playing exercise, or the basis of an assignment in which students are challenged to develop a more convincing argument than those in this book.

We wish to thank the series editors, Eileen Gambrill and Robert Pruger, for inviting us to participate. We also want to acknowledge the wonderful assistance of a very special person, Rosemary Klump, who helped us communicate with all the authors and keep track of the many drafts as they arrived. In addition, we want to thank our talented secretaries who helped with retyping various sections of the book: Sharon Ikami and Holly Johnson. And finally, we both acknowledge the support and encouragement of our spouses, Sue and Ed, who made it possible for us to seclude ourselves in our own world of writing.

Michael J. Austin
Jane Isaacs Lowe

CONTROVERSIAL ISSUES

IN COMMUNITIES
AND ORGANIZATIONS

Introduction

Let the Debates Begin

As this volume is being completed in the fall of 1992, we find renewed public interest in the debate format for sorting out issues and perspectives as reflected in the debates of presidential candidates. The debate format is not new, but it is new to public discourse in the human service arena. New segments appear in our professional journals where practitioners and educators move from the back of the journal reserved for letters to the editor to the front of the journal as featured point-counterpoint debaters. These are exciting new developments to help practitioners, students, and educators sharpen our collective thinking about where we stand on controversial issues and why.

In this overview, we describe the themes of the debates and define our orientation to macro practice. Our macro practice perspective includes the domains of community organizing and administration. Our definition of community organizing includes locality development, social planning, and social action. Administration consists of interpersonal, informational, and decisional roles related to client-centered program design, implementation, and evaluation skills along with policy analysis skills. While policy practice is emerging as a new practice domain in graduate social work education, it is seen in this definition of macro practice as integral to both community organizing and administration.

The issues debated in this book are organized into four parts. The first two relate to the changing nature of communities and the dilemmas confronting

1

community organizers. The second two parts address the changing nature of human service organizations and the dilemmas confronting administrators.

The debates in Part I focus on issues of community empowerment and the various focal points for community organizing, such as building coalitions or building grassroots membership-based organizations; enhancing collective community leadership or promoting the charismatic leader; linking community organizations with political parties or independent political activism; and the issues surrounding specialized services for women, gays and lesbians, and the poor. Part II includes selected dilemmas confronting community organizers, such as the relevance of using tactics from the past, the future of community organizing as an area of social work practice, the value of quick and dirty community needs assessment strategies, and the role of minority group organizers in minority communities.

In Part III the debates address the changing nature of human service organizations. Arguments include the role of privatization, the value of service coordination and client control of agency policies, and the quality of work life.

The fourth and final part on the dilemmas confronting human services administrators includes such themes as non–social work administrators, client-oriented administrators, marketing versus program development, and staff response to centralization and decentralization.

Defining Macro Practice

The relationship between the practice of community organizing and the practice of social administration can be viewed from the campus as well as the field. In the field, the history of community organizing and administration can be traced to the settlement house movement at the turn of the century, where organizing efforts to meet the needs of immigrants, workers, and neighborhood residents were followed by administrative efforts to develop and manage services of all kinds (Garvin and Cox, 1979). The history of these two practice domains on campus is more recent as both struggled for legitimacy through the use of elective courses and occasional field placements during the period of 1930–1960. The first formal programs of courses and field work in community organization and administration began to appear in schools of social work in the early 1960s, usually as second-year specializations. Over the past thirty years, the specializations have grown either in the form of macro practice (Meenaghan, 1987; Brandwein, 1987) or into separate areas of practice, research, and education (Moroney, 1987; Gilbert & Specht, 1987; Wenocur, 1987; Perlmutter, 1987; Friesen, 1987; Sarri, 1987; Berger & Nash, 1984; Kruzich & Friesen, 1984).

When the specialized practice programs were launched, Kramer (1966) addressed the issue of integrating community organization and administration. He identified the following shared knowledge and methodologies: (1) concern with enabling a group of people to accomplish a social goal, whether it is the staff's fulfillment of the agency's program objective or a citizens committee's attempt to solve a community problem; (2) concern with organizational and community decision making, planning, allocation, and mobilization of resources, and coordination of efforts to achieve desired goals; and (3) involvement in fact finding, analysis, evaluation, organizing, education, reporting, promotion, social action, budgeting, finance, policy formulation, and programming. He also suggested that there are reciprocal career lines whereby social workers shift back and forth from one area of practice to another in the course of their professional careers.

For some, the evolution of community organization and social administration can be viewed as a struggle between preparing practitioners to organize the poor and oppressed and preparing practitioners to manage new and existing services. From this perspective, the values, knowledge base, and techniques related to community-based social class struggle are seen as different from the values, knowledge base, and techniques related to managerial efficiency and effectiveness (Erlich & Rivera, 1981; Lauffer, 1981; Patti, 1981). For others, the evolution of two practice domains reflects larger societal forces including the availability of community organizing jobs emerging from the flood of social legislation of the 1960s and the availability of managerial jobs related to the accountability era of the 1970s and 1980s (Austin, 1986; Hayden, 1988; Janson, 1987; Ziter, 1983).

In the light of the brief overview of macro practice, it is important to define the key elements of this practice domain. First of all, community organization practice is viewed as an interventive method reflecting what Rothman (1987) has described as locality development, social action, and social planning. Rothman describes the goal of locality development as community capacity building and integration based on the processes of self-help. It involves a broad cross section of people involved in determining and solving their own problems through group discussion and consensus building. The primary practitioner skills include facilitating the work of small task-oriented groups (e.g., catalyst, coordinator, educator). In contrast, the goals of social planning include community problem solving with respect to specific problems (e.g., delinquency, housing) based on a task-orientation that features fact gathering and rational decision making. The primary practitioner skills include data gathering and analysis, program planning and implementing, and advocating for consumers amidst the power structure of formal organizations. The third dimension of community organizing involves social action that addresses the goal of shifting power relationships and resources in pursuit of basic institutional change. The activist strategies include crystallizing issues and organizing people to take action through conflict, confrontation, and negotiation. The primary practitioner skills involve negotiation, advocacy, brokering, and political partisanship. While these three components of community organizing have emerged as specializations in their own right, it is their similarities and differences that are seen here as the essential fabric of community organization practice.

Second, administrative practice is viewed as an interventive method used to achieve organizational goals and objectives by enabling and directing the work of paid staff and lay leaders to transform social policy into services and to maximize organizational performance in serving clients (Rapp & Poertner, 1992; Edwards & Yankey, 1991; Holland & Petchers, 1987; Davis-Sachs & Hasenfeld, 1987; Weiner, 1982; Patti, 1981). The three major components of this method include interpersonal roles, informational roles, and decisional roles (Mintzberg, 1973). The interpersonal roles include figurehead (e.g., performing ceremonial duties), leader (e.g., personnel management duties of hiring, training, motivating, promoting, and dismissing staff), and liaison (e.g., relationship building with persons outside the agency). In contrast, the informational roles relate to monitoring (e.g., seeking information on internal operations and external events), disseminating (e.g., sending factual and value information to staff), and being a spokesperson (e.g., transmitting information to the agency's environment). The third set of roles involves decision making. These include entrepreneur or innovator (e.g., designing and initiating organizational change), disturbance handler (e.g., responding to situations and changes beyond one's control), resource allocator (e.g., overseeing the agency's allocation of human and financial resources), and negotiator (e.g., negotiating with other organizations or individuals).

Why should skilled community organizers be well-grounded in administrative practice, and why should skilled administrators be able to display competent community organizing capacities? While both practice domains rely heavily on the macro practice perspectives of system thinking, students of these domains sometimes reflect different temperaments and life experiences. The organizer interested in expanding the number of food banks in a community (locality development), organizing rate payers to counteract the rate increases of utility companies (social action), or staffing a community-wide United Way task on developing shelters for battered women (social planning) is different, in some ways, from the assistant director of a family service agency. The assistant director is involved in supervising staff (interpersonal), managing the client and financial information system (informational), and writing grants and negotiating interagency service contracts as new programs are developed (decisional). The organizer tends to view the world through the issues and problems *in the community* that need attention, whereas the administrator tends to view the world through the issues and problems *in the organization* that need attention. Sometimes their life experiences are significantly different; an organizer may enter the profession as a result of life experiences related to *social issues and causes,* and the administrator may enter the profession or gain promotion as a result of providing direct services to clients related to individual *client needs and the functions of service delivery* (Hart, 1984).

Irrespective of temperament and life experiences, the societal forces of the 1990s and beyond appear to be requiring a greater breadth of skill and competence of those engaged in macro practice. The experiences over the past decade with cutback management (Austin, 1984) suggest that the administrator of the future will need to be far more community-oriented in lobbying for social legislation through coalition building (social action), promoting greater interagency collaboration in the community as well as enabling the growth of self-help groups (locality development), and engaging in strategic planning for the agency in relationship to its environment based on client and community data (social planning). Similarly, the community organizer of the future, whether operating from the base of a grassroots organization or under the auspices of an existing agency, needs to be able to effectively supervise staff and volunteers (interpersonal), document and analyze community needs (informational), and engage in fund raising and institution building (decisional). The commonality of problem solving, program development, and negotiating in both practice domains has been highlighted by Rothman, Erlich, and Teresa (1981) in the following practitioner activities: (1) systems analysis, (2) promoting innovation, (3) changing organizational's goals, (4) fostering participation, and (5) increasing effectiveness of role performance. It is this vision of the future, based on recent changes in the field of social welfare, that serves as the foundation for returning to a greater integration between the practice domains in the 1990s and beyond.

Building an Integrated Macro Practice Framework

Based on the definitions and concepts of Rothman (1979) and Mintzberg (1973), it is possible to construct a framework using the three role clusters of community organization practice (i.e., locality development, social action, and social planning) and the three role clusters of administrative practice (i.e., interpersonal, informational, and decisional activities). The complexity of integrating these roles into one framework is not to be underestimated.

The emerging framework seeks to identify the knowledge and skill areas relevant to an integrated approach to educating the future "organizer-manager" (Austin, 1986). The nine components of the framework represent a content analysis of both practice domains and can be identified as follows:

1. Group process and supervisory management skills
2. Resource development and marketing skills
3. Negotiation and participatory management skills
4. Interorganizational planning and leadership development skills
5. Community/policy analysis and information systems skills
6. Program implementation and financial management skills
7. Lobbying and coalition-building skills

8. Media relations and public speaking skills
9. Planned change and conflict management

Two major themes underlie this framework, namely, practitioner temperament and value dilemmas. The temperament issues of leadership style and work activity style are addressed first. The development of the left or right hemisphere of one's brain may have much to do with one's temperament for community organization and social administration. Mintzberg (1973) speculates that planning may reflect the logical, rational side of the left hemisphere, whereas managing may represent the intuitive, process-oriented side of the right hemisphere. The "organizer-manager" requires capacities emanating from both spheres of the brain to maintain a balance of temperament needed for macro practice. Using Mintzberg's perspective, community and organizational effectiveness lies in a blend of "clear-headed logic" and "powerful intuition," which are also known as a blend of a "process" and "task" orientation.

A second theme underlying the framework for the "organizer-manager" involves value dilemmas. How can one take the social action skills of a neighborhood organizer who uses partisanship and power politics and blend them with the administrative budget-building skills of a manager accountable to a board of directors? While some argue that the values and constraints related to client advocacy represent a fundamentally different world from the accountability values of agency management, we suggest that the worlds are not so far apart. If one assumes that agencies and grassroots organizations are established primarily to serve the needs of a client or consumer group, then the issue appears to be the capacity of the "organizer-manager" to handle differences. For example, let's assume that the "organizer-manager" of a grassroots association for retarded citizen sits across the negotiating table from an "organizer-manager" of a local agency serving the developmentally disabled. And let's also assume that they have different agendas (e.g., one wants more neighborhood-based group homes and the other wants improved in-home services) and that they have been educated in the ways of principled negotiation (Fisher & Ury, 1981). While both parties value maximizing services to the developmentally disabled, they may differ on priorities and the means for achieving their priorities. It seems critical that both parties recognize "difference" as a legitimate component of value tensions in human service work.

The educating of future "organizer-managers" needs to include opportunities to learn how to understand and manage such differences. Other value tensions may relate to lay-professional differences, client-specific versus client population differences, or system maintenance versus system change differences. Handling these differences and understanding these tensions are important capacities for "organizer-managers" to acquire irrespective of which side of the table they may occupy.

This book uses the debate format as one more approach to understanding and managing difference. Analyzing and understanding competing values and perspectives is an important component of educating future macro practice social workers. If we in the profession of social work do not confront and deal with controversial issues in our own "backyard," they will probably be addressed in other arenas by macro practitioners who are not social workers. The controversial issues and debates in this volume should contribute to the process of strengthening macro practice and the integration of community organizing and administration.

References

Austin, M. J. (1986). Community organization and administration: Partnership or irrelevance. *Administration in Social Work, 10*(3), 27–39.

Austin, M. J. (1984). Managing cutbacks in the 1980s. *Social Work,* 29(5), 428–434.

Austin, M. J., Brannon, D., & Pecora, P. J. (1984). *Managing staff development programs in human services agencies.* Chicago: Nelson-Hall.

Berger, C. S., & Nash, K. B. (1984). Developing roles for macro practitioners within the health field. *Administration in Social Work, 8,* 67–76.

Brandwein, R. A. (1987). Women in macro practice. A. Minahan (Ed.), *Encyclopedia of social work.* Silver Spring, MD: National Association of Social Workers.

Davis-Sachs, M. L., & Hasenfeld, Y. (1987). Organizations: Impact on employees and community. A. Minahan (Ed.), *Encyclopedia of social work.* Silver Spring, MD: National Association of Social Workers.

Edwards, R. L., & Yankey, J. A. (Eds.). (1991). *Skills for effective human services management.* Silver Spring, MD: National Association of Social Workers.

Erlich, J. L., & Rivera, F. G. (1981). Community organization and community development. In N. Gilbert & H. Specht (Eds.), *Handbook of social services.* Englewood Cliffs, NJ: Prentice-Hall.

Fisher, R., & Ury, W. (1981). *Getting to yes.* Boston: Houghton.

Friesen, B. (1987). Administration: Interpersonal aspects. A. Minahan (Ed.), *Encyclopedia of Social Work.* Silver Spring, MD: National Association of Social Workers.

Garvin, C. D., & Cox, F. M. (1987). A history of community organizing since the civil war, with special reference to oppressed communities. In F. M. Cox, J. L. Erlich, J. Rothman, J. E. Tropman (Eds.), *Strategies of community organization,* 4th edition. Itasca, IL: F. E. Peacock.

Gilbert, N., & Specht, H. (1987). Social planning and community organization. A. Minahan (Ed.), *Encyclopedia of social work.* Silver Spring, MD: National Association of Social Workers.

Hart, A. F. (1984). Clinical social work and social administration: Bridging the culture gap. *Administration in Social Work 8,* 71–78.

Hayden, W. (1988). A curriculum model for social work management. In P. R. Keys & L. H. Ginsberg (Eds.), *New management in human services.* Silver Spring, MD: National Association of Social Workers.

Holland, T. P., & Petchers, M. K. (1987). Organizations: Context for social service delivery. A. Minahan (Ed.), *Encyclopedia of social work.* Silver Spring, MD: National Association of Social Workers.

Jansson, B. (1987). From sibling rivalry to pooled knowledge and shared curriculum: Relations among community organization, administration, planning and policy. *Administration in Social Work, 11*(2), 5–18.

Kramer, R. M. (1966). Community organizing and administration: Integration or separate but equal? *Education for Social Work, 2,* 48–56.

Kruzich, J. M., & Friesen, B. J. (1984). Blending administrative and community organization practice: The case of community residential facilities. *Administration in Social Work, 8,* 55–66.

Lauffer, A. (1981). The practice of social planning. In N. Gilbert & H. Specht (Eds.), *Handbook of social services.* Englewood Cliffs, NJ: Prentice-Hall.

Meenaghan, T. M. (1987). Macro practice: Current trends and issues. A. Minahan (Ed.), *Encyclopedia of social work.* Silver Spring, MD: National Association of Social Workers.

Mintzberg, H. (1973). *The nature of managerial work.* New York: Harper and Row.

Moroney, R. M. (1987). Social planning. A. Minahan (Ed.), *Encyclopedia of social work.* Silver Spring, MD: National Association of Social Workers.

Patti, R. J. (1981). Social welfare administration. In N. Gilbert and H. Specht (Eds.) *Handbook of social services.* Englewood Cliffs, NJ: Prentice-Hall.

Perlmutter, F. D. (1987). Administration: Environmental aspects. A. Minahan (Ed.), *Encyclopedia of social work.* Silver Spring, MD: National Association of Social Workers.

Rapp, C. A., & Poertner, J. (1992). *Social administration: A client-centered approach.* New York: Longman.

Rothman, J. (1984). Models of community organization and macro practice perspectives: Their mixing and phasing. In F. M. Cox, J. L. Erlich, J. Rothman, J. E. Tropman (Eds.), *Strategies of community organization,* 4th edition. Itasca, IL: F. E. Peacock. 1987.

Rothman, J., Erlich, J. L., & Teresa, J. G. (1981). *Changing organizations and community programs.* Beverly Hills, CA: Sage Publications.

Sarri, R. (1987). Administration in social welfare. *Encyclopedia of social work.* Silver Spring, MD: National Association of Social Workers.

Weiner, M. R. (1982). *Human services management: Analysis and application.* Homewood, IL: Dorsey Press.

Wenocur, S. (1987). Social planning in the voluntary sector. *Encyclopedia of social work.* Silver Spring, MD: National Association of Social Workers.

Ziter, M. L. P. (1983). Social policy practice: Tasks and skills. *Administration in Social Work, 7,* 37–50.

Should Community-Based Organizations Give Priority to Building Coalitions Rather Than Building Their Own Membership?

EDITOR'S NOTE: Community organizations exist to get things done. They are made up of people who are willing to work together to solve their problems and bring about change. All community organizations need to recruit members and secure financial and other resources to achieve their goals. Thus, at the center of this debate are the following questions: Should a community organization focus on building its own constituency, resources, and "base of power" to solve problems and achieve desired outcomes? Or, should a community organization join a coalition to solve problems and achieve desired change? The answers to these questions involve defining the purposes of the organization, the organizing tactics, and the strategies for social change and assessing whether the organization can have its biggest impact on a specific issue by working alone or as part of a coalition.

Tim Sampson is a professor in the Department of Social Work Education at San Francisco State University. He is active in the faculty union there. He is a board member and trainer with the Center for Third World Organizing (CTWO). His roots are in the welfare rights movement, and he has been involved with grassroots community and labor organizing for more than thirty years.

Beth B. Rosenthal, M.S., an independent consultant/trainer, specializes in organizational, community, and coalition development. She has organized and staffed dozens of coalitions and collaborations and was executive director of a multiethnic, multiservice neighborhood coalition for its first six years. She has designed and administered research-based programs to address urban poverty, immigrants, homelessness, conflict resolution, leadership development, and community empowerment. She has served on the faculty of the City University of

New York's York College and Hostos Community College and has been a field instructor for seven universities, training professional students for community organizing, research, and administration. In collaboration with Terry Mizrahi, she has been involved in a research and training project, ''Coalitions: Enhancing Capacity and Effectiveness,'' since 1985.

Terry Mizrahi, Ph.D., is a professor at the Hunter College School of Social Work and Director of the Education Center for Community Organizing in New York City. Since 1966, Dr. Mizrahi has held positions as Assistant Professor at Virginia Commonwealth University, organizer with the Lower East Side Neighborhood Association, and field coordinator for the Federation of Protestant Welfare Agencies. Her scholarship, training, and research expertise are in the areas of medical sociology, organizational and community development, program evaluation, and health care policy and practice. Areas of her research include professional socialization, interdisciplinary collaboration, and coalition building. She has written *Getting Rid of Patients: Contradictions in the Socialization of Physicians* (Rutgers, 1986) and coedited *Community Organization and Social Administration: Advances, Trends and Emerging Principles* (Haworth, 1992).

YES

BETH B. ROSENTHAL AND TERRY MIZRAHI

We believe that community-based organizations have a greater impact on issues by joining forces and building coalitions. Coalitions are increasingly recognized and used as mechanisms for service coordination, problem solving, advocacy, and social change. A coalition is an organization composed of independent organizations that engage in collective activity to influence external institutions while maintaining their own autonomy. A coalition is time limited, characterized by dynamic tensions, and operated as a conflict-resolution mechanism. Coalitions, as forms of collective political behavior, are part of both social movements and social movement organizations. They are also forms of interorganizational relations related to ''action sets'' and ''organizational fields'' (McAdam, McCarthy, & Zald, 1988; Whetten, 1981; Benson, 1975; Aldrich & Marsden, 1988).

The recent proliferation of coalitions reflects the reality that organizations in the 1990s must function with increasing sophistication and interdependency to be effective. Local issues usually represent larger patterns: social and economic problems that affect individuals and communities are often intertwined and compounded, and funding for advocacy and direct services is increasingly being allocated to entire neighborhoods or program consortia rather than to individual agencies.

The sheer number of organizations and funding streams handling different issues demands new strategies for advocacy, service delivery, and information sharing. Complex, overlapping issues and constituencies require connections between diverse organizations and multiple, rather than single, approaches to problem solving. Organizations recognize that they must coordinate and cooperate with each other to be effective, address service gaps, avoid duplication, and ensure their own survival. In the political arena, coalitions have become the locus of social movement activity as vehicles that can incorporate the multiplicity of players and perspectives.

Coalitions are used for a range of organizational and political purposes. Specific uses include:

1. resource procurement or resource dependency
2. political advocacy
3. organizational legitimation
4. management of the external environment
5. response to government threats or intrusions
6. interorganizational exchange
7. influencing policy and political economy

In certain situations, coalitions promise a greater degree of success, greater power vis-a-vis a third party, divisible outcomes, and other benefits than can be attained by a single organization. Coalitions can reduce environmental uncertainties, minimize losses, defeat competing coalitions, provide protection and legitimacy, and preserve resources.

Structured correctly, coalitions are open and egalitarian and appeal to and involve many different stakeholders—individuals, grassroots groups, religious organizations, academic institutions, business, government, labor, community-based organizations, and others. They are also viable multicultural efforts that integrate minority and majority groups, new immigrants and more settled residents, and traditionally powerless groups and those more powerful.

Coalitions have accomplished impressive outcomes that are virtually impossible for organizations to achieve singly. They have been found to be highly effective in addressing a broad range of issues, including housing, justice, economic development, health care, social services, environmental issues, women's rights, immigration policy, racism, domestic violence, and more. Coalitions have developed and strengthened social services, changed policies, introduced or defeated legislation, produced material gains through the welfare system, created new funding streams for emerging problems, bolstered local economies, and significantly changed public awareness about critical social issues (Mizrahi & Rosenthal, 1990).

Advantages of the Coalition Model

Organizational Development

Organizations today operate in a field with others who share community location, target population, issues, or funding sources. Organizations can increase their effectiveness by recognizing and maximizing these connections. Coalitions provide a channel for ongoing communication and coordination among service providers, funders, researchers, social change allies and targets, government agencies, and elected officials. Organizations can develop a greater understanding of client and community needs and existing resources by seeing the whole picture. Coalitions also engender an increased sense of the larger spheres in which organizations operate and give them access to key allies, players, and targets they might not meet otherwise. Networks, exposure to new ideas, and mentoring are among the secondary benefits of regular intergroup involvement.

Coalitions are often a preferred vehicle for intergroup action because they preserve the autonomy of member organizations while providing the necessary structure for unified effort. Enabling people to link special interests and share information and diverse expertise, coalitions permit organizations to clarify their differences and incorporate various skills, levels of experience, and roles for participation. They allow groups that are at different stages of their own internal development to have equal say.

Tangible benefits also accrue from coalition participation. Organizations can continue to focus on what they do best and preserve their own resources while relying on others for related tasks and expertise. Moreover, by sharing their own knowledge and experiences, organizations increase their credibility and visibility. Through coalitions, organizations can also acquire power, information, publicity, new perspectives, contacts, resources, and access to other constituencies. Coalitions enable organizations, without straying from their mission, to enter creative new ventures and pilot projects with other groups. These can involve the addition of jointly shared staff, centralized data/client information, and space. Such activities help even small grassroots groups to expand without paying for all the overhead alone. Another benefit of such collaborations is the ability to diversify projects, membership, and constituencies.

Service Coordination and Expansion

Government and private funders recognize the need for collaboration to minimize duplication and increase coordination among service providers with shared target populations. Federal, state, and private funding initiatives in the 1990s mandate collaborative approaches for human services, health, and criminal justice programs including aging, substance abuse prevention, AIDS, children and families, public health, and prenatal care, among others. Funders have also formed their own coalitions to focus on certain issues or geographic areas they support in an effort to coordinate and evaluate the collective impact of their grants.

Coalitions encourage a view of families and communities that is holistic and comprehensive. Knowledge of target populations and areas is amplified by information sharing through coalitions of activists, neighborhood residents, service providers, researchers, and evaluators. Families are better helped by greater service coordination or case management at the provider level than by a panoply of social services from different providers, each operating in ignorance of the others, developing fragmented treatment plans for problems that are really indivisible, and multiplying paperwork and bureaucracy. Similarly, underserved communities require many different supports for stabilization and revitalization. Coalitions can be vehicles for communities to engage in comprehensive planning and development efforts that integrate different resources, assets, and perspectives. They can help providers and consumers identify and advocate for needed services and programs and can result in improved material conditions and resources.

Political Action

The temporality, mutability, and flexibility of coalitions has made them vehicles for social change activists and human services in the post-1960s era. Economic and political conservatism since the 1980s has reduced opportunities for mass social movements and forced neighborhood and issue-based organizations to focus on survival. Under these conditions, actions and campaigns are overwhelmingly defensive and organizing is largely confined to single locales, issues, and constituencies. Through coalitions social action organizations with restricted agendas can link their work to broad-scale mobilization efforts.

Coalitions allow groups to pursue bigger targets on a larger scale, address power inequities, shape public ideology, and build solutions to complex problems together. Bridging differences, coalitions can help diverse groups develop a common language and ideology with which to shape a collective vision for social change. Coalitions, in fact, function as incubators for social movements on women, the environment, anti-oppression/multicultural strategies, peace, education, health, and antiviolence, among other issues.

They enable groups to mobilize quickly in case of emergencies such as racist incidents, budget cuts, and imposed plans for neighborhoods, which require collective response. Such beginnings often lead to lasting collaborations to ensure that external targets remain accountable. By using coalitions to engage in political advocacy, organizations share the risks, gain some measure of protection, and take a stand without necessarily being publicly identified. Coalitions can advance the social change agendas of individual organizations by mobilizing action and support and attracting resources and visibility for issues.

Professional Education, Training, and Practice

Professionals in social work, urban planning, and public administration are increasingly being called on to participate in or give leadership to coalitions. Staff of neighborhood and issue-oriented groups, social service directors, government officials, and business, human service, and labor leaders frequently find themselves operating in focus groups, collaborations, and other sorts of coalition efforts. Leaders of such coalitions have been identified as policy entrepreneurs, boundary spanners, and brokers (Sink & Stowers, 1989; Marsden, 1992) and require expertise for these roles.

In preparing human service professionals for macro practice, we must take into account the future career tracks of our graduates. Wages for grassroots organizers are usually too low to retain professionally trained people. Moreover, human service agencies do not generally hire organizers because of political risk and conservatism (Wenocur & Weisner, 1992). While the social work profession should continue to promote organizing as a career, its emphasis should be to encourage and train professionals for leadership positions in the type of organizing they are likely to assume at the interorganizational level. Knowledge and skill in forming and sustaining collaborations is necessary if social workers and other human service professionals are to be effective. Skills in planning, negotiating, bargaining, conflict resolution, multiparty decision making, exchange, consensus, leadership development, resource development, and multilevel systems of accountability which are critical to coalition building are also relevant to human service professionals within their own organizations and communities.

Coalition building entails holding a diverse group together while attempting to influence an external social change target. This requires additional knowledge and skills from those used to organize single-issue grassroots groups or manage an agency with one mission, board, and service base. Because the competencies needed for interorganizational coalition building span practice methods, they are suitable for a macro track (Austin, 1986), which pools and shares resources across methods of community organizing, planning, administration, and policy (Jansson, 1987).

Building coalitions is consistent with social work values of progressivism—working toward democracy, social and economic justice, diversity, and peace. Models of intergroup cooperation are essential if we are to counter parochialism and provincialism and to minimize self-interest, competition, and intolerance. Social work schools are natural locations for curricula and professional development, research, evaluation, and planning models on coalitions. Academicians, researchers, and scholars with a focus on coalitions can meet a critical need for more precise knowledge on this burgeoning form of organizing.

Conclusion

The increased use of coalitions by a wide variety of practitioners for the purposes of organizational development, service coordination and expansion, and political action demonstrates the relevance of this form for organizational effectiveness.

To strengthen the use and effectiveness of coalition work, funders and professionals need to learn more about this model and provide the required resources, training, and leadership. In cultivating practitioners and providing research and technical assistance to organizations and communities, the social work role for the 1990s should be to champion and support coalitions.

REFERENCES

Aldrich, H. E., & Marsden, P. V. (1988). Environments and organizations. In N. J. Smelser (Ed.), *Handbook of sociology* (pp. 361–392). Newbury Park, CA: Sage.

Austin, M. J. (1986). Community organization and social administration: Partnership or irrelevance? *Administration in Social Work, 10*(3), 27–39.

Benson, J. K. (1975). The interorganizational network as a political economy. *Administrative Science Quarterly, 20*(1), 229–249.

Jansson, B. S. (1987). From sibling rivalry to pooled knowledge and shared curriculum: Relations among community organization, administration, planning and policy analysis. *Administration in Social Work, 11*(2), 5–18.

Marsden, P. (1992). Social network theory. In E. F. Borgotta and M. L. Borgotta (Eds.), *Encyclopedia of sociology, 4,* 1887–1894.

McAdam, D., McCarthy, J. D., & Zald, M. N. (1988). Social movements. In N. Smelser (Ed.), *Handbook on Sociology* (pp. 695–737). Newburg Park, CA: Sage.

Mizrahi, T., & Rosenthal, B. (1990). The dynamics and development of social change coalitions: A study of 40 local, regional and state coalitions. Unpublished paper.

Mizrahi, T., & Rosenthal, B. (1992). Managing dynamic tensions in social change coalitions. In T. Mizrahi and J. Morrison (Eds.), *Community organization and social administration: Advances, trends and emerging principles.* New York: Haworth Press.

Rosenthal, B., & Mizrahi, T. (1990). Coalitions: Building strength from diversity. *NY Ragtimes.* New York: New York Regional Association of Grantmakers, Spring, 1–3.

Sink, D. W., & Stowers, G. (1989). Coalitions and their effect on the urban policy agenda. *Administration in Social Work, 13*(2), 83–89.

Wenocur, S., & Weisner, S. (1992). Debate 19: Should community organization be based on a grassroots strategy? In E. Gambrill and R. Pruger (Eds.), *Controversial Issues in Social Work* (pp. 288–300), Boston: Allyn Bacon.

Whetten, D. A. (1981). Interorganizational relations: A review of the field. *Journal of Higher Education, 52* (1), 1–28.

Rejoinder to Ms. Rosenthal and Dr. Mizrahi

TIM SAMPSON

Reading the Rosenthal/Mizrahi argument in praise of coalitions reminded me of the fable of the emperor's new clothes. They offer wondrous clothing, but will the emperor (organizer or social worker) who chooses these materials wind up with little to wear? The arguments that coalitions are proliferating, are a more sophisticated approach to the issues of the 1990s, and are more financially rewarding for social workers than grassroots organizing don't have much substance.

Treating coalitions as a single alternative to building a membership base, instead of offering a varied set of strategic possibilities, confuses rather than illuminates their use. They say, "*In certain situations* [emphasis added], coalitions promise a greater degree of success." Granted, but what are these conditions? I submit that a key condition relates to organizations that have already built a strong membership base of power.

Another confusing aspect of the Rosenthal/Mizrahi presentation of coalition advantages is their frequent reference to service coordination, resource procurement, relationship with funders, minimizing duplication, and organizational survival. These are useful features of coalition work, but the focus of my argument is not on services, coordination, resources, or survival but rather on building power for social change. If justice is the goal, then organize. If services and coordination are desired, then coalition may well be the strategy of choice.

Ms. Rosenthal and Dr. Mizrahi point out the value of coalitions for multicultural work. They talk about quick mobilizations in the face of emergencies that can lead to lasting collaborations. My experience is contrary to both of these. Most coalitions tend to lack diversity rather than foster it. Racism, sexism, and classism are all too frequently present in coalitions as they are in the rest of society. And quick mobilizations rarely result in either much immediate success or lasting coalitions.

Finally, coalitions are touted as "incubators for social movements." I believe that the opposite is more often the case. It is groups, organizations, and individuals who "march to a different drummer" to form social movements. Then others join in coalitional relations. Coalitions have an important place in social change strategy. But building new grassroots organizations and developing the membership base of existing organizations is the critical, essential step in working for change.

The processes of building grassroots organizations are no less complex than coalition building. Social workers and others should not be seduced into seeing coalitions as better, more advanced, necessary for impact, or, even worse, as a short-cut to the complex process of building a membership base. For as the late Fred Ross, an organizer's organizer, said, "short-cuts usually end in detours which lead to dead ends" (Ross, 1989). Coalitions often seem like short-cuts or the only way. There is another way!

REFERENCE

Ross, F. (1989). *Axioms for organizers.* San Francisco: Neighbor to Neighbor Education Fund.

NO

Tim Sampson

In organizing we are always seeking to build our own organization *and* to work in coalitions with others to win on issues (Sampson, 1984). However, there are always serious questions about emphasis and choices to be made about scarce resources in community organizing. These questions include: Why are we working on this issue? What is the state of our organization? Where are we in the fight? What coalition partners are possible/available to us? What are the organizing possibilities and obstacles relating to our own constituency?

The raison d'être of organizing is power. And power is at the heart of building membership as well as coalition building. To have impact on issues takes power. When you are in a fight on an issue, it is tempting to try the short-cut of "borrowing power"—that is, to find other organizations that have some power and seek to add that power to yours to win on the issue. Sometimes this is feasible and works. Often the other organizations either don't have very much power to add to yours or are not very interested in the issue as you have defined it. Further when the fight is over you may not have built and advanced your own organization. In addition you may now have an obligation to work on the issue agenda of other organizations whether or not this addresses the needs and interests of your constituency.

People—and their active participation—are the principal power that community-based organizations of low, moderate, and middle income have. If our focus is on building our own organization, then we need to define the issue and choose the strategy and tactics so we can engage more people who are the critical power ingredient.

The development of people—the relations among them, their leadership, their skills, their analysis—is what community organizing is about. The issues serve as vehicles for that development rather than as its rationale. Impact on issues is only one aspect of organizing. While people organize to have a voice in decisions on issues that affect their lives, they also organize to act on their values, to build community with others, to change the way they look at and understand the world—to learn about how things work and how they can change them. This is an ongoing process that transcends particular issues and proceeds even if there is limited impact on a particular issue.

Limits of Coalitions

Coalitions frequently are built on the assumption that having an impact on an issue (winning) is the most important thing *and* that your organization lacked sufficient power to win on its own or sufficient time to build sufficient power on its own. This may or may not be the case. Arguing against coalition is like opposition to apple pie. But the limits of coalition are less well known than its merits, and hence close examination of these should be useful.

Often we uncritically assume that the mere endorsement of another organization adds strength to our cause. Endorsements certainly encourage us. Sometimes they add legitimacy to our struggle. But often there is little in the way of power brought to bear by such common and often nominal statements of support. These days there is often insufficient experience to be able to distinguish between real and nominal support.

Mike Miller (undated) has enunciated the essential math of coalitions: $0 + 0 = 0$. Or more often: a little plus a little does not equal much more than a little. Prefontainé (1973), in discussing the properties of human relations, reminds us that when you add one human being to another human being you don't get two—rather you either get less than two if they diminish each other or more than two if they strengthen each other. Hope springs eternal that linking our forces together will increase our power. But the operative word here is *link*. The adage that a chain is only as strong as its weakest link is another aspect of coalition math.

Coalitions are useful if the goal is to overcome competition and diversion. But if lack of power is the critical problem, bringing together weak forces is not as likely to work as is focusing on building membership. Indeed, building one's own organization is the quintessential step in forming successful coalitions. When you proceed from strength you chose coalition partners with a clearer sense of what they can deliver because you know better what *you* can deliver. The coalition/alliance process then becomes something different from a collection of low power partners.

Dispelling a Myth

It is a myth that organizations are built around issues. Organizations are built by developing people's skills in relating with other people. The one-on-one organizing method so successfully developed by Ernesto Cortes and the Industrial Areas

Foundation (1990) has made all of us in organizing keenly aware of this central ingredient. Similarly, people come together and act when they are in touch with and reflect on the values that are most important to them. The organizing process is profoundly one of learning. People want to study, think, and analyze in relation to both the issues and the process. They want to learn new skills, try new behaviors, and have new experiences. In addition to the relationships between individuals, a central goal of grassroots organizing is to develop a collective structure of people involved in planning, deciding, acting, and evaluating together. While issues are part of the activity around which these organizing processes take place, making an impact on these issues is only part of how we measure progress in community organizing.

When an organization grows we can see more people getting actively involved, more people taking responsibility for the organization's work, more people reflecting on their experience and connecting it with their values, and more people learning about what is going on and what they can do about it.

Community-Based Agencies

In social work there is often confusion between grassroots community organization and community-based agencies. A grassroots community organization seeks to represent constituencies in a particular community and to build an organization as a means to advance the interests of the people of that community. An agency—even a community-based agency—exists to offer services. It *may* involve people from that community in giving the services and it may advocate for people in the community, but it rarely organizes people in the community to build and exercise power apart from the service mission of the agency.

In one sense a good community-based agency is an active coalition of clients, families, and community/neighborhood institutions such as churches, unions, businesses, staff, board, suppliers, and so on. It may resemble a community organization, but its focus is on the kind of services it was set up to provide and it often fights most and hardest to protect and expand these services.

Conclusion

Given the scarce resources of time and money, grassroots organizers must focus attention on building community organizations. Strengthening such organizations, especially through the active engagement of *more* people and the development of existing leaders and members, is a top priority. As a result, members will be able to impact on issues—if not on a current issue then on the next one. Strengthening grassroots organizations through membership development opens up possibilities of alliances and coalitions. My main argument is: first build membership by organizing, then build coalitions based on strength.

Most often these days we seem to try to unite the limited organizations we have instead of expanding our efforts to organize the unorganized and develop a membership base of grassroots organizations. The genius of John L. Lewis and the CIO organizers was to understand that it was time to bring millions more people into the labor movement. Today's unions are beginning to understand that we cannot "impact our issues" by the limited coalition represented by the AFL-CIO or even by new alliances with community forces and constituencies. Rather, we must again organize the unorganized *and* develop our own unions by engaging our members. Community organizing must not be content with a coalition of limited forces. We need to change the 0 + 0 = 0 equation of coalitions. Building more grassroots organizations, developing their membership base, and bringing many more people into them must take priority over coalition building.

REFERENCES

Industrial Areas Foundation. (1990). *Organizing for change: I.A.F. fifty years* (pp. 33–34). New York: Industrial Areas Foundation.

Miller, M. (Undated). Discussion paper on national/regional coalitions. San Francisco: Organizer Training Center.

Prefonitainé, N. (1973, Summer). What I think I see: Reflections on the foundations of social policy. *Canadian Public Administration, 16*(2), 300.

Sampson, T. (1984). Coalitions and other relations. In L. Staples (Ed.), *Roots to power: A manual for grassroots organizing.* (pp. 209–211). New York: Praeger.

Rejoinder to Professor Sampson

BETH B. ROSENTHAL AND
TERRY MIZRAHI

We agree with Professor Sampson that there are some limitations on the use and effectiveness of coalitions. We do not suggest that coalitions are panaceas for all situations, but that they are extremely useful when a proliferation of different organizations are operating in a field or organizing on the same issue, particularly when those organizations display differences in amounts of power and effectiveness. Coalitions tend to form under certain conditions: when organizations want to achieve a greater impact on an issue than they could by working alone, when they want to work on an issue, but do not want to allocate a lot of their resources to it, when they seek protection or less visibility, or when they need a more diverse base to win.

We agree that groups should "coalesce from strength." To have an impact on external change targets, coalitions must amass the correct constellation of resources and power and have access to appropriate targets and supporters. Coalitions are most effective when comprised of organizations that have achieved enough maturity and internal development to enable them to participate responsibly in an interorganizational effort. While organizations that have not yet developed their own leadership, membership base, and credibility may not be major players in coalitions, their participation in coalitions is not only possible, but desirable.

In his concern that "a chain is only as strong as its weakest link," Professor Sampson infers that "weak" organizations, those with few resources or members, may damage others in a coalition. We take issue with his definition of weak organizations, as well as his reluctance to see their merit as coalition members. "People power" may, as Professor Sampson asserts, be the most important factor in a grassroots organization's strength, but organizations also possess many other assets that can be vital resources for coalition work. Young, emerging organizations or groups with limited financial resources or membership can all play a role in coalitions. Groups with any amount of "people power" may be able to provide a volunteer to make phone calls, an organization's name on the letterhead or signature on a petition, access to a group of parents, or a personal contact with an important ally.

The beauty of the coalition is its ability to incorporate groups that are at different stages of their own organizational development. Participation in coalitions does not detract from organizational development; in fact it may enhance it. While pursuing their own growth and progress, organizations that participate in coalitions are also engaged with others, gaining exposure and access to the bigger picture and bringing back new information, networks, and approaches to energize their own efforts.

Professor Sampson creates a false dichotomy between "nominal and real support." Sometimes "nominal support"—support in name only—is a big plus. Linking a group or cause with others through a coalition, endorsing a position, or writing letters of support for a new project can significantly increase an organization's legitimacy. "Real support" can come in forms other than "people power" or financial resources. Organizations can gain additional support from sharing their own issues and perspectives with other coalition members, who in turn may incorporate and publicize these positions. The clout of a coalition can open doors and gain exposure for its members. This added credibility may help coalition members to attract new constituents. Thus, while coalitions do not necessarily "organize the unorganized," they *can* deliver power to their members.

And speaking of organizing the unorganized, the grassroots organizing approach endorsed by Professor Sampson assumes a romanticized notion of "the people" who supposedly agree and work together in harmony. Homogeneous membership organizations may, indeed, mobilize a solid base of like-minded people. If they are to be effective, they need to accommodate a variety of people, orientations, values, and cultures. Coalitions unite diverse actors and organizations in a geographical or functional community without forcing people to feel like "one big, happy family" or to expand their own organization beyond its natural boundaries.

Coalitions may include community organizations with paid social work staff as well as indigenous grassroots organizations that are community led and volunteer run. We agree with Professor Sampson's distinction between these two types of organizations. Grassroots organizations are more directly connected to the needs, leadership, and interests of community residents than are funded community-based agencies. Funded agencies may be providing needed services and expertise to the community. These two types of organizations have distinct resources to bring to a coalition. They also may have conflicting interests and loyalties. Communities will be stronger if they form coalitions that encourage these groups to work together while recognizing and dealing with their differences. While grassroots groups can organize to get a bigger piece of the pie, coalitions can expand the pie for everyone.

We share Professor Sampson's view that the development of people is a fundamental reason for organizing. Gaining experience in coalition building brings leadership development to another level, analogous to the difference between building a family and being an active part of the community. Through coalition work people learn to negotiate a variety of resources and to shape collective plans for bigger arenas and multiple issues. Coalition participants develop special skills to deal with the interface between their own organization and other groups: mediating, bargaining, coordinating disparate components, consensus decision making, and multilevel communication. They also acquire an ability to mobilize on an issue while keeping the coalition together and having it remain accountable to its membership.

In conclusion, knowledge and experience in coalition building is increasingly necessary for professional growth, agency survival, program development, and organizational credibility. Today, coalitions are "where the action is" politically and economically. With scarce resources for organizing, increased technology for networking, and greater efficiency through coordination, we will see more coalitions. In addition to being a *means* of accomplishing specific goals, successful coalitions can become *models* of interorganizational cooperation and understanding. These models embody a collective vision of justice and equality and create a new landscape for organizational and community development.

Should Charismatic Leaders Be Recruited by Grassroots Organizations to Promote Social Change?

EDITOR'S NOTE: The development of leaders is a central task for grassroots community organizations. Many community organizations have been identified with the name of a single charismatic leader, whereas others have been identified with a group of leaders. The debate over the type of leadership that should be recruited depends heavily on the theoretical and practical approaches the organizer adopts as well as on the strategies and tactics that guide social change. One of the central themes in the debate about grassroots leadership is the concept of empowerment. Some would argue that charismatic leadership inhibits the development of grassroots leaders as well as the organization. Others argue that it is precisely this type of leadership that mobilizes the masses and empowers them to act on their own behalf. Yet, charismatic and collective leadership have often operated in conjunction with each other. Is the question then one of complementarity rather than exclusivity in mobilizing and organizing for social change?

Richard A. Cloward says YES. He is a professor at the Columbia University School of Social Work. His books include *Regulating the Poor, Poor People's Movements, The New Class War,* and *Why Americans Don't Vote.* He is the recipient of the Dennis Caroll Award of the International Society of Criminology; the C. Wright Mills Award and the Founders Award of the Society for the Study of Social Problems; the Bryant Spann Award of the Eugene V. Debs Foundation; the Herman D. Stein Excellence in Social Work Education Award from the Mandel School of Social Work, Case-Western Reserve University; and an Honorary Doctorate of Humane Letters from Adelphi University.

Jacqueline B. Mondros, D.S.W., argues NO. She is Professor and Associate Dean at Barry University School of Social Work. She teaches and publishes in the area of community organization and has organized several multiracial community groups in the Northeast.

YES

RICHARD A. CLOWARD

From one perspective, I am a poor choice to deal with the question of collective versus charismatic leadership because I think the most historically familiar forms of popular mobilization by poor people have not been led at all—neither by collective leaders nor by charismatic ones. From another perspective, however, I am a good choice for this debate, since I think some poor people's mobilizations are led by charismatic leaders, although never by collective ones.

Riots are one of the most frequent forms of uprisings by the poor, and they are leaderless by any reasonable definition of the term. The main conclusions reached by historians who set out in the post–World War II period to recover "history from below"—such as E. P. Thompson (1974), E. J. Hobsbawm (1981), George Rude (1964), Charles Tilly (1975; 1986), and Charles, Louise, and Richard Tilly (1975)—is that "the riot is the characteristic and ever-recurring form of popular protest" (Rude, 1964, p. 6). Preindustrial food riots, grain seizures, land invasions, and machine smashing thus have rough parallels in the modern period with urban riots, mob looting, and rent riots. E. P. Thompson (1974) thought that poor people were naturally drawn to riots because they afforded protection from repression. Writing about the English crowd's "capacity for swift direct action," he said:

> To be of a crowd or a mob was another way of being anonymous, whereas to be a member of a continuing organization was bound to expose one to detection and victimization. . . . The 18th century crowd well understood its capacities for action, and its own art of the possible. Its successes must be immediate, or not at all. It must destroy those machines, intimidate those employers or dealers, damage that mill . . . before troops come on the scene. (p. 401).

What the whole of this literature reveals, in short, is that neither collective nor charismatic leadership is requisite to mass protest among the poorer classes. They are capable of acting without either. The reason this is so is that poor people are capable of acting without first forming organizations that require some kind of acknowledged leadership. Poor people are not organized formally, but they are organized. They are related to one another through the institutional patterns of everyday life; they develop a sense of common identity in everyday life; they forge shared definitions of grievances and antagonists; they have the ability to communicate; and so on. In other words, poor people possess the requisites for collective action in the absence of formal organization.

Moreover, the means of collective protest are always available and do not depend on organization or leadership. The most popular means has been property destruction, especially incendiarism. Arson, whether burning the fields and manor houses in the preindustrial world or the shops and utilities in the streets of the urbanized world, requires technological rather than organizational resources, and not much of the former, either.

Many analysts and most organizers disparage these historically common forms of popular action, defining them as inchoate and ephemeral. The political power inherent in mass numbers is said to be dissipated because people fail to see the need to come together to form enduring mass-based organizations. They may even believe that riots and incendiarism are counterproductive. The response of civil rights organizers to the ghetto riots of the 1960s was to see nothing but political peril. They thought rioting might destroy the legitimacy of the struggle for civil rights and might doom chances of winning civil rights concessions. (Many historians and political analysts looking back at the 1960s take the same view, so that the riots are not so much analyzed as regretted.)

Accordingly, the main role played by various organizers during the rioting was to try to quell it. When riots broke out in Birmingham in June 1963, Morris says that civil rights leaders "hit the streets at once in order to persuade members of the black community not to engage in violence" so as to "save the agreement" with the economic elites of Birmingham with whom an agreement was being negotiated (Morris, 1984). McAdam (1982) correctly notes that the early riots triggered a veritable "northward stampede by organizers to establish organizational footholds in the ghettos as a means of regaining control over a movement that was slipping away from them" (p. 191). McAdam (1982) considers that Jacobs and Landau "accurately summed up the situation" when they explained that "neither SNCC nor any other group has found a form of political organization that can convert the energy of the slums into political power" (p. 191). And Oberschall (1973) expresses the same outlook when he concludes that "the single most important failure of the middle-class black and the civil rights organizations was their failure to mobilize and to organize the lower-class community" (p. 213).

The implication, of course, is that popular mobilizations—such as riots and incendiarism—do not have positive political salience and do not contribute to winning great victories. But that implication is wrong. Consider the correlation between the nationwide strike waves in the 1930s and the passage of the Wagner Act. Is it possible that the greatest strike waves in American history and the passage of the most important labor legislation in our history was mere coincidence? Or consider the correlation between urban rioting and passage of the Civil

Rights Act of 1964 and the Voting Rights Act of 1965. Is it possible that the greatest popular uprisings in the twentieth century (by any measure, that is what the ghetto riots were) and the enactment of the most important legislation of the century pertaining to blacks (which is what the civil rights acts were) was mere historical coincidence? Or did the riots signify to political leaders that aspirations for civil and political rights had become so urgent, so inflamed, that nothing short of granting the legitimacy of those aspirations would succeed in restoring civil order?

Here it should be said that ruling elite factions fear nothing so much as the appearance that their subjects have gotten out of control. One can never know whether popular disturbances will spread, or whether competing elite factions will try to take advantage of civil disorder to advance their own claims to power. (For these and other reasons, ruling groups always much prefer to deal with organizations because they know that people enmeshed in organizational networks are likely to be under control.) Perhaps one may therefore be forgiven for suggesting that if efforts by civil rights organizers to harness the northern urban ghettos had in fact been undertaken early and successfully in the 1960s, there might indeed have been no riots and there might have been no civil rights legislation. This is only one of many examples that could be given of the way popular political mobilization is disparaged, even marginalized.

Turning now to charismatic leadership, it has been undeniably important in the history of some (but only some) popular uprisings. Think of the most celebrated mobilizations by poor people historically. Names—revered names or despised ones, depending on the perspective taken—are always associated with them: Debs, Lewis, and Reuther (among others) with the industrial worker's movements; Garvey, Malcolm X, McKissick, and Brown (among others) with black nationalist movements; Randolph, Rustin, King, Farmer, Parks, Hamer, and Moses (among others) with the civil rights movement; Grey (among others) with New York City rent strikes; Wiley, Tillmon, and Sanders (among others) with the welfare rights movement.

But now a qualification on the importance of charisma. Despite the crucial roles played by these charismatic individuals, they were more the creatures of, than the creators of, popular mobilizations. Frances Fox Piven and I portrayed this time-order of events in *Poor People's Movements.* For example, the surging strike waves among industrial workers in the 1930s were not organized by unions or led by charismatic union leaders. Existing charismatic union leaders, like John L. Lewis of the Mineworkers, had to run to catch up and to keep up with the mushrooming picket lines. On this point, Hobsbawm (1978) has since agreed: "Mass union organization, in the US of the 1930s as in all analogous 'explosions' of labor unionism with which I am familiar, was the *result* of worker mobilization and not its cause" (p. 4). One saw the same mass mobilizations, unled and unorganized, in the case of housing and welfare protests in the 1960s. By the time Jesse Grey announced the Harlem rent strike in 1964, thousands of tenants had already stopped paying rent, as even the most casual perusal of the upward trends in rent delinquency statistics revealed; and by the time Wiley announced the formation of the National Welfare Rights Organization in 1966, applications for welfare had already nearly doubled over 1960, as monthly welfare department statistics quite clearly revealed. Separately, but in concert, people were already on the move.

Once a popular mobilization is under way, however, charismatic leaders and formal organizations do typically come to be associated with them. "Social movement entrepreneurs," to use a term popularized by McCarthy and Zald (1973), recognize that popular mobilizations are in progress, so they rush to form organizations, and they often emerge as charismatic leaders in the process. But when the history of such events is recorded, the time-order usually gets reversed, so that the organizations and leaders are erroneously credited, retroactively, for the popular mobilizations themselves. Examples are legion: Lewis and the Congress of Industrial Organizations are credited with inciting the worker strike waves in the 1930s; Grey and Wiley, respectively, are credited with inciting the housing and welfare movements of the 1960s. Thus poor people—whether or not led by charismatic leaders—are denied their proper place in the annals of struggles for justice.

REFERENCES

Hobsbawm, E. J. (1981). *Bandits.* NY: Pantheon.

Hobsbawm, E. J. (1978, March 23). *The New York Review of Books,* p. 25.

McAdam, D. (1982). *Political process and the development of black insurgency, 1930–1970.* Chicago, IL: University of Chicago Press.

McCarthy, J. D., & Zald, M. (1973). *The trend of social movements in America: Professionalization and resource mobilization.* Morristown, NJ: General Learning Press.

Morris, A. (1984). *The origins of the civil rights movement.* New York: Free Press.

Oberschall, A. (1973). *Social conflict and social movements.* Englewood Cliffs, NJ: Prentice-Hall.

Rude, G. (1964). *The crowd in history.* New York: John Wiley and Sons.

Thompson, E. P. (1974). Patrician society, plebeian culture. *Journal of Social History, 7*(4), 401–408.

Tilly, C. (1975). Food supply and public order in modern Europe. In C. Tilly (Ed.), *The formation of national states in Western Europe.* Princeton, NJ: Princeton University Press.

Tilly, C. (1986). *The contentious French.* Cambridge, MA: Harvard University Press.

Tilly, C., Tilly, L., & Tilly, R. (1975). *The rebellious century.* Cambridge, MA: Harvard University Press.

Rejoinder to Professor Cloward   Jacqueline B. Mondros

Professor Cloward begins his argument by discussing the significant changes brought about by "leaderless" uprisings, compared to changes brought about by formal community organizations. This is a point we need not debate. Riots and uprisings have sometimes been successful in bringing about change, and community organizations have sometimes failed to do so. But riots are not always successful (witness the spring 1992 riot in Los Angeles), and formal organizing does not always result in insignificant change. For example, the Community Reinvestment Act of 1978 was an outcome of the work of a coalition of neighborhood groups. Clearly, change springs from many sources. As Professor Cloward himself acknowledges, change most frequently emerges from the decisions of elites who, for one reason or another, find the change to be in their self-interest (Piven & Cloward, 1979).

Professor Cloward and I also agree on the limited prospects for enduring social change. On several occasions I have heard him describe social change as a "process of two steps forward and one step back," and I agree. Though he argues that the urban riots of the 1960s resulted in the Civil Rights Act of 1965, he would not, I think, dispute the fact that almost thirty years later economic indicators show few changes in the conditions of poor African-Americans, conditions that led to the riots in the first place. Nor have bankers become the responsive civic-minded lenders we had hoped for, the Community Reinvestment Act notwithstanding.

The question is not one of how change occurs, but how to increase the odds that it will be continued. While we may agree generally about the role of community organizations in creating change, we may have somewhat different perspectives on their significance. These organizations, as Professor Cloward says, "keep hope alive" by identifying, legitimating, and intensifying grievances and identifying those areas where influence is possible. People who participate in community organizations gain important skills: they learn to make collective decisions, design strategies, recruit and maintain relationships with others, reveal heretofore concealed information, and negotiate with powerholders. The use of these skills and the small, though not insignificant, changes that ensue enhance people's sense of power. Surely Professor Cloward would not minimize the advantage of creating such a skilled and empowered group of people, if only to have them available when the historical moment emerges. It has been argued, for example, that the leaders of the civil rights movement received their preprotest "training" from their involvement in the black churches of the South (Lincoln & Mamiya, 1990). Also, many people active in today's community organizations, including organizers, cut their teeth in the protest movements of the 1960s. Should such cross-fertilization be disparaged or enhanced?

Where Professor Cloward and I do part company is on the issue of whether or not protest should be led by charismatic leaders. I have some question about protest movements, in fact, ever being led by a single charismatic leader. Names do become associated with protest movements, but in every movement cited, there were other lesser-known leaders as well. King had Jackson, Abernathy, Mays, Young, Bond, along with many lesser known colleagues. Wiley had DeLeuw, Day, and most notably Cloward himself. Alinsky had Chambers, Harmon, Trapp, Gaudette, Von Hoffman. Even in what are perhaps history's most successful protest movements—the rise of Judaism and Christianity—there is evidence of collective leadership. Where would Christianity be without Paul and Peter, and Judaism without Joshua and Aaron? We really should not confuse the visibility of a leader with the work of many.

I also question Professor Cloward's portrayal of the organizer as a charismatic leader. Organizers who are committed to the goals of empowerment don't make key decisions; they certainly don't define what grievances are legitimate, what issues are to be taken up, what strategies are to be pursued. Nor do they control leadership. A smart organizer would not prevent a magnetic, popular, and skillful person from assuming a key organizational role. In fact, a skilled organizer would do precisely what Professor Cloward seems to disparage. He or she would find a way to discover people's institutions, grievances, hopes, plans, and natural leaders, and use his or her skills to help achieve the goals. The very nature of organizing requires us to "jump on the bandwagon" to help people play their tunes better. It is, of course, helpful for an organizer to be likable, but I have known many mild-mannered and unassuming ones who are very effective at developing magnetic indigenous leaders.

While this debate is perhaps entertaining, even revealing, it is unlikely to resolve the issues discussed here. A quick look at our references suggests that Professor Cloward and I represent different traditions, both with an interest in protest activity and organizing. His is steeped in the study of the history of protest movements; mine comes from my interest in the details of the practice of organizing. Both traditions seek to understand organizing and both wish it well, and, in my view, they have been pursued separately for too long. What we need is not a debate, but a mutual exploration of past and current protest movements. The contributions of less visible leaders of historical protest movements, and their relationship to the more visible leaders, need to be examined. Today's community organizations must be compared with those of history to understand similarities and differences. We need, particularly, to know how leadership is defined and employed in protest and how organizers work in times of tumult and in times of quiet. Such study would inform how community organizers pursued change in each particular historical period and social context. That would satisfy us both, I am sure.

REFERENCES

Lincoln, C. E., & Mamiya, L. H. (1990). *The black church in the African American experience.* Durham, NC: Duke University Press.
Piven, F. F., & Cloward, R. (1979). *Poor people's movements.* NY: Pantheon Books.

NO

JACQUELINE B. MONDROS

Those who have written about community organizing have struggled with the question of who should lead and be most visible in the organization. Should the organizer speak for the group? Should the organizer seek to recruit a specially talented and skillful individual or a particularly prestigious one to take on the organization's leadership roles? Should the organizer himself accept a "low profile" and recruit members who, though not charismatic or prestigious, are indigenous to the community and will collectively decide and act for the organization? How organizers answer these questions depends on their views about the relative advantages and disadvantages of charismatic and collective leadership and the principled desiderata of grassroots community organizations. A collective leadership better serves the goals, daily rigors, and political environments of protest organizations, and, moreover, its impact endures.

Defining Charismatic and Collective Leadership

According to Weber, charismatic leaders are "self-appointed leaders who are followed by those who are in distress and who need to follow the leader because they believe him to be extraordinarily qualified" (Gerth & Mills, 1946, p. 52). Often appearing during times of crisis, charismatic leadership is antithetical to institutional and permanent leadership. The charismatic leader is a radical who offers his followers an alternative to the traditionally oppressive hierarchy and power structure. Followers are thus emotionally and cognitively attracted to the charismatic and depend on him or her to effect radical change. According to recent writers, charismatic leaders can be found in many social systems (Conger, 1989).

Charismatic leadership is, however, by its nature ephemeral. Only constant success will sustain it, and the search for new leaders begins as success wanes

(Downtown, 1973). If the movement is to survive the charismatic, legitimate structures and rules must be established. The necessity to institutionalize the success of charisma, otherwise known as the *routinization* of charisma, transfers leadership from the individual to the institution (Gerth & Mills, 1946). The institution is then imbued with the legitimacy of the original charismatic until, of course, another radical seeks to reform it. If the charisma has not been institutionalized, or the leader fails or is otherwise incapacitated, the movement withers and dies.

Collective leadership consists in a group of people with no distinctive abilities or "vision of the truth." They share responsibility for problems and the work of the organization and decide, direct, and represent the functions and objectives of the organization (Heifetz & Sinder, 1988). As Heifetz and Sinder describe it, this type of leadership emerges not from position, not from special gifts, but from involvement in the work of the organization. The activity of leadership is to mobilize groups to do work (i.e., define problems, generate solutions, and locate responsibility for defining and solving problems). Leaders guide. They do not provide answers, they interpret and stimulate engagement. They participate in a process of learning and compromise that produces programs that are owned collectively rather than by any single individual.

The Nature of Community Organizations

Community organizations are defined as self-generated (as opposed to legally mandated) associations of people who create organizations to wrest power resources from established individuals and institutions and create change (Grosser & Mondros, 1985). This definition is broad enough to encompass a range of types of grassroots organizations and styles of organizing. Community organizations share at least three common characteristics.

First, these organizations generally work on what Heifetz and Sinder (1988) identify as complex, sometimes messy problems that are not easily amenable to technical solutions, nor are they within the domain of a single leader. Both problems and solutions need to be broadly understood and require the participation of those with a stake in them (Heifetz & Sinder, 1988). The problems with which community organizations contend (e.g., homelessness, drug abuse, welfare reform, crime, and housing) all require involvement by members of the community.

Second, even in the best of times, such organizations are easily defeated. The social, economic, and political environment is seldom amenable to change from below. Indeed, it has been argued that the contribution of grassroots organizations to social change is small compared to the forces committed to the maintenance of the status quo (Piven & Cloward, 1977). For an organization to survive and effect change in a hostile economic and political environment, it must be established to cope with the often painstaking and slow process of making change. It must also be able to endure the many obstacles and the inevitable setbacks associated with the organizing effort.

Finally, most students and practitioners of organizing urge that instrumental social change is not the only goal of community organizations. Virtually equal importance is given to developing leadership by building the skills and resources that allow people to achieve results and have a growing sense of confidence in their ability to act. That goal is now called *empowerment* and is a central feature of organizing put forward by Sieder (1956), Pray (1948), and McClenahan (1922) to Alinsky (1972), Staples (1984), and Kahn (1992), and those in between.

Collective leadership better serves the goals, mitigates the daily rigors, and accommodates the political environments of grassroots community organizations.

Collective Leadership and Goals

In some ways the debate about charismatic versus multiple leadership is inherently linked to the debate about the purposes of grassroots organizing. If one accepts that the principal aim of grassroots organizing is to attain instrumental changes, then whatever type of leadership that most effectively realizes those changes is sought. On the other hand, most organizers believe that empowering people by developing leadership is equally important.

The goal of empowerment presupposes collective leadership. It assumes that many members, not only the skillful few, will be developed as leaders. As they argue, compromise, decide, and exchange both routine and visible roles and tasks, members learn they too can develop leadership skills. Empowerment is not an abstract goal; it is experienced in action and in detail.

By its very nature, charismatic leadership depends on the dependency of followers; the charismatic is looked to for all decisions, answers, and actions (Gerth & Mills, 1946). The effect of the dominant individual often diminishes members. As one person assumes all the roles and visibility, others begin to question their own contribution to the enterprise. Lacking roles, members' investment will wane (McLuhan, 1964). If the gains can be made without them, why is their involvement necessary (O'Brien, 1975; Olson, 1965)? And perhaps, most important, when all the glory accrues to the charismatic, despite the hard work of others, people begin to feel manipulated, used, and undervalued. This is especially true when the charismatic is the organizer, whose personal circumstances are often different, and not nearly as dire, as those of the members of the group.

Thus, empowering people does require collective leadership. As members' opinions and ideas are elicited, encouraged, and valued, they learn the organization depends on them. They experience themselves as leaders rather than followers. The best grassroots leader or organizer does not assume the mantle of leadership, but rather mentors others to behave on equal footing (Heifetz &

Sinder, 1988). The grassroots leader stimulates tasks and abilities that enhances the leadership of others (Alinsky, 1972).

Collective Leadership and the Rigors of Organizing

The inherent ephemeral and fragile character of charismatic leadership may bring ruin to protest groups. Transitory leadership is intrinsically antithetical to building an organization that endures a long change process. There is always the danger that the charismatic may move, perish, or become co-opted by competing power holders. Few community organizations can sustain the constant success necessary for the charismatic to continue to lead. Any setback may put the organization on the path of looking for a new leader with a new answer, rather than sustaining commitment among members to continue seeking change. And, if "routinization of charisma" occurs, the organization may find itself bereft of the new ideas, skills, and energy that community organizations need to make it over the long haul.

Collective leadership, on the other hand, deals with these problems by supplying a constant flow and ever larger number of competent people. If a leader becomes ill, estranged, moves out of the community, or becomes otherwise engaged, replacements usually are available. The protest organization is not inherently dependent on a single individual's efforts, and therefore survives the departure of an important individual.

A cadre of active leaders attenuates the need for *constant* success. The organization can survive some reversals without dismissing the entire leadership structure. People support each other through the trials and troubles of organizing, rather than seek to place blame. As members of the decision-making group, they are less likely than otherwise to feel manipulated. Factors, other than the need for success, sustain their involvement. The factors that sustain their commitment include ego satisfaction of media attention, being the spokesperson, negotiating with a powerholder, developing camaraderie among members, and learning new skills (Mondros & Wilson, 1986).

Finally, if leadership opportunities are open and accessible, there is always room for new people with ideas, energies, concerns, and personal networks. The influx of new leaders with resources and energy helps the organization resist the parochial, the mean-spirited, and the shortsighted. New blood keeps the organization vital and relevant.

Collective Leadership and Political Environment

The final set of rationales supporting the case for collective leadership is the organization's ability to "win" in a complex and hostile external environment. The kinds of problems most community organizations usually tackle require collective leadership. They are issues of public policy, problems on which people disagree about definitions and solutions. The organizations' agendas usually oblige debate and collective decision making. As Heifetz and Sinder (1988) argue;

> In public policy situations . . . the defining and solving comprise significant political and social learning processes as the constituencies involved sort out their orientation, values, and potential tradeoffs. No "leader" can magically do this work. Only the group—the relevant community of interests—can do this work. It must do the sorting and learning necessary to define what constitutes a problem. It must make the adaptations and adjustments to the problem situation that most solutions require. Solutions in public policy generally consist of adjustments in the community's attitudes and actions. Who else but those with stakes in the situation can make the necessary adjustments? (p. 187–188)

The hostile political environment in which protest organizations work offers a further rationale for collective leadership. A charismatic leader is easily discredited or co-opted. Very frequently, the charismatic is "red baited" or otherwise disparaged, and a serious blow is dealt to the protest movement. It is simply more difficult for the powerful to "shut down" protest if there are many leaders. The numbers alone make leaders less vulnerable to personal attacks. Then, too, numbers of competent leaders allow the organization to diversify their targets, to pin down and negotiate with several power holders at once (Alinsky, 1972). Such diversification does not depend on a single individual being everywhere and responsible for all organizational activity.

In sum, the purposes, exigencies, and environments of grassroots protest organizations require collective leadership. Without a cadre of capable people, community organizations cannot achieve their goals of empowerment for change.

REFERENCES

Alinsky, S. (1972). *Rules for radicals.* New York: Vintage Books.

Conger, J. (1989). *The charismatic leader: Behind the mystique of exceptional leadership.* San Francisco: Jossey-Bass.

Downtown, J. (1973). *Rebel leadership: Commitment and charisma in the revolutionary process.* NY: The Free Press.

Gerth, H. H., & Mills, C. W. (1946). *From Max Weber: Essays in sociology.* New York: Oxford Press.

Grosser, C. F., & Mondros, J. B. (1985). Pluralism and participation: The political action approach. In S. Taylor and R. Roberts (Eds.), *Theory and practice of community social work* (pp. 154–178). New York: Columbia University Press.

Heifetz, R. A., & Sinder, R. M. (1988). Political leadership: Managing the public's problem solving. In R. Reich (Ed.), *The power of public ideas* (pp. 179–203). Cambridge, MA: Ballinger Publishing.

Kahn, S. (1992). *Organizing: A guide for grassroots leaders* (2nd ed.). New York: McGraw-Hill.

McClenahan, B. A. (1922). *Organizing the community.* New York: Century Company.

McLuhan, M. (1964). *Understanding media: The extension of man.* New York: McGraw-Hill.

Mondros, J. B., & Wilson, S. M. (1986). Recruitment and involvement of community leaders: What's happening out there now? *Journal of Sociology and Social Work, 14*(3/4), 203–221.

O'Brien, D. (1975). *Neighborhood organization and interest-group processes.* Princeton, NJ: Princeton University Press.

Olson, M. (1965). *The logic of collective action: Public goods and the theory of groups.* Cambridge, MA: Harvard University Press.

Piven, F. F., & Cloward, R. C. (1977). *Poor people's movements.* New York: Pantheon Books.

Pray, K. (1948). When is community organization social work practice? *Proceedings of the National Conference of Social Work.* New York: Columbia University Press.

Sieder, V. (1956). What is community organization practice? *The social welfare forum, proceedings, National Conference of Social Work, St. Louis, 1956.* New York: Columbia University Press.

Staples, L. (1984). *Roots to power: A manual for grassroots organizing.* New York: Praeger Publishers.

Rejoinder to Professor Mondros　RICHARD A. CLOWARD

Professor Mondros argues for collective leadership. But the history of poor people's mobilizations shows no evidence of it. How can we explain this divergence of opinion? Have I read the history wrong? I think not. We differ because we have in mind entirely different historical circumstances.

I have in mind periods, such as the 1930s and 1960s, when people took to the streets in great numbers—great waves of strikes, great marches of the unemployed, great rent riots, great waves of civil disobedience, and great ghetto riots. These are the times when great victories were won—the Wagner Act in 1935 or the Voting Rights Act in 1965. These are also times when organizers don't count for much. Organizers certainly don't decide whether riots should be led or unled or whether charismatic leaders should or should not head movements.

What organizers can do in such periods is to help people do what they are already doing, and that means mobilizing rather than organizing. There really isn't enough time to do organizing in the sense of building organizations. These periods are episodic; mass unrest never lasts. If welfare applications are rising, take advantage of the moment to mobilize millions more to apply; if rent delinquencies are rising, take advantage of the moment to mobilize millions more to stop paying rent. Much of my historical and analytical work (with Frances Fox Piven) is devoted to showing how the fiscal and political crises resulting from such mobilizing strategies as ''flooding the rolls'' (Cloward & Piven, 1966) or ''bankrupting the slum housing system'' (Piven & Cloward, 1967) might supply the leverage to win major policy concessions, whether a federalization of welfare or massive housing subsidies.

Professor Mondros, by contrast, has in mind the periods that follow times of great tumult—periods such as the 1940s and 1950s, or the 1970s and 1980s. These are reactionary periods, full of menace. In such periods, there is little readiness among people to take the streets. They instead endure fatalistically. Or, as Richard Flacks (1988) would say, people concentrate on making their everyday lives. Nor are great victories possible. Organizing in these periods is therefore small-scale, and goals are limited to localistic objectives defined as winnable by small numbers of people. The main hope in these periods is to keep the ideal of mass mobilization alive.

Periods of relative quiescence require different organizer roles. One obviously can't mobilize, since people are not mobilizing. A strategy tailored to such times is required—door-knocking, canvassing, persuasion, education, painstaking membership building and organization building, and endless other organizer-intensive activities. Indeed, it is precisely because people are prepared to do so little in these periods that organizers are required to do so much. Grassroots organizations usually experience rapid turnover of membership, requiring constant door-knocking and canvassing to replenish the ranks. Or they collapse once organizers leave, as the most cursory reading of the history of poor people's organizations reveals. Naison's (1986) account of tenant organizing in New York City during the 1930s ends by noting that the city-wide structure that coordinated local tenant organizations ''proved fragile'' once its unemployed organizers left:

> Never did City-Wide's fund-raising produce over one thousand dollars per year . . . . The slum tenants . . . lacked the resources to subsidize it, or the political skills and inclinations to build the kind of stable organizations that could give City-Wide real permanence. City-Wide survived on the politically-motivated idealism and skills of underemployed professionals, both of which were vulnerable to shifts in political climate and improvements in the economy. (p. 127)

And it is precisely because people are prepared to do so little that organizers inherit the latitude to make key decisions, such as deciding the kinds of leadership to be recruited.

Still, it is my strong impression that it is charisma that prevails even in these reactionary periods. And it is not primarily indigenous charismatic leaders who prevail, but charismatic organizers. Without charismatic organizers, few grassroots protest organizations would form at all in these periods. As for the organizations that endure, they are overwhelmingly headed by organizers who are themselves charismatic; for example: Chavez and Ross (and others) in the farm labor organizing struggle; Chambers (and others) in the organizing projects fostered by the Industrial Areas Foundation; Rathke and Kest (and others) in ACORN's many projects; and Booth (and others) in the disparate strands of the citizen action movement.

Even the contemporary strain of grassroots organizing theory and practice in which the role of charisma is so eschewed was itself initiated by a charismatic leader, Saul Alinsky. As for my friend and colleague Jacqueline Mondros, I've been personally involved in some organizing ventures with her, and she's pretty charismatic herself.

REFERENCES

Flacks, R. (1988). *Making history: The radical tradition and the American mind.* New York: Columbia University Press.

Cloward, R. A., & Piven, F. F. (1966, May 2). A strategy to end poverty. *The Nation.* Reprinted in Cloward, R., & Piven, F. F. (1974). *The politics of turmoil.* New York: Pantheon.

Naison, M. (1986). From eviction resistance to rent control: Tenant activism in the great depression. In R. Lawson (Ed.), with the assistance of M. Naison, *The tenant movement in New York City, 1904–1984.* New Brunswick, NJ: Rutgers University Press.

Piven, F. F., and Cloward, R. A. (1967, December 2). Rent strike: Disrupting the slum system. *The New Republic.* Reprinted in Cloward, R. A., & Piven, F. F. (1974). *The politics of turmoil.* New York: Pantheon.

DEBATE 3

Should Grassroots Community Organizations Be Linked to a Political Party to Promote Social Change?

EDITOR'S NOTE: The concept of empowerment refers both to the process by which individual and collective power is developed and acquired as well as to the capacity for effective action. Grassroots community organizations seek to empower their constituencies to help individuals and communities solve problems, change their situations, and mobilize for social action. Thus, the focus of empowerment strategies should be on the individual and the social environment. The critical question for grassroots organizations is: What are the most effective strategies for empowering individuals, groups, and communities? Recognizing that problems in communities are increasingly complex and interrelated, what role does "politics"—the electoral process and political parties—play in helping grassroots organizations empower citizens so they can participate as agents for social change?

Mark G. Hanna, D.S.W., and Buddy Robinson say YES. Mark Hanna is an associate professor of Social Work at California State University-Fresno, where he chairs the social policy sequence and teaches community organizing. He and Buddy Robinson have collaborated on a national survey of community organizer training and on a book in progress titled, *Strategies for Social Change Practice in the 1990's: Direct Action and Transformative Approaches to Community Organization.*

Buddy Robinson is Staff Director of the Minnesota Senior Federation–Northeast Coalition, a 5,000-member community organization in Duluth that develops senior citizen leadership and works on consumer issues. He has eighteen years of community organizing experience with a variety of constituencies in three states.

Michael Reisch takes the NO position. He is the Director of the Department of Social Work Education and Professor of Social Work and Public Administration at San Francisco State University. With a multidisciplinary educational background in law, history, and social work, Professor Reisch has published widely on the history and philosophy of social welfare, social policy, and community organization theory and practice. Among his publications are *From Charity to Enterprise: The Development of American Social Work in a Market Economy, The Political-Economy of Social Work in the 1980s, The Future of Non-Profit Management and the Human Services,* and numerous articles on community organization theory and practice. He has over twenty-five years' experience as a community organizer and as a director of local and statewide advocacy organizations. In addition, he has served as a campaign manager and consultant to local, state, and Congressional candidates for twenty years.

YES

MARK G. HANNA AND BUDDY ROBINSON

As we present the affirmative position on this question, it is important to first set straight our terms of discussion. A grassroots community organization is not a formal unit of government such as a county social service department, nor is it an internationally or nationally chartered religious, labor, trade, professional, or service organization such as the YWCA or Lions Club. From here on, however, the definition gets more difficult. We are most concerned with two organizational characteristics: the autonomy of local organizations to chart their own direction and the nature of the membership base, principally individual or group membership (belonging by virtue of one's participation in a primary organization); for instance, all members of congregation "X" are de facto members in "United Neighborhood Organization" or "UNO," as the church is one of several dues-paying "units" of UNO. Another cumbersome variation would be the local and statewide chapters of "citizen" organizations, such as nationwide organizations that claim large numbers of "members," despite the fact that the participation of nearly all these members is restricted to donating nominal "dues" which are solicited door to door, while policy operations are dominated by a small cadre of paid (or underpaid) staff.

More traditionally, grassroots community organizations are associated with small, single- or multi-issue organizations initiated by and through the efforts of unpaid citizens who live in or near the geographic boundaries within which the problem, need, or concern is manifest, such as neighborhood improvement, shelter/housing, neighborhood watch, escort and senior assistance, civic participation, and so on. Whether such organizations are developed around a program of service, advocacy, education, or civic/political rights, what all have in common is the requirement for the development of sufficient social, economic, and political resources to accomplish their identified goals. Without *power* (defined as the ability to act in the absence of agreement on the part of authoritative decision makers), grassroots community organizations, of whatever stripe, will be marginal to the larger forces of social change, forever restricted to the "curb and stoplight" variety of organizing.

It is our contention that one of the most direct and productive approaches to developing power for effecting social change comes from concerted, systematic development of linkages with established political parties. Let us look briefly at the major reasons why community organizations do not develop such linkages, and then consider why and how such linkages might be nurtured for the future.

Frequently mentioned reasons for not developing linkages from grassroots community organizations to political parties include fear of being swallowed up by dominant political forces, fear of being punished by winners when one backs the losing party, fear of losing tax-exempt status because of engaging in partisan political activity, a concern about getting caught in a mode of dependency in which the politician "solves" the problems, a disdain for party politics, a fear of dividing constituents over partisan issues and the consequent loss of focus on central issues of the organization, and not enough time or resources to play in the political arena. We view such reasons as being of two types: problems of autonomy and problems of membership.

Problems of autonomy really come down to wanting to keep what one already has; to preserve and maintain the status quo, the epitome of self-interest: *survival.* "Who needs political parties to mess around in our internal policies or to begin to make demands on our resources during elections, which is the only time party organizations are interested in grassroots organizations?" Or, "My board would never allow this organization to get involved in partisan politics because we would lose our 501(c)(3) tax-exempt status and could never qualify for government or foundation grants again."

There are statutes, precedent, and case law constraining political activity on the part of community organizations, but these are rarely central to the decisions of community organizations to engage or not to engage in partisan political work. Most board members don't have the foggiest notion of what activities are legal or illegal and make decisions on misinformation or narrowly ideological perspectives. There are straightforward reporting requirements that, if understood and met, permit a number of creative solutions to these initial constraints. More central to the autonomy problem is the perception that party organizations are out of control and completely unaccountable to the 800,000 tax-exempt and church–nonprofit organizations in the United States and the additional six to seven million community organizations (Skidmore, 1990).

It is true that party organization in the United States is completely out of control. With the diminished voter identification with either the Republican or

Democratic Party and the rise of the insurgent Independent Party candidacy of Ross Perot, there may be no worse time to be advocating for the linkage of grassroots community organizations to political parties to empower citizens as social change agents. Our two-party system in the United States has been transformed into a cult of personality with maximum feasible distortion and misrepresentation of the needs and concerns of citizens. Hostility dominates where cynicism and alienation have not taken hold. Politicians are viewed as vapid caricatures whose sole interests are personal advantage and manipulation of passive, uninformed voters. Nonetheless, we assert strenuously that it is in the vital long-term interests of grassroots community organizations to combat such disintegration and to move massively to reengage party organizations in the blood, sweat, and tears of common citizens struggling for decency and justice.

The cost to our nation stemming from the loss of vitality to political parties is great. The loss has been the erosion of the republican legacy (which has its flaws, but which is a different issue) and the essential centralizing tendencies of government enterprise, including fair representation of minority populations and their interests which have been trammeled by the power of elites at the local and state levels, whether in educational opportunity, civil rights, or equal political rights.

Second, we have seen the rapid fragmentation of political interests, once effectively aggregated by parties, faithfully attending to the traditional functions of recruiting political candidates, shaping the national policy agenda, and organizing the government to make policy. In short, the traditional function of parties as linkage institutions between citizens and policies has been short-circuited by the plethora of special-interest organizations and their associated political action committees (PACs). A few hundred such PACs in 1971 have grown to over 18,000 in 1986, with combined contributions (mostly to federal congressional candidates) of over 300 million dollars (Welch, Gruhl, Steinman, & Comer, 1986).

Now, we are forced to get a little bit partisan in our observations. Although there are more than enough PACs to go around for trade, professional, labor, and social welfare organizations, it is the conservative PACs that have been the most successful at raising money and channeling it to politicians who represent their interests. Corporate and trade PACs, along with the most well-heeled professional PACs, account for the preponderance of PAC funds. Liberal interests have not attained the kind of dominance in the promotion of their economic or social interests, and the inability of the Democratic party to hold the White House can be viewed as one consequence of the imbalance among ''competing'' interest groups for the attention and support of political candidates.

Contrary to the trends at the national level, the party identification of entering M.S.W. students is predominantly Democratic (62%), not ''no partisan identification'' (19%)(California Social Work Education Center, 1992), and a national sample of persons attending nonacademic organizing/social change training continues to be Democratic (Hanna & Robinson, 1992a). Maybe such diehard Democrats know something the new independents (and former Democrats) don't. Perhaps it is remembered and understood that social welfare budget cuts under Reagan and Bush have devastated public welfare programs which took a generation to develop and that Republican economic policy has crippled our civilian infrastructure, adding another trillion dollars to the national debt.

Whatever the reasons for continued Democratic Party identification among social change activists, it should be understood that renewed linkages with political parties are an essential ingredient in any long-term strategy to turn away from the "PAC" disease which eats away at grassroots political culture and democratic process. Weak political parties only strengthen the grip that PACs have on politicians. There can be no higher priority for grassroots community organizations than to develop informal and formal linkages with party organizations. A number of examples of such linkages may serve to illustrate the point.

Several linkages of an unofficial sort to a political party occur often in community organizing, with beneficial results. These informal connections appear even in groups that carry a charitable-purpose 501(c)(3) designation. [The IRS rules allow a 501(c)(3) to spend up to 20 percent of its budget on legislative lobbying, although direct endorsement or opposition of a political party or candidate is forbidden.]

Community groups that routinely engage in legislative activity (and in particular, statewide organizations that annually promote an agenda in their state legislatures) commonly develop working relationships with legislators and aides who evolve into stable allies. Many left-progressive citizen groups frequently find liberal legislators, usually Democrats, of a like mind on a range of issues. These alliances on issues result in a de facto relationship with elements of the Democratic Party. This by no means constitutes blind loyalty, and community groups assiduously reserve the right to battle any Democratic legislator who opposes their issues. By the same token, they are perfectly willing to work with Republican lawmakers who side with them. In this way, an organization's technical neutrality is maintained. It does not, however, diminish the overall trend of the long-term relationship with Democratic elected officials. The policy-influencing function often carries over to participation in precinct caucuses and district party conventions, where platform issues are generated.

A more indirect method of influencing the political process is voter registration drives, aimed at low-income populations. Community organizations can undertake these in conjunction with their public education on issues and also in anticipation of an upcoming election season. The Texas Industrial Areas Foundation (IAF) groups, working primarily with underrepresented Mexican-American constituencies, were instrumental in a roundabout way—through their voter registration activities—in helping Ann Richards win the gubernatorial race in 1990.

In the case of election campaigns, indirect connections surface also, again even in the case of 501(c)(3) groups that technically are barred from participating. The informal tie is simply the individual participation of active members and staff people on the election campaigns of legislative allies. In the case of visible officers and paid staff, this activity is necessarily on their own time and without using the name of the organization. The net effect, however, can be significant. This campaign volunteering helps ensure ongoing access (which, for wealthier interest groups, would be obtained instead by means of campaign contributions). Another linkage to elections is the conducting of candidate forums and the publicizing of candidate positions and voting records. As long as all candidates are given equal opportunity to respond, overt neutrality is preserved. But, by clearly juxtaposing the organization's issue positions with those of the candidates, it becomes quite obvious who the group's allies and opponents are. The organization's members can draw their own conclusions on entering the voting booth.

Some community organizations engage in open, formal electoral activity, which is permissible with an IRS 501(c)(4) (social welfare) nonprofit tax status. The most typical manifestation is direct assistance to an ally's election campaign as part of an overall legislative strategy. Bob Creamer, executive director of Illinois Public Action Council (IPAC), explains that it's foolish to lobby the legislature without also trying to affect its composition. Citizen action statewide groups have frequently plied this course for both state and congressional positions—Democrats, of course—and their door-to-door canvassing operations have proved very useful. In close elections, the canvass is especially adroit at identifying swing voters who are then targeted for repeat messages. The highly visible assistance for Democratic candidates creates a clear image of connection to the party. A few citizen action organizations (including IPAC and Connecticut Citizen Action Group) have additionally run candidates for state office from their own ranks. This strategy helps ensure the pursuit of the group's agenda and provides a ready-made relationship of accountability.

One last form of direct linkage is to overtly attempt to shape the party's platform or representation rules through delegates and mass action. One major attempt in recent history bears mentioning. The Association of Communities for Reform Now (ACORN), a multistate organization, intended to seriously affect the Democratic national platform in 1980 at the party convention, but shifted its plan to demand the creation of a party commission to improve the participation of low-income people. (The commission was created, only to have its recommendations rejected by the Democratic National Committee two years later.) ACORN's tactics included getting some of its members elected as convention delegates, lobbying state delegations, and staging a mass "counterconvention" and demonstration.

Such illustrations underscore the erroneous perception that engaging in partisan political work from a base of grassroots organizations is an impediment to increasing membership and participation. The close association of citizen action to the Democratic Party has actually been a key to the success of its fundraising/membership work, as political candidates, seeking support of citizen action or emerging from within the citizen action organization itself, reinforced the identity of the party and the organization. This is not to say that citizen action or any other form of organizational coalition or alliance will not have had to painstakingly build its reputation and strength and stand on its own two feet before it can approach electoral and party work. Quite to the contrary, grassroots community organizations must not substitute party linkage for hard work. But without the savvy and vision (and examples of success and failure) that our above illustrations provide, grassroots citizen organizations might never thoughtfully consider the possibilities for broadened horizons.

Formal party linkages are often confused with the "bandwagon" approach to elections and politics where citizens (and citizen-controlled, democratically structured organizations) become co-opted or manipulated into taking the party line. Our approach to formal linkages recognizes both the legal limitations of 501(c)(3) and 501(c)(4) status as well as the severe limitations on staff to engage in electoral political work. We are interested in proactive political work, including the identification of political issues, the recruitment of political candidates, the strategic development of alliances with other grassroots community organizations (in the same way that a variety of public service labor organizations—state employees, teachers, university faculty, and county employees might develop a joint PAC), the development of political research capability (within reach of most multi-issue community organizations, organized along the lines of the Midwest Center for Labor Research), and the active participation in voter registration, campaigns, elections, and follow-through with political accountability sessions. Citizens gain power when they stop restricting their activity to volunteer charity work and self-help and walk out into the light of unified political action; when they expand their organizational agenda to include a "public" dimension that involves citizens in the representation of their own interests and the shaping of the policy agenda of those candidates who seek the support of grassroots organizations. If it is true that grassroots citizen organizations cannot compete with the high-stakes "organized money" interest groups (and we think this is true), then such citizen organizations must rely on "organized people" as the base of political interest groups and the power such interests represent to the task of revitalizing political parties, especially the Democratic Party.

It is a mistake to think that grassroots organizations can somehow "go it alone" in the world of big league politics, just as it is a mistake to think that attention to local issues on the part of grassroots organizations will lead to incrementally induced social change. Social and cultural myopia are as much a part of the parochial landscape of grassroots organizations as they are institutionalized impediments at the national level. But it is equally perilous for political parties to ignore several interesting and potentially important approaches to active promotion of citizen democracy, simply because such approaches may require up-front investment of resources without immediate "payoff" in election results.

Party organizations must invest some of their money in the development of longer range political education that promotes dialogue and genuine understanding of complex problems, rather than invention of simplistic slogans. Resurrection of political parties will not occur from the national to the local level. It will be the vitality of local citizens, in free association around common interests (not simply "issues"—interests are those unifying themes that lie beneath issues and answer the question "why" do we want this or that), that will determine the future of parties in America. To deal effectively with the vast scale of political organization in the United States and with the consequent debilitation of political institutions, the new mediating institutions will be organized from a local base, but there must be a system of elected representation that resembles our current structure. The difference will be that many states will adopt term limits for their legislatures, thereby weakening the power and stability of incumbency and the entrenched special interests they represent. Therefore, broad-based community organizations will need to anticipate new windows of opportunity at the state level. More and more, state party organizations will rely on organized grassroots constituencies to put forward candidates and ideas for consideration. Already we see evidence that grassroots organizations, even largely church-affiliated constituents of the broad-based organizing projects, are exerting influence over office holders and policy agendas.

We anticipate an assemblage of broad-based community organizations that will go beyond a mere "mobilization of bias," which occurs when people understand their own self-interests and have the resources to act on them. Contemporary forms and functions of political parties must be transformed through pressure exerted from just such broad-based citizen organizations. Central party resources need to support and nurture another important dimension of political work, which only grassroots organizations can initiate. This dimension might be considered "prepolitical" or educational.

Here we are talking about embracing a five-stage process that begins with recognition of the value/sentiment systems within which ethnic and cultural identity is developed. The second stage involves promoting (still within informal social affiliation networks) dialogical inquiry about areas of immediate interest to citizens. There is a third stage of developing critical consciousness of the contradictions that exist between the day-to-day reality of citizens and a common reference for the way things "ought to be" (against a scriptural or constitutional promise). Fourth, through a recognition of such contradictions and examination of avenues for redress of grievances, people enter into a more explicit period of political socialization. During the fifth stage, mobilization of bias (more than during any previous stage) broad-based community organizations (and revitalized political parties) get into the business of mobilizing citizens for overtly partisan political activity. There are at least three methodologies: study circles, citizenship schools, and religiously centered base ecclesial communities (BECs) that are suited to the development of the first three stages of the above process. Political parties and grassroots community organizations would be well-advised to learn more about these three "prepolitical" methods as proven, yet under-utilized vehicles for long-term development of political culture.

Study circles, notably illustrated by the Swedish Study Circle Movement which heralded universal literacy and modern Swedish democracy, have been inextricably linked to the apparatus of government, to several political parties, and to labor organizations. All of these actively sponsor and invest large sums of money to develop and sustain over 350,000 study circles, each consisting of eight to fifteen people who voluntarily meet at least weekly in democratically orga-nized discussion groups around a diverse set of topical areas. A substantial proportion (over 35 percent) of such circles eventually move into some kind of "political" or civic action, even if initially meeting about cultural or nonpolitical issues (Oliver, 1990).

Citizenship schools are another example of an educationally focused plan for the development of political culture. The model pioneered by Myles Horton at the Highlander Folk School in Monteagle, Tennessee, during the 1940s through the 1960s Civil Rights Movement used many of the same pedagogical elements found in the study circle approach, including nonprofessional teachers, strict equality among participants, and placing a premium on nondirective, participant-initiated discussion. The principal difference between the two methods was Horton's central commitment to social action within the context of reflection on real-life situations experienced by participants. It was during this time that the Southern Christian Leadership Conference (SCLC) successfully utilized the approach to promote literacy among, and to register tens of thousands of, African-American voters and to introduce these people to democratic, politi-cal culture. In California, a young Cesar Chávez was doing similar work, along with Fred Ross, Sr. and the Industrial Areas Foundation, to develop the Commu-nity Service Organizations (CSOs), based on a mix of literacy and voter registra-tion as well as legal advocacy for the growing and long oppressed farm worker population (Horton, 1990).

The third educationally focused approach to promoting citizen empower-ment can be seen in the Latin American inspired base ecclesial communities, long associated with Liberation Theology. Although current adaptations found in the United States seem largely restricted to use among first-generation Mexican Catholic immigrants, the approach seems to have untapped promise among a variety of disenfranchised, "prepolitical" groups. The essential components of the method involve a regular meeting of a small group of families (three or four) around readings or discussions of religious scripture. But the readings are intended to prompt a three-stage process of seeing one's reality, reflecting on this reality in light of scriptural teachings (most often from the perspective of a "preferential option for the poor"), and acting as a community of faith. It is the action phase (or the absence of one) that is the basis for much of the criticism directed toward this approach by proponents of direct-action methods of organizing and by political parties. "Action" for participants in a base ecclesial community may indeed be "weak" by comparison. But the point is that political parties, in collaboration with grassroots community organizations, need to develop forums appropriate to the varying degrees of sophistication and political socialization among new immigrant groups (whose size and electoral importance will be growing exponentially during the next fifteen years). If such organizations restrict opportunities for participation to only those people who are ready or who can be "mobilized" for sporadic activist-type campaigns, then we weaken the potential base of support for community organization, and we certainly continue the erosion of political parties.

It is likewise in the interests of grassroots community organizations to understand the context of political power as it applies to the micro and macro issues which are their concern. As was stated at the outset, few grassroots citizen organizations will ever develop the power to operate at national or perhaps even statewide levels (although there are some very exciting developments for organizations with the resources and staying power to build alliances among similarly minded groups; such alliance building realistically can be expected to take many years). But after the initial consolidation of a broad, diverse, continuously rotating citizen leadership and membership base, local successes, and development of a clear vision for the organization, it will be up to the organization to signal its political preferences for elected and appointed positions. Although such preferences will be explicitly driven by the candidates' positions on "our" issues, it is precisely "our" issues that must become part of the party machinery from the precinct and county organizations to the state house. Grassroots community organizations may not frequently "barnstorm" the Democratic Platform Committee like ACORN tried to do, but it will not take politicians long to figure out that citizen organizations can be formidable proponents when the quid pro quo is understood and honored on both sides.

Much of the success of building effective quid pro quo relationships derives from enhanced public politics, when citizens become organized for power, when they recognize the need for a variety of forums for political socialization and education, and finally when they can deliver more than steam and promises on election campaigns. For too long citizens have passively (but willingly) consented in the forfeit of democracy through laziness and habituation. Empty rituals of candidate support (as long as a candidate smiles and mutters pleasing words) need to be replaced. Citizen membership must develop internal accountability to itself for turning out the troops, for meeting deadlines, for articulating a clear, limited agenda. Politicians will jump through hoops for any group that means what it says and does what it intends. It is not such a long step from there to the point where grassroots citizen organizations have the legitimacy and access to participate in the party rule-making and candidate selection. When reciprocal demands are made on party organizations to assist grassroots organizations with initiating transformative programs within grassroots communities, parties will be forced to respond or they will be held up to public ridicule by skillful citizen organizations. This kind of public action on the part of organized citizens is a reality this very day in communities across the United States. The models are available, the technical and organizing talent is developing, and the need could not be more evident. There will be no knight in shining armor to do it for us, not even if they come from Texas.

REFERENCES

California Social Work Education Center (1992, April 1). "1991 Entering MSW Student Demographics & Characteristics in California: A Preliminary Report of Survey Findings." Berkeley, CA: University of California at Berkeley, School of Social Welfare.

Hanna, M., & Robinson, B. (1992a). "Report to Participating Training Centers and Survey Respondents: Overview of Selected Data From 1990–91 Organizer Training Participant Survey." Fresno, CA: California State University-Fresno, Department of Social Work Education.

Hanna, M., & Robinson, B. (1992b). *Strategies of social change practice* (unpublished manuscript).

Horton, M. (1990). *The long haul.* New York: Anchor Books.

Oliver, L. P. (1990). *Study circles.* Cabin John: Seven Locks Press.

Skidmore, R. A. (1990). *Social work administration.* New York: Prentice-Hall.

Welch, S., Gruhl, J., Steinman, M., & Comer, J. (1986). *American government.* New York: West.

Rejoinder to Professor Hanna and Mr. Robinson
MICHAEL REISCH

It is difficult to argue with many of the underlying assumptions of the position presented by Hanna and Robinson, particularly their definition of grassroots organizations and much of their analysis of the political process in the United States today. Most of their argument, however, attempts to demonstrate the *legality* of political involvement for grassroots organizations and fails to make a case for the *efficacy* of linkages between grassroots organizations and political parties. My rebuttal of their position, therefore, focuses on several aspects that might be termed "wishful thinking" if their implications were not so serious.

These involve: (1) the sources of power and autonomy for grassroots community organizations; (2) the relationship between issue-oriented advocacy and electoral politics, specifically the difference between political action as a tactic and linkage with a political party; and (3) the role of political parties in the non-elective aspects of political work.

Sources of Power and Autonomy

Hanna and Robinson appear to argue that grassroots community organizations cannot obtain power unless they "borrow" it from established sources. They further assert that such organizations resist associating with political parties out of a self-interested fear of losing their autonomy. This argument overlooks two basic aspects of organizing in the United States: (1) affiliation with another organizational entity is not in the best interests of a grassroots group unless it has already established its own power base; and (2) the history of community organizing in the United States is replete with betrayals of grassroots organizations by political parties. What Hanna and Robinson view as self-interest may, in fact, be a healthy dose of justifiable paranoia.

Advocacy and Electoral Politics

Hanna and Robinson seem to equate participating in the political process with working with established political parties. Neither research nor the author's personal experience as an activist justifies this equation. In fact, the effectiveness of advocacy organizations is closely associated with independence from political parties or their leaders. While grassroots organizations can work successfully with politicians on specific issues, their influence declines when linkage with a political party makes it easier for politicians to take them for granted or to discount their arguments because of a known affiliation with the political opposition.

Political Parties and Political Work

Finally, Hanna and Robinson cite several examples of successful political work by grassroots organizations and mistakenly attribute their success to affiliation with established political parties. In fact, the success of the groups to which they refer owed little to the assistance of political parties; rather, their strength came from their ability to establish a separate political identity that did not rely on traditional centers of power and authority. As much as Hanna and Robinson might wish otherwise, there is no evidence that political parties have or will devote substantial resources to "the development of longer range political education that promotes dialogue and genuine understanding of complex problems.'' Only independent grassroots community organizations—in coalition with like-minded groups—have the will to take such action.

Hanna and Robinson imply that separation from political parties requires grassroots organizations to "go it alone." Current and past organizing efforts reveal, however, that the choice is not between success through linkage with political parties and failure through misguided autonomous action. Other options exist, and it is one component of community empowerment to develop and implement them. Power, to paraphrase the British sociologist Tom Bottomore, is the ability to determine alternatives. And grassroots community work is about nothing if it is not about power.

NO

MICHAEL REISCH

In the midst of a Presidential election year, it is tempting to link the fortunes of emerging grassroots community organizations to a political party to capitalize on the increased interest in social and economic issues that often accompany national campaigns and to try to hitch the wagon of nascent or struggling organizations to the potential ascendancy of a party's candidates. Both history and current reality, however, reveal that such a strategy is contrary to the best interests of grassroots community organizations and, in several fundamental ways, contradicts their basic goal of empowering their constituents. While the context is ripe for grassroots involvement in electoral politics, grassroots organizations are far more likely to promote social change from outside the political system, rather than through direct involvement with a political party.

There are numerous powerful arguments against such involvement. They can be summarized as follows:

- Grassroots community organizations and political parties have fundamentally different, often irreconcilable, orientations and goals.
- The relationship between grassroots community organizations and political parties is not reciprocal, making affiliation with such parties contrary to the best interests of grassroots community organizations.
- Linkage to political parties has a negative impact on the development and maintenance of grassroots community organizations and their social change agendas.
- Participation in political "business as usual" potentially compromises the integrity of community organizers working with grassroots organizations.

Differences in Orientation

"The political system encompasses all the forces that struggle for social control and orientation, [and] the establishment of social priorities and social goals" (Quirion, 1972, p. 90). As one of the contenders within this system, grassroots organizations require long-term stability, a distinctive ideology, large amounts of tangible resources, broad geographic representation, and a growing cadre of organizational leaders to succeed in their social change efforts. However, the better they attain these elements to serve the interests of the communities that they represent, the more the satisfaction of community needs runs contrary to those of established political parties. This is because the nature of the political system in the United States is designed to promote certain goals that are antithetical to those of grassroots organizations: the preservation of elite rule; the exclusion of new elements and new leaders from the political process; and the separation of political parties from their constituents except when asking for contributions or votes.

Grassroots organizing is rooted in the fabric of peoples' everyday lives and experiences. By contrast, mainstream electoral politics—and there is no other kind of electoral activity in the United States because of laws, the media, and corporate influence—creates institutions, symbols, and processes that are outside these everyday experiences and, therefore, more difficult for people to relate to or participate in. The absence of a class-based party system, rooted in peoples' culture, therefore, renders electoral activities not only more difficult for grassroots organizations but also in opposition to their interests. Consequently, such "organizations are faced with the choice of either going for very small, achievable victories or waging long fights with dim prospects for success over issues they really care about" (Project 2000, 1987, p. 28).

Lack of Reciprocity

The relationship between grassroots organizations and political parties is hardly reciprocal. Political parties use grassroots organizations solely to raise money, recruit volunteers, and elect their candidates and, in so doing, to maintain the political status quo. Parties are reluctant to provide grassroots organizations with real power; in fact, they have often actively resisted the establishment of political bases within grassroots organizations out of fear that such bases could develop independent political identities and influence. The experiences of the Community Action Programs in the 1960s and the Congress of Industrial Organizations (CIO) in the 1930s illustrate the fear that political parties have about the potential of grassroots groups to develop independent bases of political power that might challenge entrenched office holders or status quo oriented policies. After initial successes obtained with the support of the Democratic Party, both of these change efforts were undermined by party leaders when they began to pressure the political system for fundamental structural change.

Second, in the 1990s, political parties are less and less important in the United States political process. The decline of their influence is reflected in opinion polls, the volatility of the electorate, the general anti-incumbency mood of voters, and peoples' growing distrust of the political process itself. As their organizational strength is decreasing, now is not the time for grassroots organizations to form linkages with them. Ironically, such linkages would, in all likelihood, rejuvenate the parties through the infusion of new resources which, in turn, would merely preserve the status quo that grassroots organizations want to change.

Last, in the United States today, there is no political party with sufficient power to make it attractive as a political ally that is independent of the influence of corporate power and money. Affiliation with existing parties, therefore, would require grassroots organizations to either abandon most, if not all, of their social change agendas or engage in a process of ongoing political dishonesty. "It would seem, then, that an electoral party of the kind we have in the United States . . . is not the best consciousness-raising tool" for grassroots organizations, nor is it the best way to build mass support for grassroots issues (Jezer, 1982, p. 37).

Impact on Grassroots Organizations

The perpetual barriers to success for grassroots organizations—shortage of resources, government obstacles, and lack of a strong social base—are not removed by affiliation with political parties, which are primarily concerned with electing candidates and maintaining or expanding their political power. Simply put, political parties in the United States are not interested in pursuing anything other than mainstream political agendas. Grassroots organizations that form close ties to such parties must sacrifice their social change goals or face marginalization in the political process (Browning, Tobb & Marshall, 1990). In addition, through their affiliation with political parties, grassroots organizations run the risk in today's political environment of being painted into the "special interests" corner and, thereby, diminishing the opportunities to expand their base of support. This is a particular risk for racial and ethnic minority communities.

Political parties also operate on principles that are contrary to the empowerment objectives of grassroots organizations. The political process in the United States feeds off of electoral victories which, in turn, increasingly require enormous amounts of money and a high degree of technical expertise to achieve. Most of the millions of dollars raised for political campaigns by political parties goes to incumbents who spend it on "hired gun" consultants, not grassroots organizing (Federal Election Commission, 1992). The contributions themselves are designed to guarantee the influence of contributors (largely political action committees organized by corporate interests) on future policy decisions.

The traditional political process also excludes noncitizens from the most meaningful activities (voting and running for office) and is, therefore, particularly disempowering in immigrant and refugee communities that are, or should be, the focus of much current community work. (The question formulated for this debate—which refers to *citizen* empowerment—is an unintentional reflection of this disempowering process.) Electoral politics, therefore, does not foster the direct involvement of constituents so essential to the success of grassroots organizations and to the empowerment of its members.

In addition, the broadening of constituencies without a clear ideological framework to connect them—which electoral politics requires for success— generally leads to a phenomenon known as "issue substitution." This is a particular risk for those grassroots organizations in racial and ethnic minority communities for which the "deracialization" of issues amounts to an abandonment of their cause. The 1992 Democratic Party platform was an excellent example of the dilution of historic concerns for social reform in the interest of broadening the party's electoral appeal to a particular category of voters— middle-income, white males—whose concerns for social reform does not complement those of underrepresented populations.

The political success of grassroots groups, especially those comprised of racial and ethnic minorities, is closely tied to "incorporation," not merely winning office. "Incorporation is a complex phenomenon, shaped by the political character of both the group achieving incorporation and the coalition it is being incorporated into" (Stone, 1988, p. 618). Particularly at the local level where grassroots organizations exist, long-term success for racial and ethnic minorities is closely linked to their ability to become part of the dominant economic and political coalitions that control government. Yet, without a significant transformation of the political system and its major entities (parties), political incorporation inevitably co-opts grassroots efforts and renders them powerless. William Gamson's study (1975) of "challenging groups" in United States history demonstrates this all too well. Involvement in political parties, therefore, diminishes the likelihood of true incorporation occurring by draining off scarce resources and diverting grassroots organizations from the type of activities that create alternative centers of power, "while leaving them no closer to the levers of power" (Parenti, 1982, p. 25).

Reliance on political parties by grassroots organizations to achieve social change also leads to the creation of a class of leaders who enter politics for their own benefit, rather than for the interests of constituents. It also leads to the celebration of individual accomplishment (election to office) rather than group achievement (institutional change) and subtly replaces the community-oriented values of many grassroots groups with values that promote individualism. The experience of the Chicano community in the United States is but one example of this phenomenon (Acuna, 1981).

In the case of the African-American community, reliance on political parties as a vehicle for social change has often resulted in the withering away of traditional breeding grounds for new leaders, in such institutions as the church and movement groups. It has also resulted in a general disenchantment with the political process within minority communities and a growing disbelief in the possibility of change occurring in any constructive ways. Last, electoral politics, according to one minority activist, "functions as a distraction or a substitute for real organizing and real leadership development . . . and gives [the] illusion . . . that changes will be made through the election of someone else and not through building independent power" (Thigpen, 1988).

By contrast, successful political work by grassroots groups occurs outside the structure of political parties to exert greater influence on their policies and their activities and to overcome the resistance to change exhibited by traditional economic and political elites. The success of activists in Santa Monica and Berkeley, California, in Madison, Wisconsin, and in Vermont demonstrates the efficacy of this approach to social change.

Conclusion: Grassroots Organizing and Political Work

In considering whether to affiliate with political parties, grassroots organizations should pose the following questions:

> Will participation provide opportunities for raising political consciousness commensurate with the effort it demands? . . . Can [grassroots organizations] invest a major portion of [their] meager resources in [such activities] without neglecting other, more enduring forms of political work. . . ?
> . . . By entering electoral politics, does one lend a certain legitimacy to the political game one is trying to expose? (Parenti, p. 26)

By cooperating with political parties in the United States, community workers run the risk of becoming subtle agents of the established political system. Social workers engaged in community work "must be concerned with the ideology that supports . . . existing political institutions, [as] these institutions often perpetuate the systematic exclusion of the poor from the power network" (Quirion, 1972, p. 90). Instead of adapting our practice to the rules and interests of the status quo, organizers "have to project a vision of the . . . future that will reinvigorate democracy, rebuild larger loyalties, and inspire a new public morality. . . . [This requires] a return to themes of democratic participation and non-violent social change"—themes that are generally not reflected by political parties in the United States (Project 2000, p. 28).

The strength of grassroots community organizations lies in their ability to exert pressure on political parties through nontraditional means, beyond "politics as usual." This would involve work to broaden and diversity these organizations by focusing on specific issues, especially those ignored by political parties today. It would involve the creation of a decentralized infrastructure and institutional diversity—through, for example, the establishment of alternative centers of power—rather than becoming ancillary parts of established power structures. It would require the development of a diverse cadre of leaders and organizers, beyond the handpicked group selected by the party system. This would constitute true empowerment of grassroots organizations. Finally, it would involve the development of an organizing agenda that viewed electoral politics as *one component* of a broad, multilayered strategy for social change and not the all-consuming, short-term activity that, all too often, serves as the graveyard for the desperate hopes of people.

REFERENCES

Acuna, R. (1981). *Occupied America: The Chicanos' struggle for liberation*, New York: Harper and Row.

Browning, R., Tabb, D., & Marshall, D. R. (1990). *Racial politics in American cities*. New York: Longman.

Federal Election Commission, (1992). *Report on campaign spending*, Washington, DC: US Printing Office.

Gamson, W. (1975). *The strategy of social protest*, Homewood, IL: Dorsey Press.

Jezer, M. (1982, October). Citizens' Party: Can it live up to its name? *The Progressive, 46*(10) 36–38.

Quirion, H. (1972, September). Community organization and political action in Montreal. *Social Work, 17*(5) 85–90.

Parenti, M. (1982, October). The left: Do we party? *The Progressive, 46*(10) 23–26.

Project 2000. (1987, Spring). The emerging American progressive ideology. *Social Policy, 21*(2) 23–33.

Stone, C. N. (1988). Preemptive power: Floyd Hunter's 'community power structure' reconsidered. *American Journal of Political Science, 32* 81–104.

Thigpen, A. (1988, Fall). Quoted in Electoral politics in communities of color. *The Minority Trendsletter, 1*(4), 14–16.

Rejoinder to Professor Reisch

MARK G. HANNA AND
BUDDY ROBINSON

Professor Reisch performs admirable service in laying out the familiar litany of reasons why the radical left has remained highly skeptical of building linkages to political parties. In this view, such relationships are hampered by contradictory orientations, absence of reciprocity, a deleterious effect on progressive agendas, and the ''contamination'' of community organizers by party politicos. What we find interesting is that Professor Reisch concludes his rich, nay-saying narrative by suggesting that grassroots organizational agendas should include electoral politics as one component of a strategy for social change. This end point is the beginning point for our essay.

In the same way that Professor Reisch cedes the point that ''the context is ripe for grassroots involvement in electoral politics (and that this should be one of the agenda of such organizations, rather major concessions for a nay-sayer), we cede the point that most grassroots organizations would be foolhardy to tie their fortunes to the dog-and-pony shows of the national parties.

But there is much disagreement about the feasibility and utility of grass-roots organizational linkages, formal and informal, to local and state party organizations. In fact, failure to accurately come to grips with the problems associated with scale and power in the political enterprise lies at the center of Professor Reisch's flawed arguments.

The great problem for modern democracy is precisely the difficulty of adapting a republican constitutional legacy to the requirements of vastly ex-panded constituencies (Dahl, 1990). But even as national party organizations can no longer serve as effective mediating institutions for political education and political socialization (they serve best in the mobilization of bias), neither can myriad, fractious grassroots organizations adequately serve to aggregate the simultaneous interests (shared attitudes) of hundreds or thousands of unequally developed subgroups.

If Professor Reisch is perfectly content to condemn the parties to oblivion for their sin of not being grassroots enough, then what mechanism does he suggest to potentially counterbalance the growing dominance of multinational corporations and conservative political action committees (PACs)? A new third party? Spontaneous mass uprising? Enlightened noncompetition among community organizations?

The scale of social change goals undertaken by grassroots organizations is directly proportionate to the power of these organizations, and that power, more often than not, is tied to the increasing number and diversity of persons involved. As it is perfectly obvious that PAC money runs national and statewide elections, and as it is almost exclusively at the national level that Professor Reisch focuses, the result is marginalization and trivialization of the real prospects for unified grassroots action in conjunction with party work (which we reviewed in some detail in our own argument).

Instead of carefully reviewing the successful record of voter registration among Hispanics associated with the Industrial Areas Foundation projects (everyone knows Hispanics vote overwhelmingly Democratic), or considering the record of the Illinois Public Action Council or Ohio Citizens Action (where proactive campaigns regularly identify and back Democratic candidates for state office, backed by a broad coalition of grassroots organizations), Professor Reisch gives us examples of Santa Monica and Berkeley, California; Madison, Wisconsin; and Vermont. A cursory glance at the demographics of these areas reveals that none would qualify as economically depressed or heterogeneous on many dimensions. The entire state of Vermont has fewer than half a million people, and 98 percent of them are white. So it seems quite reasonable to find an insurgent Socialist Congressman from Vermont (Bernard Sanders) or a genuine radical like Tom Hayden of Santa Monica (last seen pumping a million and change into the closing hours of his Democratic re-election campaign to the California Assembly).

What's missing from Professor Reisch's analysis is the awareness that grassroots community organizing "ain't" what it used to be. There are increasing numbers of highly skilled organizers who understand power and the use of quid pro quo arrangements as well as any highly paid campaign consultant. Such organizers, valued by their grassroots sponsoring organizations, have built reciprocal accountability into their organizational structures. As a result, they can effectively maintain autonomy while linking selectively with parties on issues and candidates. Such loyalty is not fixed in stone but is shifting and dynamic, sometimes Republican, but mostly Democratic.

In his last paragraph, Professor Reisch himself begins to outline the formula for grassroots organizations that would have an effective relationship to political parties: "focusing on specific issues," "establishing alternative centers of power" and "developing a diverse cadre of leaders and organizers." Instead of a hypothetical fantasy, this is exactly what many (but certainly not all) community organizing projects are doing right now. Three key additions to this recipe are: (1) the construction of a strong culture of accountability, both internally and in external dealings with political figures, (2) a clear analysis of both sides' self-interests so that deals can be cut accordingly, and (3) a recognition that interaction with party structures cannot be restricted to election time; rather, it must extend to continually influence public policy. As Nick Von Hoffman put it in 1962, "the ballot box is the last resort of a citizenry that has not been looking after its affairs closely enough" (Social Progress, April, 1962).

We suspect that what really drives the arguments of Professor Reisch is his concern for ideological purity. Somehow, the scenario is set wherein weak and naive grassroots organizations watch meekly as their most articulate, motivated leaders become inexorably seduced and contaminated by hopelessly compromised "mainstream" party politicos and status quo platforms. We wonder if there isn't a failure to recognize that the majority of the grassroots organizations are decidedly "mainstream" in their goals, orientation, political philosophy and personal aspirations of members. There is also an apparent failure to recognize that some groups have built enough power and sophistication to be taken seriously and have succeeded in holding local and state political figures accountable to grassroots agendas on many occasions.

As much as Professor Reisch, and for that matter ourselves, might like it to be otherwise, perhaps Alinsky was closer to the truth when he spoke of the "haves," the "have-nots," and the "have a little, want mores." We are all for the maintenance of neo-liberal bearers of the counterhegemonic ideology. But if Santa Monica and Vermont are supposed to serve as models for achievement of alternative bases of power and oppositional community, is this any plausible strategy from which to spring the revolution?

In the same vein, it is hardly surprising that Professor Reisch waxes romantic about powerless immigrants and refugees who cannot vote as being "so essential to the success" of community organizations, while blithely ignoring the vastly more numerous ranks of low-income citizens who can, but are not registered. Savvy organizations make a beeline to these people, talk issues, register them, and so earn hefty political capital for bargaining with party officials.

What we need are sufficiently resourceful, large, and diverse grassroots organizations with well-trained organizers, staying in the faces of party organizations, cutting deals, making compromises, and remembering the everyday "have-not" and "have a little, want more" needs of people in Newark, St. Louis, Jacksonville, Chicago, Los Angeles, Oakland, and a hundred other places where regular folks wake up every day.

REFERENCES

Dahl, R. (1989). *Democracy and its critics.* New Haven: Yale University Press.
Von Hoffmann, N. (1962, April). Reorganization in the Casbah. *Social Progress,* pp. 33–44.

DEBATE 4

Should Targeted Services Organized by and for Women Be Integrated into Mainstream Human Service Organizations?

EDITOR'S NOTE: During the past decade, many agencies have emerged that have targeted their services to specific groups of people—gays and lesbians, women, the homeless, the chronically mentally ill, and the disabled. These nontraditional alternative agencies have sought to meet new and existing needs by emphasizing social change, flexibility, innovation, and a commitment to a specific ideology (e.g., feminism). The leadership often has emerged from the group that the agency has targeted for services. Both established and targeted service agencies attempt to manage and resolve complex social problems. However, they approach these problems from often radically different viewpoints. Therefore, using women's services as an example, the questions that underlie this debate are: Can established health and social services agencies address issues of oppression and inequity that have often kept certain groups from receiving needed services, and can targeted health and social services more effectively meet the needs of people who may not be accepted by the larger society and address those social problems that are seen as marginal concerns to established agencies?

George W. Appenzeller, M.S.W., and Sarah L. Meadows, M.S.W., argue YES. George Appenzeller directs research and evaluation on quality issues for the state health and human services agency in South Carolina. He conducts therapeutic and recreational wilderness adventures for children with special needs.

Sarah Meadows is Director of the quality assurance program of the substance abuse agency in South Carolina. She also conducts therapeutic and recreational wilderness adventures for women.

M. Sharon Maxwell, Ph.D., Patricia Y. Martin, Ph.D., Diane Byington, Ph.D., and Diana DiNitto, Ph.D., argue NO. Sharon Maxwell is Associate Professor of Social Work at Florida State University, where she teaches in the areas of community organizing and social policy. She has done research and written publications addressing feminist movement organizations. She has helped organize shelters for battered women and services for rape survivors.

Patricia Yancey Martin is Daisy Parker Flory Alumni Professor and Professor of Sociology at Florida State University (on sabbatical leave the University of Delaware during 1992–1993). Martin teaches the sociology of gender, work, and organizations and has published widely on social welfare organizations. She is coediting a book (with M. Ferree at the University of Connecticut) on feminist organizations, has a forthcoming paper on feminism and management, and is writing a monograph on the local politics of rape processing. Her newest project concerns the changing demographics of the labor force and their implications for women and men in corporations.

Diane Byington is Associate Professor of Social Work at the University of Denver, where she teaches in the area of health policy. Dr. Byington was coauthor with Dr. Maxwell, Dr. Martin, and Dr. DiNitto of a statewide needs assessment study in Florida for rape victims.

Diana DiNitto is Professor of Social Work at the University of Texas-Austin. Dr. DiNitto is the author of texts in social policy and substance abuse as well as the author of numerous articles in social work.

YES

GEORGE APPENZELLER AND SARAH MEADOWS

Targeted women's services that deal with issues such as sexual assault, domestic violence, and peer support form an important and necessary part of the continuum of services offered in the community. But, rather than have them replace services provided by established agencies, social work should strive to have them integrated into the mainstream agencies. There are four reasons why this integration should occur: First, in this society, serving certain individuals separately from everyone else reinforces an impression of their inequality. Second, placing such services outside the mainstream segregates women's services, and their problems, in a ghetto where they can be comfortably isolated. Third, creation of a parallel system for women's services gets established agencies and organizations "off the hook," so that they no longer have the burden of being responsive to women's issues. Fourth, separate women's services are at a disadvantage in competing for increasingly scarce resources.

Social work values emphasize respect and dignity of the individual. These values have been the underpinnings of the support social workers have provided to movements such as equal opportunity in education and employment. Social workers, individually and as a profession, have supported these movements at great personal and professional cost. But the cost has been considered less important than the continued movement toward a more integrated, egalitarian, democratic society. In recent years, there has been a tendency in the nation and in social work to turn away from the integrative ideal. Instead, groups with problems that need attention have asked that attention to be given in a singular manner. Or, at least, those who hold themselves forth as representing those groups have asked for specialized (i.e., segregated) services. These groups range from the elderly to head- and spinal-cord-injured persons, as well as advocacy groups for women. All these groups believe, often with good cause, that their needs are not being met to the extent they should be by the existing service system.

Historically, in social work and in the nation, the reaction of disfranchised groups has been to push to enter the mainstream and gain access to established institutions. After all, that's where the resources are. *And, much more importantly, that is where our social and constitutional tradition serves people who have standing in the community.* Thurgood Marshall expressed this idea clearly in his 1954 argument before the Supreme Court in *Brown v. Board of Education.* He argued that if the Court were to sustain the legality of segregated schools ''. . . the only way to arrive at this decision is to find that for some reason Negroes are inferior to all other human beings.'' The Court, of course, agreed and declared that ''separate educational facilities are inherently unequal.'' It may be argued that the same inequality applies to any service that is considered to be the responsibility of the society as a whole.

Organizations, on the whole, resist change. This resistance holds true in regard to women's issues as well as many others. However, once change occurs, and becomes institutionalized, the mainstream organization itself becomes the protector. Only a strong outside influence can undo that which has occurred. For example, in the 1970s and 1980s, there was a long and difficult battle to establish humane and effective procedures for hospitals and police to conduct investigations of rape. In many jurisdictions, that battle has been won and protocols are now a routine part of doing business. Independent rape crisis centers and advocates helped win better treatment for victims. But so did hospital administrators, law enforcement agencies, private organizations, social service agencies, and many others. To now say to these supporters, ''Thanks for your help, but we're taking our targeted services and going over there to operate'' would be to reject the broad community support that made those services possible. Putting services into a ghetto would thus strip the services of the protection of the larger organizations. At the same time, it would provide an opportunity for reactionary forces to watch, isolate, and eventually eliminate targeted services.

When targeted women's services are provided in a separate but parallel system, it becomes easy for mainline organizations to ignore women's needs. The organizational conscience begins to atrophy. They no longer have to respond to these annoying problems because they have no responsibility. Moreover, they no longer have any perceived obligation to support this type of programming. Why should they? Someone else is taking care of it. This organizational tendency appears particularly acute in the health care establishment. Despite the advocacy provided by the women's health care movement, which began in the 1960s, women continue to receive a lower quality of care from physicians and hospitals than their male counterparts (Muller, 1986). It is important to utilize the values of social work practice to challenge the complacency of organizations. Broader awareness of specialized needs of women can be incorporated into mainstream social work practice (Valentich, 1992). Social workers can and should provide leadership within mainstream organizations to see that this occurs, just as we have challenged racism and other forms of injustice and insensitivity.

Targeted services are at a distinct disadvantage in competing with mainstream organizations for scarce resources. In more prosperous times, established agencies can afford to support funding applications by women's and other special interest groups. However, when the resource pie itself is shrinking, established organizations usually have more broad community support for their continuation. Many women's shelters established in the 1970s were heavily dependent on Comprehensive Employment and Training Act (CETA)-funded positions. When that program ended, some shelters had to close because communities were unwilling to provide ongoing funding. Rape crisis centers founded with Law Enforcement Assistance Administration (LEAA) and other specialized grants later received local government support. However, as the federal support for local government has diminished in recent years, the local competition for funds has increased. Often, the targeted services are the losers (Davis & Hagen, 1988). Large institutions have also been hurt by the economy, but they can shift resources so that services can survive within the structure.

Independent, single-issue organizations serve an important role in the service delivery system. That role often is taking risks that established organizations cannot or will not take- for political reasons or because of inertia. Specialized organizations can innovate, change rapidly, test, experiment, prove, and advocate. But once the innovation, change, experimentation, testing, or advocacy has occurred and a viable service option had been established, it is time for the specialized organization to turn over the reins to someone else. The new organization should have the stability and the resources necessary to nurture and expand the services that have been developed.

There is a natural life cycle to special-interest movements such as that which has created targeted women's services. A notable example of this life cycle is the movement for handicapped rights, which began with peer support, continued through advocacy for specific services, and resulted in political action. This movement has matured through integration into the mainstream of service delivery. This access and mainstreaming were recently institutionalized in law through the Americans with Disabilities Act. Once case law is established, services and access will be part of the fabric of institutional and community life. The movement, as such, will no longer be viable. It will have achieved its mission. The movement for targeted women's services must follow that same course, or it will find itself simply fading away.

REFERENCES

Davis, L. V., & Hagen, J. L. (1988, December). Services for battered women: The public policy response. *Social Service Review, 62*(4), 649–647.
Hagen, J. L. (1990). Designing services for homeless women. *Journal of Health and Social Policy, 1*(3), 1–16.
Muller, C. (1986, Summer). Women and men: Quality and equality in health care. *Social Policy, 17*(1), 39–45.
The guide to American law, Vol. 2 (pp. 179–182). (1983). St. Paul, MN: West Publishing.
The Boston Women's Health Book Collective. (1984). *The new our bodies, our selves.* New York: Simon and Schuster.
Valentich, M. (1992, Summer). Toward gender-sensitive clinical social work practice. *Arete, 17*(1), 1–12.

Rejoinder to Mr. Appenzeller and Ms. Meadows

SHARON MAXWELL, ET AL.

In responding to the argument presented by Mr. Appenzeller and Ms. Meadows against having the targeted services organized by and for women replace those provided by mainstream human service organizations, it might be said that our respective arguments, like ships, have passed in the night. Our research strongly supports the efforts of rape crisis centers (RCCs) to continue providing what in some communities is the only targeted service to rape survivors; in others, critical services are not offered with either the same commitment or philosophical framework from which to understand the rape experience. We maintain that mainstream human service organizations that process rape survivors have a generalist mandate that, unfortunately, dilutes their efforts in responding to the specific needs of rape survivors.

There appear to be major points of disagreement in our respective arguments. First, we maintain that providing services for rape survivors separately from "everyone else" in no way creates an impression of inequality. To the contrary, as described in our NO argument, rape crisis centers have emerged as a way of reacting to widespread abuse and rejection of rape survivors by the very mainstream human service organizations, such as hospitals and law enforcement agencies, that are mandated by society to process them (Burgess & Holmstrom, 1979). This "second assault," as it has become known, may be less tolerable by now to some in mainstream organizations, but by no measure has it become eliminated or even significantly reduced. The presence of a rape crisis center in a community puts ongoing pressure on these organizations to respond appropriately to rape victims' needs. We are not arguing that targeted rape services can provide all interventions necessary on behalf of rape victims; indeed, we recognize that the nature of rape mandates involvement by mainstream organizations such as hospitals and law enforcement agencies. Our research suggests, however, that when the functions most often provided by rape crisis centers become integrated into more mainstream organizations the needs of victims become less well served.

Further, we found that rape crisis centers appear to lose some of their focus—for example, their outreach, their community education activities—and thus their effectiveness the more they become affiliated with social service, health care or mental health center organizations (Byington, Martin, DiNitto, & Maxwell, 1991). This is due in no small part to the fact that RCCs serve rape survivors by engaging not only in direct service activities but also by engaging in social change activities and in community organizations. It is these latter two foci that appear to become diluted on affiliation with more mainstream organizations and thus the organizations themselves are less able or less willing to address the structural precipitants of rape.

Second, targeted services to rape survivors from our perspective are neither parallel service systems nor vehicles for getting established agencies' organizations "off the hook" with respect to womens' concerns. This "off the hook" fallacy is not in any manner supported by research. In fact, the contrary is indicated—that is, the presence of an active rape crisis center (RCC) in a community serves a critical purpose in being a conscience for more established agencies to do right by rape victims. It is often when a rape crisis center is not present that the recurring lack of response to rape survivors goes unchecked.

Rape survivors who report their assault (roughly one in ten) are processed by law enforcement agencies that investigate the assault or by hospitals, which are used most frequently as merely the site at which the rape kit examination is performed. (Note: this is an activity done to aid in the prosecution of the assailant, not an activity done on behalf of the victim. Prosecutors, if the assailant is to be prosecuted, will then process the victim as a "witness.") Thus, the mandate of these agencies with respect to the crime of rape dictates their interaction with the victim. It thus should be obvious that RCCs do not attempt to perform processing functions in any type of parallel service system. Few RCCs are equipped to perform the rape exam, and those that do are most frequently affiliated with larger human service organizations. Obviously, no RCCs allege to perform law enforcement or prosecutorial functions.

What RCCs do perform are activities directed on behalf of the victim within a feminist framework that sees empowerment and the regaining of control over the victim's life as the critical needs of the rape survivor. Rape crisis centers hold distinctive political views of and about rape that are derived from their origins and alignment with the larger women's movement, rather than from a mainstream psychopathological interpretation of rape.

These distinctions in philosophy and service provision contradict any notion of rape crisis centers offering a parallel service system. These services, for the most part, are unduplicated services *not* provided by established agencies or by mainstream human service organizations. As our NO argument states, rape crisis centers are unique among organizations dealing with the issue of rape in their community education activities; their emphasis is on crisis intervention, psychosocial and advocacy support, and the overall amount of contact they have with rape survivors (Maxwell, 1987).

Finally, while we agree that separate women's services are at a distinct disadvantage for resources, we argue that this is no excuse for not providing targeted services for women. That such services are recognized as being at such a disadvantage acknowledges the oppression of women and those organizations devoted to women's concerns by larger societal forces. Our research suggests that those rape crisis centers that have faced dwindling resources and merged with mainstream human service organizations have changed both their foci and their emphasis on service delivery and that this change has been less favorable to the needs of rape victims (Byington et al., 1991).

We acknowledge that many rape crisis centers are quasi-volunteer, but this organizational status does not appear to detract from their organizational performance. Despite having low budgets, few paid staff, and heavy volunteer reliance, rape crisis centers have managed to interact with many more rape survivors than have their mainstream counterparts and have provided the extensive community education and services previously described (Maxwell, 1987; Byington et al., 1991).

While it may be true that at times movement organizations are successful at identifying injustice and instituting appropriate responses to the extent that service integration can occur, it is unlikely that this will occur in the near future with respect to services targeted for women. Indeed, the current political backlash against women calls for even more specialized services and continued support for those existing targeted services such as our example of rape crisis centers.

REFERENCES

Burgess, A. W., & Holmstrom, L. L. (1979). *Rape: Crisis & Recover.* MD: Brady.

Byington, D. B., Martin, P. Y., DiNitto, D., & Maxwell, M. S. (1991). Organizational affiliation and effectiveness: The case of rape crisis centers. *Administration in Social Work, 15*(3),

Maxwell, M. S. (1987). Rape crisis centers and mainstream human service organizations: Community education and service. Ph.D. dissertation. Tallahassee, FL: Florida State University.

NO

M. Sharon Maxwell, Patricia Y. Martin, Diane Byington, and Diana DiNitto

To better understand why targeted services organized by and for women, such as rape crisis centers, should not be replaced by mainstream or established human service organizations it is necessary to understand how and why such targeted services have emerged. Using rape crisis centers as an example of such targeted services, this argument presents a comparison of the differences between feminist movement organizations, such as rape crisis centers, and mainstream human service organizations and a description of the history of the anti-rape movement and the emergence of rape crisis centers out of this movement and their resulting structural arrangements. It also discusses the unique contributions of feminist organizations to the needs of rape survivors and to societal reform.

Feminist movement organizations (FMOs) are entities developing out of the women's movement in the last twenty-five years that provide social services, medical care, and educational activities to or on behalf of women, while also acting as vehicles for social change (Riger, 1984; Maxwell, 1987; Martin, 1990; Feree & Hess, 1985). Rape crisis centers are particular examples of FMOs that developed out of the anti-rape movement in the 1960s (O'Sullivan, 1978). Feminist movement organizations differ from mainstream human service organizations in their commitment to providing services aimed at empowering women as well as in their commitment to challenge societal attitudes about the existing role of women. Rape crisis centers are a type of feminist movement organization—as are feminist health centers, birthing centers, and battered women shelters—that represent alternative responses for women in need of specific social or medical services.

Mainstream human service organizations (HSOs) are health, social service, and criminal justice agencies sanctioned by the community to perform a specific activity with or on behalf of the general public, such as those activities conducted on behalf of rape survivors by law enforcement agencies or hospitals (Hasenfeld & English, 1974). Feminist movement organizations recognize that mainstream HSOs frequently are administered from a perspective that devalues the experience of women and fails to respond to the needs of rape victims.

Based on our research, we conclude that rape victims are better served in communities with specialized rape crisis centers (RCCs). RCCs provide a range and quality of services to victims that other organizations rarely offer; also, mainstream human service organizations treat rape victims better when an RCC is located in the community. Few communities that lack a rape crisis center treat victims in responsive or expert ways. We found that freestanding rape crisis centers are the most helpful to victims, followed by RCCs affiliated with governmental social and health care organizations; RCCs affiliated with community mental health centers are least effective (see Byington, Martin, DiNitto,

& Maxwell, 1991). What dynamics and conditions lie behind these claims? Why do we favor the continuation of specialized rape crisis centers over the view that mainstream human service organizations can now take over? Our answers are based on research on 130 Florida organizations that process rape victims. Twenty-five are specialized RCCs—with seven different affiliated homes—and the remaining 105 include police, sheriffs, hospital emergency rooms, state prosecutors, physicians and health clinics, children's service agencies, and similar organizations (see Martin, DiNitto, Norton, & Maxwell, 1984; Maxwell, 1987; Byington et al., 1991).

What Is Service to Rape Victims from the Purview of Rape Crisis Centers?

In our view, services to rape victims must be broadly defined. RCCs serve rape victims by engaging in social change and community organization as well as direct service—treatment and advocacy—activities. For example, RCCs undertake community education and social change work to increase general awareness of the structural precipitants of rape and to alter understandings of rape crimes; they teach rape victims that their rape is a result of men's collective privilege and women's collective oppression; and they engage in a range of practices to help victims receive the best services and support, including those provided by mainstream organizations.

The anti-rape wing of the new women's movement of the 1970s and 1980s viewed the domain and mission of RCCs as multifaceted. They viewed the ultimate explanation for rape crimes as women's inequality and oppression. To stop rape, society—especially men and the structures of privilege and advantage for men—must change. Women's inequality must be eliminated; men must stop tolerating rape in other men; and women (and girls) must be valued equally as much as men (and boys). Anti-rape groups claimed that society misconstrues rape crimes and blames female victims for failing to control male sexuality and aggression. Citizens fail to understand that rape is a hostile act directed by men at women in a show of domination, control, force, and humiliation. RCC activities claimed that many mainstream human service organization staff members endorse the same myths and flawed understandings of rape as citizens do. Thus, rape crisis centers tried (and try) to reach these staff, teach them about rape, and lobby them to change their practices and behavior. Long before a rape victim is directly served by a processing organization, rape crisis center activities promote a conception of rape that attributes it to women's inequality and attempt to change processing organizations and the community. We view these proactive, social change efforts as a service to all women in society, especially the victims of rape. Many rape crisis centers work especially hard at communicating their understandings of rape crimes to mainstream processing organizations.

How Did Rape Crisis Centers Emerge?

Concerns about the treatment of survivors of sexual assault became a dominant issue in the women's movement by the mid-1960s when feminists began meeting in consciousness-raising groups to compare their experiences of being victims of discrimination, spouse abuse, and sexual assault (Connell & Wilson, 1974; Rose, 1977). Rape speak-outs followed, drawing public attention to expose the mythology associated with the occurrence of rape. As a feminist analysis of rape emerged—one that viewed rape as serving both a social and political function to keep women powerless—feminists adopted the position that feminist action (i.e., women taking responsibility for the well-being and survival of other women) was imperative to address the problem of rape.

Out of this action in the late 1960s and early 1970s emerged the first rape crisis centers. These early rape crisis centers were seen as specialized feminist movement organizations established to deal with the specific needs of rape survivors as well as to sponsor social change activities aimed at changing prevailing beliefs about rape (Maxwell, 1987).

Early rape crisis centers were for the most part freestanding, feminist organizations unaffiliated with sponsoring mainstream organizations. By adopting a feminist approach to the issue of rape, these early centers also adopted structural and staffing arrangements that reflected their opposition to traditional hierarchical structures. Feminist analysis of rape was an integral part of the philosophy of the early centers and provided the framework from which to train center volunteers and deliver services (Gornick, Burt, & Pittman, 1983). As FMOs, rape crisis centers viewed rape assistance as a political activity (Martin, DiNitto, Byington, & Maxwell, 1992; Largen, 1981; Gornick et al., 1983) and often took measures to avoid being identified as mainstream human social service providers.

While most early rape crisis centers were freestanding organizations, there was also an early trend for anti-rape movement members to push for the establishment of rape crisis centers within local hospitals or other human service organizations (Gager & Schurr, 1976; Hicks & Platt, 1976). By the mid-1970s, rape crisis centers were being sponsored by churches, YWCAs, and other social service organizations (Connell & Wilson, 1974; Largen, 1976; O'Sullivan, 1978; Byington et al., 1991).

Despite differences in organizational form, certain activities were and remain common features of rape crisis centers: hotlines or crisis telephone services, information and referral, counseling, advocacy, public education, lobbying, and sensitivity training for law enforcement agencies. While not all rape crisis centers provide this entire continuum of interventions they remain the organizations within communities that provide the greatest number of activities for rape survivors (Maxwell, 1987; Byington et al., 1991).

Why Are Rape Crisis Centers Better?

As women's movement organizations, RCCs understand rape as a political issue involving social injustice and the need for fundamental social change (see Gornick, et al., 1983). Their conceptions of the services that rape victims need is feminist; they see empowerment and the regaining of control over her life as the overarching need of a rape victim (Koss & Harvey, 1991). RCC activities hold political views of and about rape that are derived from their women's movement origins and alignment rather than from standard materials in psychology or mental health curricula.

Maxwell (1987) examined the activities of rape crisis centers as compared with the activities of mainstream human service organizations that also deal with rape issues from a secondary data analysis of Martin et al. (1984). Specifically, the emphasis placed on community education activities by these two types of organizations, the foci of their community education messages, the targets of their community education activities, the emphasis they place on intervention activities, and the extensiveness of their outreach efforts were compared.

Rape crisis centers were found to do far more community education presentations (presentations or demonstrations made by a member of an organization to inform others about rape-related issues) than did staff of mainstream HSOs such as prosecutors, staffs of ERs, or social service agencies (Maxwell, 1987). Byington et al. (1991) also reported that freestanding rape crisis centers, those unaffiliated with other organizations, were more likely to be involved in education activities aimed at rape prevention and that the lowest rape prevention intensity was found in rape services provided through community mental health centers.

This emphasis by rape crisis centers on community education is consistent with the activities of feminist movement organizations and different from community education activities of mainstream HSOs. In the emerging years of the anti-rape movement, rape crisis centers emphasized the importance of community education in challenging inappropriate institutional responses and stereotypes about rape.

Rape crisis centers also employ community education messages with a social change foci more than mainstream human service organizations (Maxwell, 1987). These messages confront myths and stereotypes about sexual assault, discuss appropriate intervention strategies with rape survivors, and highlight the prevalence of date/acquaintance rape.

In their community education activities, rape crisis centers target different audiences than do mainstream HSOs. Rape crisis centers are more likely to reach staff of established human service organizations in their educational activities in an effort to effect institutional changes in how these HSOs respond to rape survivors, particularly those HSOs charged with processing rape survivors. Additionally, rape crisis centers are more likely to reach out to potential rape victims such as school children, university students, and civic/women's groups as well as the general public. Rape crisis centers are unique among organizations dealing with the issue of rape in their efforts to reach out to both the staff of other organizations and to potential victim gaps with their community educational activities (Maxwell, 1987).

Rape crisis centers emphasize psychosocial/medical activities, primarily crisis intervention, as well as support services, primarily advocacy (Maxwell, 1987). Hospital emergency rooms concentrate on providing medical treatment and performing the rape kit examination, whereas law enforcement agencies and prosecutors emphasize processing activities that are closely associated with their social mandate for interacting with rape survivors. Despite research in the past decade that supports the use of more psychosocial/medical and support activities by mainstream HSOs when interacting with rape survivors, these organizations often have not increased their emphasis in these areas. In the presence of an active rape crisis center in a community this might not be problematic; in the absence of a rape crisis center or in the event mainstream HSOs do not utilize the services of a rape crisis center, then this lack of psychosocial emphasis may well hinder a survivor's ability to successfully recover from an assault.

Rape crisis centers also have contact with far more rape survivors than do mainstream human service organizations in communities where they exist (Maxwell, 1987). While this is not surprising, it is important to note that many rape crisis centers are quasi-volunteer programs (Byington et al., 1991; Maxwell, 1987). That these rape crisis centers are able to reach as many rape survivors as they do with relatively low budgets, few paid staff, and heavy reliance on volunteers is in and of itself a testimony to their commitment to the anti-rape movement. Mainstream human service organizations that process rape survivors may require survivors to agree to prosecute, to notify law enforcement, or to pass some other litmus test before services are provided. Most rape crisis centers operate an "open door" policy with respect to rape survivors and provide services whether the survivor intends to report, prosecute, or in any fashion interact with mainstream human service providers.

REFERENCES

Burgess, A. W., & Holmstrom, L. L. (1979). *Rape: Crisis & recovery.* Bowie, MD: Brady.

Byington, D. B., Martin, P. Y., DiNitto, D., & Maxwell, M. S. (1991). Organizational affiliation and effectiveness: The case of rape crisis centers. *Administration in Social Work, 15*(3), pp. 83–103.

Connell, N., & Wilson, C. (1974). *Rape: The first sourcebook for women.* New York: New American Library.

DiNitto, D., Martin, P. Y., Byington, D., & Maxwell, M. S. (1986). After rape: Who should examine rape survivors? *American Journal of Nursing, 86,* 538–540.

DiNitto, D., Martin, P. Y., Maxwell, M. S., & Norton, D. B. (1989). Rape treatment programs: Delivering innovative services to survivors. *Medicine and Law, 8,* 21–30.

Ferree, M. M., & Hess, B. (1985). *Controversy and coalition: The new feminist movement.* Boston: Twayne Publishers.

Gager, N., & Schurr, C. (1976). *Sexual assault: Confronting rape in America.* New York: Grossett & Dunlap.

Gornick, J., Burt, M., & Pittman, K. (1983). *Structure and activities of rape crisis centers in the early 1980s.* Washington, DC: The Urban Institute.

Hasenfeld, Y. & English, R. A. (1974). *Human service organizations.* Ann Arbor, MI.

Hicks, D. J., & Platt, C. (1976). Medical treatment for the rape victim: The development of a rape treatment center. In M. J. Walker and S. L. Brodsky (Eds.), *Sexual assault* (pp. 53–59). Lexington, MA: Lexington Books.

Koss, M., & Harvey, M. (1991). The rape victim: *Clinical and community interventions.* CA: Sage Publications.

Largen, M. A. (1976, Summer). Grassroots centers and national task forces: A history of the anti-rape movement. *Aegis, 46–52.*

Martin, P. Y. (1990). Rethinking feminist organizations. *Gender and Society, 4,* 182–206.

Martin, P. Y., DiNitto, D., Norton, D. B., & Maxwell, M. S. (1984). *Sexual assault: Services to rape victims in Florida.* Tallahassee, FL: Department of Health and Rehabilitative Services, State of Florida.

Martin, P. Y., DiNitto, D., Byington, D., & Maxwell, M. S. (1992). Organizational and community transformation: The case of a rape crisis center. *Administration in Social Work 15*(3), 123–145.

Maxwell, M. S. (1987). Rape crisis centers and mainstream human service organizations: Community education and service. Ph.D. dissertation. Tallahassee, FL: Florida State University.

O'Sullivan, E. (1978). What has happened to rape crisis centers? A look at their structures, numbers and funding. *Victimology, 3,* 45–62.

Riger, S. (1984). Vehicles for empowerment: The case for feminist movement organizations. *Prevention in Human Services, 3*(2–3), 99–117.

Rejoinder to Dr. Maxwell, et al.

GEORGE APPENZELLER AND SARAH MEADOWS

Dr. Maxwell and her associates base their argument on the assumption that mainline health and social service organizations are too sexist to develop policy to provide the services women need. They contend that the oppressors of women are in control of all organizations except those established in the last twenty-five years by women politicized in a certain way. This view of the issue ignores many of the values and much of the practice knowledge of professional social workers.

The ending of oppression through clinical and organizational interventions is a fundamental goal of all social workers, wherever they may practice. Clinically the desired outcome is to empower the victim to become independent of the oppressor. With organizations, the desired outcome is to empower the organization to end oppression internally and to support the ending of oppression externally. Dr. Maxwell and her associates seem to assume that professionals in mainline health and social service organizations are unable, or unwilling, to carry out this fundamental social work goal with and for female sexual assault victims.

The emphasis placed by our counterparts on cultivating the political awareness of victims seems to overlook another value: that we should help people where they are, not where we are. Before people can be free, an assured source of food, shelter, clothing, and physical security must exist for themselves and those for whom they are responsible. Many, if not most, victims of sexual assault are without this assurance. Until these needs are satisfied, victims are in no position to strive for self-actualization through awareness of their natural rights. And these basic needs are satisfied in the old, established agencies.

The dependence of rape crisis services on a volunteer work force, cited as a strength by Dr. Maxwell, is also problematical. Although volunteers can enlarge the scope of awareness in the community, long-term dependence on volunteers to carry out complex support and social services may often deny clients the opportunity to receive the services most appropriate to help them with their problems. Trained staff in mainline organizations value the need for professional services, augmented by volunteers.

Dr. Maxwell and her associates do not present a compelling argument on the benefit to be gained by victims if rape crisis services continue to be on the fringe of the service delivery system. Victims deserve competent professional services and are more likely to get them from mainline agencies. If oppression is to be ended, the major battles must be fought and won in the mainline agencies. In these settings are the clients, the resources, and the professionals who can make women's services a legitimate part of the mainstream.

Should Health and Human Services Be Decentralized into Neighborhood Social Health Centers Managed by the Community?

EDITOR'S NOTE: The debate about whether health and human services should be centralized or decentralized has been ongoing. During the 1960s the major thrust was to decentralize services into communities. Community leaders were given responsibility for controlling and managing health and human services. During the 1970s and 1980s services were not only centralized, but also were increasingly cut due to budget constraints. However, during the past several years, interest has increased in moving human and health services back to the communities. Given the intractability of many social problems and the fragmentation of health and human services designed to deal with them, several questions must now be addressed: Are decentralized neighborhood service centers that combine health and human services the preferred model for managing interrelated and complex social problems because they can respond more quickly and effectively to the changing needs of clients and the social environment? Are centralized services better able to deliver efficient services, make greater use of scarce resources, and meet the needs of a wide variety of clients by adhering to established guidelines and procedures? Which form of service delivery is most likely to empower clients?

Jacqueline Azzarto, Ph.D., argues YES. She is Assistant Professor of Social Work at Skidmore College and Adjunct Assistant Professor of Family Medicine at Albany Medical College. Her research focuses on the ways physician and medical institution maintain family-like functions in the lives of the elderly and the disadvantaged. Her work has been published in medical and social work journals.

Mary F. Smith, M.S.W., Ph.D., answers NO. She is Associate Professor and Post-Graduate Coordinator in the Department of Family Practice at Albany Medical College. Dr. Smith has twenty-five years of professional social work experience in the field of adolescent and community mental health and in graduate medical education. She has written in the areas of residency stress, caregivers of the elderly, teaching strategies, and hearing screening in a clinical setting.

YES

JACQUELINE AZZARTO

The delivery of health and human services in neighborhood-based, community-managed programs is a concept that we rarely see actualized. I, however, have had the privilege of spending a year researching and practicing in a family health center in a small upstate New York urban community. This organization embodied many of the principles of ideal community care. Inspired by the professional dedication and quality service I observed, I will argue that social workers should be promoting policies that support the neighborhood social health center.

The most obvious reason for supporting neighborhood social health centers is that they improve access to medical and psychosocial care. Access to care has many components that involve the client, the environment, the "system," and the provider. Some of these include: financial constraints; language and literacy barriers; transportation problems; culturally defined perceptions of illness; conflicts among patients, family, and friends regarding the interpretation of symptoms; bureaucratic regulations; and unwelcoming behavior on the part of service providers. It is my contention that many of these barriers could be reduced and in some instances eliminated in the environment of a neighborhood social health center.

To begin with, travel to and from neighborhood health centers is not a problem for residents of the neighborhood. Most centers, however, have a catchment area that extends beyond the neighborhood. Helping clients who have travel problems, in my experience, is expertly done by community members who work at the center. They know the tricks of navigating public transportation and arranging rides. They are sometimes willing to deliver a client personally. In the center where I worked everyone did their part to get the clients to their appointments. In addition, some services were delivered "on the streets." Outreach workers provided education and prevention programs to high-risk, hard to engage clients. The most effective services were delivered by an indigenous outreach worker from the "hill" community where the clients lived.

Another aspect of client access is the embarrassment that patients feel concerning their inability to pay and their problems with language and reading. It is my opinion that these concerns are best handled by workers who look and act like the clients. This is not to say that trained professionals are insensitive to the feelings of clients, but the actual disclosure of delicate issues may be easier when one thinks that the listener might have experienced the same problem.

Indigenous service providers, as well as clients, can "be themselves" in the environment of the social health care center. In being themselves they can help the professionals who are not from the neighborhood better understand the clients and their lives. At case conferences in the health center in which I worked it was not unusual for a community staff member to fill us in on facts about the client and his or her situation that we might never have known otherwise. What might have seemed like gossip in a different context was valuable information, because behavior factors are important in assessing and treating client problems in that context. Community employees not only help clients feel more comfortable at the center, but in these instances they are improving treatment at the center. They provide us with knowledge that is best acquired in neighborhoods— knowledge of life-styles, ethnicity and culture, unique problems and resources, strengths and weaknesses (Rubin & Rubin, 1992).

My next argument for the support of community social health care centers deals with the issue of empowering members of the neighborhood, as opposed to rendering them passive recipients of center services. "Of the people, by the people and for the people" is a basic democratic principle that inspires and empowers us all. However, many poor people have been denied the right to govern themselves and have been relegated to the position of societal dependents. Social workers are committed to helping the poor rise above this position. According to the National Association of Social Workers, it is an essential attribute of a democratic society that each individual realize full potential and assume responsibility through active participation in society (National Association of Social Workers, 1958). For members of the neighborhood, this translates into getting involved in the center. Getting involved can take many forms, some of which I observed at the family health center. One can volunteer or participate in groups. One can help with a particular project or just "hang out." But being involved instills a sense of belonging, and accomplishing a task improves self-esteem. It empowers the individual. It helps the community member cultivate skills that can be applied to other areas of their lives, such as developing assertiveness, improving communication, managing stress, resolving conflicts, and bargaining (Van Den Berg & Cooper, 1986).

Empowerment of clients can be viewed as the feminist perspective on power, as compared to the patriarchal perspective which emphasizes control and subordination. Processes involving the use of patriarchal power promote dichotomies that lead to conditions of the "haves and have nots" (Van Den Berg & Cooper, 1986). Social workers at times are unaware that they are conceptualizing power in a traditional patriarchal way. I support Van Den Berg's and Cooper's position that the profession should be more proactive in the advancement of feminist principles which reconceptualize power as a widely distributed energy of influences, strengths, and responsibilities. Such influences, strengths, and responsibilities felt in a neighborhood social health care center create an organization that fulfills the feminist vision. Since the majority of social work practitioners and clients are women we have an obligation to realize that ideal.

My final comments address issues concerning the actual management of the social health center. If one were to compare the current bureaucratic structure of many social and health care programs with a more collective-democratic model (Rothschild-Whitt, 1979), bearers of social work values would have a difficult time defending the formalized rules, social control, and specialization that are characteristic of bureaucratic systems. Although democratic management involving community leaders may be a more time-consuming and inefficient alternative to an autocratic style, one could argue that involvement in decision making encourages greater cooperation and compliance on the part of our hard to reach clients. We will always be confined by the bureaucratic limitations of larger systems, but a community-managed program that is creative in its implementation of policies might well serve clients more effectively and more compassionately than a traditional clinic or social service department. Although community leaders may not possess the technical and professional skills necessary for optimum management, I assert that high-tech expertise can be purchased in the marketplace. Naturally acquired knowledge of the community and its people, on the other hand, is a priceless commodity when faced with the task of designing and delivering high-risk services. In addition, according to Neugeboren (1985), in any organization it is impossible for top-level management to have extensive expert knowledge. What is more important for legitimacy is that management stand for justice. Who could better represent justice for the people than community leaders themselves?

The Department of Health in Toronto (Labonte, 1992) has put forth an empowerment model for the delivery of health care that emphasizes "power with" versus "power over" the people and stresses the importance of a true partnership between the community and the health care delivery system. In each of the five steps in the model (personal care, group development, community organization, coalition advocacy, and political action) community management is intrinsic to implementation. Particularly in the area of group development and community organization, the importance of recognizing and working with community leaders is the essence of the concept. In group development the natural leaders help build a stronger sense of community, which can become organized to become a political voice. The role of the professionals is that of providing expertise, whether it be medical knowledge and skill or public health research. Labonte emphasizes that unlike people who respond to tears, institutions respond to statistics. Professionals can respond to the tears of their patients, but they must also help community managers produce the studies and the statistics that will legitimize their appeals to funding sources, medical institutions, and government.

In conclusion, it is important to note that the concept of decentralized community-managed social service agencies has been cast in shadows of controversy since the failure of the War on Poverty. Grassroots community action agencies of the 1960s, however, were focused on curing the poor rather than caring for them. Community organizers believed they knew best. In addition, they were plagued with innumerable implementation problems, not the least of which were insufficient funds, radical upper-class workers, and unrealistic expectations. Given these failures of the past, social workers of the 1990s who support the promotion of community-managed neighborhood social health care centers must be more diligent. We must be careful to approach implementation with rationality and practicality. It is not enough to say "We tried that once." What we must say now is, "Try, try again." The work is critical because the issues of empowerment of communities and the improvement of health care for the poor are too important for social workers to give up on the effort.

REFERENCES

Labonte, R. (1992). *Uniting for healthy communities.* Presentation at the 120th Annual Meeting of the American Public Health Association in Washington, DC.

National Association of Social Workers. (1958). Working definition of social work practice. *Social Work, 3*(2), 3.

Neugeboren, B. (1985). *Organization, policy and practice in human services.* New York: Longman.

Rothschild-Whitt, J. (1979). The collectivist organization. *American Sociological Review, 44,* 519.

Rubin, G., & Rubin, I. (1992). *Community organizing and development.* New York: Macmillan.

Van Den Berg, N., & Cooper, L. (1986). Introduction. In N. Van Den Berg and L. Cooper (Eds.) *Feminist visions for social work.* Silver Springs, MD: NASW.

Rejoinder to Dr. Azzarto   MARY F. SMITH

I agree completely with the framework of the biopsychosocial approach to the delivery of human services as presented by Dr. Azzarto. I also agree that prevention is the key to good health care and that medicine should be concerned about caring, not just curing.

One of the common definitions of health is the absence of disease. According to Dobelstein (1990), policy analysis assumes that "health policy is a composite effort to maintain or to restore equilibrium, so as to prevent or remedy disequilibrium, usually understood as disease'' (p. 150). Prevention, therefore, is the key to a successful health policy and delivery system. In my opinion, centralized health and human service centers are concerned with both care and cure, with prevention and treatment, and with research and education. In particular, most such health facilities have primary care departments where patients are treated as individuals who are part of a family system and part of the community constellation. Their needs are met by experts in the field of health and human services; the treatment staff are professionally trained, rather than on-the-job trained; the emphasis is on caring and prevention; and the facility is mandated to serve the needs of patients from all social and economic backgrounds. No one feels slighted in the care they receive.

Centralized health centers can and do place much emphasis on prevention and patient education. To illustrate, smoking cessation programs are held regularly and are open to all interested in participating. Fitness and wellness programs, stress management seminars, parenting classes, and care giver support groups are just a few of the diversified services one can find in a centralized facility. All are welcome to partake, not just the poor or minority clients. Traditionally, they are not subject to the changing interests of a few vocal citizens, or to space allocation problems, or to unavailable expertise as is often the situation with local neighborhood centers. Moreover, centralized services provide more security and consistency in approach.

The practical considerations mentioned by Dr. Azzarto including access to medical and psychosocial care, language and literacy barriers, transportation issues, and family concerns, are certainly important when discussing the merits of centralized versus decentralized services. Centralized facilities employ people from the community who know how to manage the various systems. They are caring and concerned individuals who have expertise in specific areas. They also relate and identify with the clients asking for and receiving services.

Several years ago a debate occurred in a local community concerning centralization versus decentralization of alcohol and substance programs. Many neighborhood communities and groups were very interested in such services close to home. They used several of the arguments presented by Dr. Azzarto to try to convince the funding sources that the monies should go to their community. These people were genuinely concerned with the problem and they successfully fought to have services established in their locality. What they did not foresee, however, was that other citizens in the larger region would not feel comfortable or safe going into some of the disadvantaged neighborhoods. In essence, clients who were not socioeconomically or educationally deprived, but who were in need of the alcohol and substance abuse services, would not have access to these neighborhood services.

Consequently, the decision was made to create a centralized agency that was accessible by public transportation and was located in a neutral area that was devoid of the stigma or ill reputation of a "disadvantaged" neighborhood. The services were available for all those who needed them. The staff were professionally trained, some were bilingual, and many knew about the characteristics of the various surrounding neighborhoods. All clients were welcome and were made to feel comfortable. They were there for the same reason, and they coalesced as a group. This centralized program is still flourishing more than twenty years since its beginnings.

At about the same time that this alcohol program developed, a neighborhood mental health program was conceived by some dedicated local citizens. This program was designed to meet the mental health needs of a particular community; involved local leaders; rented convenient office space; and hired and trained neighborhood people to work in the facility. Twenty some years later, even though the need for mental health services goes unabated, this neighborhood facility no longer exists. Unfortunately, the leaders who conceived the program were no longer living in the community, the vocal minority shifted their priorities, and lack of staffing became a major problem.

This history of decentralized neighborhood health and human services is consistent with the experiences of many other communities. These centers do not maintain their initial impetus, they are not available to all who may need their services, and they do not withstand the test of time.

Finally, Dr. Azzarto frames very nicely the feminist vision of empowerment versus dependency issues. Social workers should be concerned with the values of self-determination, human dignity, and autonomy. Advocating and assuming responsibility for societal changes may intrinsically be a feminist principle, but in no way should these principles be limited to gender qualifications.

REFERENCE

Dobelstein, A. W. (1990). Social welfare. Chicago: Nelson-Hall Publishers.

NO

MARY F. SMITH

As a social worker during the social activist period of the late 1960s and 1970s when the movement toward community-based health centers flourished, and as a specialist in tertiary health care, I feel particularly qualified to comment on the centralization versus decentralization of services. To understand both sides of this issue, one must look at both community organization principles and social welfare policy, with emphasis on the actual delivery of health and human services.

Since the controversial issues in this book illustrate a variety of community organization principles, I shall not elaborate on these tenets other than to encourage one to become familiar with both the micro and macro levels of community organization perspectives. Without this balanced view, it is too easy to succumb to values of one side or the other without looking at the total picture. In addition, as Neugeboren (1985) suggests, there is a cyclical nature to the debate of centralized versus decentralized organizational structures. Students in this field should gain an appreciation of the historical perspective of the development of community organization principles before deciding whether either or both perspectives meet their personal and professional goals, values, and expectations (Garvin & Cox, 1987; Rubin & Rubin, 1992).

To argue for centralization of health and human services, I shall address the formation of social welfare policy, as well as the delivery and management of social services.

Social Welfare Policy

An analysis of social welfare policy from a benefit-allocation framework should focus on four major dimensions: allocation, provision, delivery, and finance (Gilbert & Specht, 1974). Regarding health and human services, all individuals should have full access to services needed. There is no question of "who" gets "what" proper care; rather, how is the care provided and who manages the funding sources available.

The issue of centralized versus decentralized services, therefore, is an integral part of the delivery and funding dimension of social welfare policy. No one, I believe, would disagree with the universal right of all people to receive proper health services. This argument is not intended to justify this basic human need, but rather to discuss the best possible way of delivering these services. It is my belief that community control and participation, local initiatives, and self-determination principles can be incorporated into a centralized plan that also includes a high level of expertise; the guarantee that all minority issues will be addressed, not just those of a few community majority leaders; specific guidelines will be followed; and the greater possibility that privacy and confidentiality of services received will be maintained in a centralized system.

Expertise

There is no doubt that centralized services are provided mainly by professionals possessing the necessary requirements for licensing in their area of expertise. For example, in the health industry, medical education in the United States is regulated and standardized by various credentialing agencies at both the national and state levels. It is the general belief that, if trained in the United States, most physicians will be exposed to similar learning opportunities and to a very high level of expertise in training. This is borne out in the difficulties that foreign medical student graduates have in obtaining graduate training positions in approved United States residency programs and in getting clearance to take licensing examinations in various states. It appears to be the consensus among the health care providers that American medical graduates are better trained physicians than those of other countries.

Tertiary care health centers are usually large facilities that cover a wide geographical area; have the latest technological advances in medical sciences; serve the entire community and region; have access to specialized units such as trauma centers, burn units, AIDS treatment centers, dialysis, as so on; and have in their employ American-trained medical personnel. In addition to patient care, tertiary centers emphasize research and educational opportunities. They attract well-known and excellent medical staff committed to the advancement of the medical sciences. Patients can see a distinguished professor of medicine, a prominent researcher in genetic counseling, or a leader in the field of family practice and a proponent of the value of continuity of care for an entire family, all at the same facility. In one facility, patients have complete access to all the medical care services they may need. They are assured of a level of quality care and a level of expertise not found anywhere else. Diagnostic services, treatment, and preventive medicine, as well as research and education, are the foci of these tertiary care centers. Community health centers, by definition of location and size, can not compete with this array of available services and staff.

Neighborhood community health centers provide an excellent service notwithstanding their limitations, and they serve to augment many of the tertiary care services that patients require. But, by virtue of their size and location, they can never operate as the primary or major provider of health care to the community.

Looking at other services that a neighborhood center may provide, paraprofessionals, in all likelihood, have the most direct client contact. They may or may not be supervised, they rarely have professional credentials themselves, and they may not always be aware of their own limitations. Centralized services, on the other hand, have specific and rigorous standards that must be met by professionals before they are permitted to deliver services directly to clients. Many have advanced training at the master or doctoral level and are licensed or credentialed through their respective state licensing boards.

From my own experiences as a professionally trained social worker in a centralized mental health clinic, I was one of several providers of client services. When the move was made toward the creation of local neighborhood offices, untrained community workers were hired, received some in-service training, and then became the providers of human services. Even though they were caring and concerned individuals, they lacked a level of expertise that centralized services provided.

Management

Centralized health and human services are mandated by national and state granting agencies to provide care to all those in need. These funding sources promulgate guidelines, require strict adherence to established procedures, and have a built-in checks and balances system of evaluation. Some may complain of the excessive guidelines and paperwork, but this level of control assures, as much as is humanly possible, that services are being provided professionally and equally throughout the targeted area. This same level of management is not available at neighborhood centers and is not consistent throughout a region.

Communities vary widely in their commitment to serving people with the most severe needs. They don't always encourage participatory planning including representation from service recipients and family members. Those in control may have certain needs and interests unlike others in the community. What happens, then, to those neighborhood individuals whose needs are not considered as important to the few in control? Where do they go to receive the care they need? The answer is very simple. Without a centralized office, these individuals are overlooked. At a given time, children may be the focus of care while the elderly, for instance, may be given less priority. Based on managerial preferences and local interests, this focus may change from time to time. In a decentralized plan, one interest group may vie with another group. With a centralized system, this is less likely to occur. Policy reform at this higher level can and does meet the needs of all interest groups. The goals of the centralized services are not easily influenced by the personal interests of a few.

In a centralized health care and human service system, prospective clients can access the tertiary care health center and are assured of receiving needed services. They are not made to feel guilty or to feel embarrassed. They do not have to deal with a neighbor who may be serving as a staff member whom they may not like. They do not have to be concerned that their presence at the facility may become food for local talk. Most importantly, they are assured they will be getting professional and expert care.

To overlook the people who manage the delivery of health and human services to the community is a grave mistake, but one that unfortunately may be overlooked by communities that wish to maintain power and control over local services. It has been my experience that local community health centers have difficulty recruiting and maintaining qualified professional health care personnel. Often, the medical director's position is not filled by a permanent person, the community governing body has difficulty attracting well-trained managers to oversee their facility, and the community is often divided into interests groups that compete for space, financial allocations, and power to control.

Evers, Farrant, and Trojan (1990) make a case for a ''multiactor'' approach to policy making that takes into account shifting boundaries and responsibilities with different actors both at the community and higher government levels. Centralization of services can accommodate both the needs of the local communities and the needs of the region by creatively using financial and professional means.

Alford (1975) states, "Community participation is a classic instance of the 'veto group' process leading to stalemate" (p. 221). The rules of decision making in a participatory process include the prevention of any major interest from being seriously damaged, often called the *purpose of consensus,* and also prevents allocating enough power to the decision-making bodies to make changes.

Finally, visions of communities can be blocked by limited interests and scope. Local groups and neighborhoods can block new activities and projects, not necessarily out of malice, but rather out of intense desires for their own particular needs to be met. Once groups are organized, they tend to fight or conflict with existing groups for attention and for funds. Priorities are often in conflict, and facilities and control issues surface at the community level. When services are centralized, priorities have already been established, funds have been allocated, and standards of delivering services have been established. (See, for example, the summary of public hearings described in Surles, 1992.) The needs of the community have already been identified and incorporated into the policy planning. There is no fear that a particular segment of the population will be overlooked because of the vocal expressions of a few. Decision making will be done on a more objective basis, thus escaping the "veto group" process that can lead to a stalemates in community participation as described by Alford (1975).

Summary

Individual and community considerations including autonomy, rights of an individual, allocation of resources, and professional administration are all aspects in favor of supporting the centralization of health and human services. Centralization of services supports the needs of all members of the community. It's fundamental principle is to promote the good for all, to do no harm, and to fairly, equitably, and expertly provide such services.

REFERENCES

Alford, R. R. (1975). *Health care politics.* Chicago: University of Chicago Press.

Evers, A., Farrant, W., & Trojan, A. (Eds.). (1990). *Healthy public policy at the local level.* Boulder, CO: Westview Press.

Garvin, C. D., & Cox, F. M. (1987). A history of community organizing since the Civil War with special reference to oppressed communities. In F. M. Cox, J. L. Erlich, J. Rothman, & J. E. Tropman (eds.), *Strategies of community organization.* Itasca, IL: F. E. Peacock Publishers.

Gilbert, N., & Specht, H. (1974). *Dimensions of social welfare policy.* Englewood Cliffs, NJ: Prentice-Hall.

Neugeboren, B. (1985). *Organization, policy, and practice in the human services.* New York: Longman.

Rubin, H. J., & Rubin, I. S. (1992). *Community organization and development.* New York: Macmillan Publishing.

Surles, R. C. (1992, February 15). *Statewide comprehensive plan for mental health services, 1992–1996.* New York State Office of Mental Health.

Rejoinder to Dr. Smith   Jacqueline Azzarto

I agree wholeheartedly with the spirit of Dr. Smith's argument that we need well-trained professionals to deliver quality care to all patients. I disagree, however, with her contention that expert care is best acquired in tertiary care centers. It has been my experience that in some tertiary care centers the focus is more often on the disease entity than on the patient. In institutions where education, research, and specialty care are the norms, patients may be viewed as interesting cases or valuable learning experiences. The very human needs and problems of some vulnerable clients can be overlooked in the quest for a "rule out" diagnosis or high-tech treatment. Given the nature of medical education, many young professionals might shy away from community health care centers because they can be frustrated by an inability to accurately assess and dramatically cure the problems our patients present to them. Those who do gravitate to primary care in this setting, however, really are experts in the complexities of human dilemmas and are truly dedicated to the *care* of vulnerable people. It is a tragedy of our society that these professionals are not financially rewarded for this expertise and dedication.

Tertiary care centers can also become complicated bureaucratic mazes to our clients. Although community health care centers are not without their paperwork and accountability procedures, the staff in local programs often serve as advocates for our clients. They help patients negotiate the twists and turns of the larger system: accessing home care and other available services, applying for Medicaid, and completing referrals to a tertiary care centers.

On the issue of accountability, Dr. Smith also takes the position that the experts know best. She believes that the needs of some special groups in the community can come before those of others and that centralized authority has the best interests of all patients built into their guidelines and system of checks and balances. Dye (1981) describes different models for understanding these public policy issues. Dr. Smith is speaking in terms of the elite model in which policy direction comes down to the masses through officials and administrators. I am utilizing the group model in which public policy compromises are negotiated by groups competing for power and influence. In actuality, neither model describes real policy as it is formulated and implemented in health care programs. However, I believe that in existing programs the values of elite policy makers are felt more strongly than those of the public for whom these programs are designed. Giving management of health centers back to the community might not establish true equality, but it will do better in accomplishing that ideal than the present patriarchal system does. Accountability to the people, in my opinion, is more important than accountability to the official hierarchy.

In conclusion, I restate my judgments concerning the existing centralized health care system. It can provide fragmented care that is not comprehensive. Many services are inaccessible to those who need them most. Accountability procedures are designed to serve decision makers, not clients. And specialty cure is more valued than primary care. Given these problems, system reform becomes a national imperative. It is my firm belief that this reform should include decentralized neighborhood social health center that are managed by the community.

REFERENCE

Dye, T. (1981). *Understanding public policy.* Englewood Cliffs, NJ: Prentice-Hall.

DEBATE 6

Should Only Gay and Lesbian Community Organizers Operate in Gay and Lesbian Communities?

EDITOR'S NOTE: During the past several years, growing evidence shows that the rights of gay and lesbian people are being increasingly threatened. Legislation directed against both groups has passed or is pending in several states, direct attacks on gay individuals have in-creased, and myths about gay and lesbian individuals continue to be perpetuated in the larger society. As a result, there is a profound need for change in the public's attitudes toward, knowledge of, and behavior toward gay and lesbian people. This debate is critically important because it raises a central question not only for gay and lesbian groups, but also for all disenfranchised groups: Is it better to work alone or with "mainstream" organizers for social change? What are the advantages and disadvantages of both approaches? Further, if organizing begins with shared interests, do gay and lesbian people share concerns with heterosexuals that enable them to work together on a common agenda for social change?

Carol T. Tully, Ph.D., argues YES. Dr. Tully is Assistant Professor of Social Work and the Director of Field Instruction at The University of Georgia School of Social Work, where she teaches research and policy analysis. She has been writing in the field of lesbian and gay issues since 1976 and has been an advocate and lobbyist for the inclusion of lesbian and gay content in social work curricula since the early 1970s.

Terry Craig, M.S.W., and Gail Nugent, M.S.W., argue NO. Terry Craig is a Talkline Supervisor for Women Helping Women Services and past coordinator for the Lesbian and Gay Community Mediation Project. She was instrumental in

86

the formation of the Lesbian and Gay Community Mediation Project and is still involved on a volunteer basis.

Gail Nugent is Director of the Community Mediation Program of Dispute Resolution Services (DRS). DRS is a nonprofit program of the Los Angeles County Bar Association that provides alternative dispute resolution services to Los Angeles County. The Lesbian and Gay Community Mediation Program is the newest of DRS's programs, and Gail assisted in the establishment of this innovative project.

YES

CAROL T. TULLY

Based on the principles of community organization (Rothman, 1974), the theoretical concepts of homophily (Rogers & Shoemaker, 1971) and homophobia (deCrescenzo & McGill, 1978; Herek, 1984, 1991) and the nature of the lesbian and gay community (Albro & Tully, 1979; Faderman, 1991; Harry & Devall, 1978), to successfully organize within the nonheterosexual community, organizers must be homosexual. In community organizing where the end result is that of social system change, the first premise is that the community must be identifiable. Since the lesbian and gay community is largely invisible within the heterosexual culture, this argument provides supporting evidence as to why, if the gay/lesbian community can be organized, only lesbian and gay persons can be successful.

Community Organization
and the Homosexual Community

It has been estimated that there are more than 26 million gay and lesbian people living in the United States, and most live in states where it is illegal to engage in what they perceive to be normal sexual activity. This loose confederation of persons, bound together by only a common sexual orientation, has been defined as a subculture by some and a community by others (Harry & Devall, 1978; Faderman, 1991; Gusfield, 1978; Murray, 1979). The gay and lesbian community typifies the primary difficulty in community organization: how has the community been identified?

Certainly, the homosexual community is not a clearly defined entity with inherent geographic or ethnic boundaries or even common characteristics. The only identifying commonality is that of a sexual orientation that deviates from the norm. Beyond this, the lesbian/gay community is as diverse as its heterosexual counterpart. And, like the heterosexual culture, the homosexual subculture has become a mental construct where the parameters are only implied (Rothman, 1974). While it may be generally agreed that a homosexual subculture does exist (Albro & Tully, 1979; Faderman, 1991; Harry & Devall, 1978), the only parts of it that are visible to the larger heterosexual culture are those parts that either gays and lesbians want revealed or that comprise types of grotesque stereotypes attributed to every minority by the majority (Faderman, 1991; Tully, 1989).

Because of the general invisibility of the gay and lesbian subculture, and hence its diverse communities, it may be assumed that the same theoretical views of community that exist within the heterosexual culture are also found within the lesbian/gay subculture. Thus, because lesbian and gay persons function within the larger, heterosexual community, organizers must examine the social systems of the larger society to discover reference points for the homosexual community. It has been fairly well established that homosexual persons interact with all facets of the social system—economic, political, educational, religious, social welfare, and familial (Faderman, 1991; Tully, 1989), and community organizers must be able to clearly articulate with which part of the gay/lesbian community they are to work. This becomes an impossibility if the community organizer is unable to identify all of the lesbian/gay community.

Heterosexual community organizers who actively work only in those parts of the gay/lesbian community that are made visible to the outside world, may naively omit the largest portion of that community. This omission can only en-gender further separation between the non–lesbian/gay organizer and the remain-der of the larger, more powerful, but hidden, homosexual subculture.

Rothman (1974) suggests the role of a community organizer is to act as a change agent in helping to create change in political and legislative behaviors, produce action within organizations, and increase citizen participation within a community. If this is so, "the community" must be an identifiable entity. Within the lesbian and gay subculture, the "community" is revealed only to those who are part of it. Thus, those who do not have membership in the subculture by virtue of sexual orientation do not have access to the extraordinarily complex systems of communities within that subculture. Therefore, they are unable to do adequate, if any, community organizing within that milieu. Some possible rea-sons for this follow.

Heterosexuals as Oppressors

Two major factors tend to contribute to the pervasive view within the lesbian and gay community that heterosexual persons can not adequately represent them—institutionalized and internalized homophobia. Institutionalized homophobia (the generalized hatred and fear of homosexuals and homosexuality that is found within every facet of society but is most prevalent within the legal and religious sectors) undergirds the entire American way of life (deCrescenzo & McGill,

1978; Herek, 1984, 1991). As a result, homosexual persons, in an effort to conform to the mores of society, may internalize this pervasive cultural value. Homophobia, the resultant anti-gay/lesbian acts that accompany it (oppression, violence, persecution, and so forth), and the perceived power base of the larger, heterosexual culture diminish the trust level between homosexuals and their heterosexual counterparts.

It has been suggested that the means to effective community organization lies in effective communication between community members and the community organizer (Warren, 1967). Assuming this is true, then what is the best way to communicate with the gay/lesbian community?

Rogers and Shoemaker (1971) have generalized that a community change agent's success is positively related to the change agent's similarity with the community. This concept of homophily (where the best communication occurs most frequently between persons who are alike) appears to be the only way for community organization to occur within the lesbian/gay community. This seems to be true primarily because of the invisible nature of the homosexual community based on the need to keep the community secret because of homophobia. Outsiders are simply not made aware of the entire complex community and know only small parts of it. Thus, to be made aware of anything but those segments of the lesbian/gay community that choose to be "out" (like groups such as ACT-UP or Queer Nation), membership in the "family" is required. This reality clearly demonstrates the concept of homophily where community organizer and members of the community share communication based on common meanings and a mutually understood subcultural language. Because of these commonalities, the exchange of ideas is likely to have greater impact in terms of changes in attitudes, knowledge, and overt behaviors (Rogers & Shoemaker, 1971). Homophobia, too, creates a sensitivity of communication between the community organizer and the community. While it may be argued that an expert community organizer who is not homosexual could effectively work within the lesbian/gay community, institutionalized and internalized homophobia will likely interfere with the process to such an extent as to make effective community organizing impossible.

If, as it has been suggested, given free choice, individuals will seek out those of similar persuasions (Rogers & Shoemaker 1971), and if the gay/lesbian community is not made known to those who are not members of it, how can heterosexuals, the perceived oppressor, effectively organize within the homosexual community? The answer is simple: they cannot.

REFERENCES

Albro, J. C., & Tully, C. T. (1979). A study of lesbian lifestyles in the homosexual micro-culture and the heterosexual macro-culture. *Journal of Homosexuality, 4*(4), 331–344.

deCrescenzo, T. A., & McGill, C. (1978). Homophobia: A study of the attributes of mental health professionals toward homosexuality. Unpublished manuscript, University of Southern California.

Faderman, L. (1991). *Odd girls and twilight lovers.* New York: Columbia University Press.

Gusfield, J. R. (1978). *Community.* Oxford: Blackwell.

Harry, J., & Devall, W. B. (1978). *The social organization of gay males.* New York: Praeger.

Herek, G. M. (1984). Beyond homophobia: A social psychological perspective on attitudes toward lesbians and gay men. *Journal of Homosexuality, 10,* 1–21.

Herek, G. M. (1991). Stigma, prejudice and violence against lesbians and gay men. In J. C. Gonsiorek and J. D. Weinrich (Eds.), *Homosexuality: Research implications for public policy* (pp. 60–80). New York: Sage.

Murray, S. O. (1979). The institutional elaboration of a quasi-ethnic community. *International Review of Modern Sociology, 9,* 165–177.

Rogers, E. M., & Shoemaker, F. F. (1971). *Communication of innovations: A cross-cultural approach.* New York: Free Press.

Rothman, J. (1974). *Planning and organizing for social change: Action principles from social science research.* New York: Columbia University Press.

Tully, C. T. (1989). Caregiving: What do mid-life lesbians view as important? *Journal of Gay & Lesbian Psychotherapy, 1*(1), 87–103.

Warren, R. L. (1967). Application of social science knowledge to the community organization field. *Journal of Education for Social Work, 3*(1), 60–72.

Rejoinder to Dr. Tully

TERRY CRAIG AND GAIL NUGENT

First, for clarification, we do not purport that heterosexuals should organize independently in the gay and lesbian community, but rather, a unified effort can be most effective in implementing social change. So on more points than not, we agree with Dr. Tully. However, we do not take the issue to the extreme. We believe, based on our experiences, that working together can be beneficial for all.

We agree that homophobia is pervasive and dangerous in our society. It is particularly prevalent in the judicial system. The lack of access gay men and lesbians have to this system, particularly with regard to their relationship issues, was the overriding reason a mediation program was pursued. We additionally were not naive about the fact that the sponsoring organization is homophobic. However, with this in mind, the Lesbian and Gay Community Mediation Project (LGCMP) was set up to operate more independently than the other projects of the

Los Angeles County Bar Association (LACBA). The LGCMP continues to have its own advisory committee, which is responsible for all decision making relevant to program operation. In fact, the committee has addressed LACBA's homophobia by being instrumental in implementing educational programs for staff and volunteers to address this. More important, the opportunity for heterosexuals to work side by side with homosexuals has encouraged people to acknowledge their biases, face their fears, and grow from their experiences. It is a model of how people can work and live together in a diverse society. Separation only fuels fear, lack of knowledge, bias, and homophobia.

The theory that social change can be accomplished only by those that are similar to the community within which they are working is one with which we are familiar. In fact, we agree and used this concept to ensure that the organizing group was comprised of gay men and lesbians, familiar with their community, thus bringing with them access to the invisible facet of it. The heterosexuals brought with them knowledge and experience in mediation and LACBA. The latter group was able to assist in manipulating the larger organization in a way that would provide the necessary autonomy to the LGCMP. Limiting such a venture to gay men and lesbian organizers would stifle creativity and the range and the depth of services available to this community.

We are aware of community organization theory and believe it has validity. Its validity, however, can be limited by relying too much on theory and not enough on new approaches. The academic system can forget that there is a world out there struggling to find real solutions, one that is learning to celebrate differences, rather than hide from them.

The notion of separation in community organization is a dangerous one. In a diverse community it limits opportunity and ultimately social change. The invisibility of the lesbian and gay community would not have been understood if only heterosexual organizers had set up the LGCMP. The gay and lesbian organizers relied on the experienced heterosexual mediators to address program needs, while their task was to reach out to their community and address relevant policy and programmatic issues. We believe that each group's expertise and talents were utilized in a side-by-side effort to address a glaring need in the gay and lesbian community—an effective use of resources in an era when resources are at a premium. Again, we believe an outgrowth of this effort was that *both* groups learned about the other.

NO

GAIL NUGENT AND TERRY CRAIG

Many individuals argue that gay and lesbian and heterosexual groups represent different constituencies and thus have different issues, while others argue that the gay and lesbian communities need to join in coalitions with the heterosexual community to advance the cause of gay and lesbian rights. These groups do not have to be separate because of their differences. Kadushin (1983) examines members of different groups working together. He discusses the extremes of ignoring differences between groups and of separating groups. He writes, "one extreme denies the significance of vital shared group experiences; the other extreme denies unique psychodynamics of individual response" (p. 303). In this debate, the argument is that heterosexual as well as gay and lesbian organizers should work together to organize gay and lesbian communities.

There are many advantages to having these groups work together. First, discomfort often felt around gay men and lesbians can be lessened through exposure to and interaction with them (Lance, 1987). Second, having only gay and lesbian community organizers operating in those communities limits the creativity, range, and depth of the services available to this population. Third, having both heterosexual and gay and lesbian organizers work together forces them to confront stereotypes and to face unwarranted fears and brings to the surface issues of common concern around homophobia, gender, and injustice. Finally, heterosexual organizers can be of help to the gay and lesbian community by focusing attention on the larger human rights issues.

Organizing communities is the first step toward promoting social change and justice. There are many approaches to organizing, such as social protest, legal advocacy, negotiation and lobbying, and community education (Biklen, 1983). Since organizers seek to empower the group or community that they are working with, the approach that is chosen depends on the situation and the desired outcome. This debate presents a case study in which dispute resolution is used as a model for heterosexuals and gay and lesbian organizers to work together. The organizations involved in this process are: Dispute Resolution Services (DRS), a primarily heterosexual organization along with a committee from the gay and lesbian community. Mediating disputes is considered a peaceful alternative to the more adversarial process of the courts. "The mediator promotes reconciliation, settlement, compromise, or understanding among two or more conflicting parties" (Parsons, 1991, p. 484).

Working Relationship

In January 1991, a committee representing the Gay and Lesbian Community Services Center of Los Angeles, Lambda Legal Defense and Education Fund, and Lawyers for Human Rights (the gay and lesbian bar association) contacted DRS for help in organizing a mediation program. Dispute Resolution Services, a nonprofit corporation of the Los Angeles County Bar Association (LACBA), is an alternative dispute resolution service that empowers disputing parties, through mediation, to work together toward a solution that is mutually beneficial.

The gay and lesbian committee wanted to discuss ideas and to seek direction in how they could develop a mediation program to specifically serve the gay and lesbian community in Los Angeles County. DRS was invited to this planning meeting as technical advisors only. At a second meeting, the process of mediation was explained to a group of forty gay men and lesbians. A decision was reached at this meeting to explore and consider the development of a mediation program under the auspices of DRS, which provided consultation to the committee.

For the gay and lesbian committee this meant the beginning of a year-long process among themselves as well as with DRS. This process consisted of power struggles, questioning who would be in control, establishing trust, and testing DRS and LACBA for homophobic attitudes. For DRS, this year-long process involved accommodating an already existing system to fit the needs and wants of the gay and lesbian community. At times, it meant withholding crucial information that would upset one or the other of the groups to avoid jeopardizing the partnership that was forming. The result of these processes was the formation of the Lesbian and Gay Community Mediation Project (LGCMP) under the auspices of Dispute Resolution Services of the Los Angeles County Bar Association.

Using DRS's Technical Assistance

Under the auspices of DRS, an organization with fourteen years of experience, the LGCMP was able to take advantage of the technical assistance and training offered by DRS (for example, setting up files, processing forms, developing intake procedures and guidelines for confidentiality, considering the ethical issues, training volunteer mediators, and finding funding resources). In addition, DRS provided the project with office space and supplies needed to get started.

By working in partnership with DRS, the LGCMP was able to model its work on a solid organization, thus avoiding many of structural problems associated with launching a program. This assistance has allowed the project to focus more readily on making services available to the lesbian and gay communities as well as educating them about the mediation process. Roel and Cook (1985) stress the need to educate people about the existence, purpose, and benefits of mediation. They claim that many disputes are unresolved because people are not aware of mediation as an option.

It is important to note that the partnership that has been established between the two organizations also gave the project the freedom to create and advertise as a distinctly gay and lesbian project. Recognizing the distinctions between a primarily heterosexual organization and one that is designed to meet the needs of the lesbian and gay communities, DRS agreed to administer this project differently from their other programs. For example, the gay and lesbian volunteer mediators and staff involved in this project have an active role in how the program is set up, advertised, and administered.

Advantages of the DRS and LGCMP Partnership

As a specifically lesbian and gay project, and at the same time being under the auspices of DRS, has proven to be advantageous. The LGCMP can offer the gay and lesbian community a safe place to be open with regard to their sexual orientation. However, if needed, the LGCMP can also honor a request to keep an individual's sexual orientation confidential.

If the LGCMP did not work in partnership with DRS, it would have been forced to continuously present itself as a lesbian and gay project. This could be a problem if a gay man or lesbian were having a dispute with a heterosexual who did not know the person's sexual orientation, and where knowing this would cause more problems. The working relationship between the two organizations enables the client to keep his or her sexual orientation confidential by using a special DRS office.

Another advantage of this partnership is the multitude of mediators who are available. In a mediation involving a heterosexual and a gay man or lesbian the LGCMP is able to use both a heterosexual mediator and a gay or lesbian mediator. Mediations are often comediated, and this mixture ensures the neutrality of the mediators.

Finally, this partnership has brought together people who might not have otherwise talked with one another. For some, this relationship has allowed them to connect words, stereotypes, and fears to actual people and, in turn, has decreased negative feelings. For others, this project has offered an opportunity to work together and organize collectively for social change.

Conclusion

The relationship between Dispute Resolution Services and the Lesbian and Gay Community Mediation Project is a good example of the advantages of having a partnership between heterosexual and gay and lesbian organizers. Not only are there benefits to the organizations, but there are also personal benefits. In struggling through the process of organizing and becoming a partnership, both heterosexuals and homosexuals have an opportunity to grow.

REFERENCES

Biklen, D. (1983). *Community organizing: Theory and practice.* Englewood Cliffs, NJ: Prentice-Hall.
Kadushin, A. (1983). *The social work interview* (2nd ed.) New York: Columbia University Press.

Lance, L. (1987). The effects of interaction with gay persons on attitudes toward homosexuality. *Human Relations, 40*(6), 329–336.
Parsons, R. J. (1991). The mediator role in social work practice. *Social Work, 36*(6), 483–487.
Roel, J. A., & Cook, R. F. (1985). Issues in mediation: Rhetoric and reality revisited. *Journal of Social Issues, 41*(2), 161–178.

Rejoinder to Ms. Craig and Ms. Nugent

CAROL T. TULLY

The excellent work described by Ms. Craig and Ms. Nugent that has evolved into the Lesbian and Gay Community Mediation Project (LGCMP) within Dispute Resolution Services (DRS; a nonprofit corporation of the Los Angeles County Bar Association) tends to enhance the argument that while some limited partnerships between the lesbian and gay subculture and the heterosexual culture can and do thrive, such exist only because the lesbian and gay community sanctions them. Ms. Craig and Ms. Nugent's activity on behalf of the gay and lesbian community in Los Angeles would not have been possible without the consent of and active involvement of those three gay/lesbian organizations that, in January 1991, sought and found help within the heterosexual culture. Even with such support, because of the unequal nature of the relationship between LGCMP and DRS, services intended for lesbians and gays fall within the auspices of the heterosexual mainstream. While the authors view this as a positive factor, how many members of the invisible gay and lesbian community are not being served because of this arrangement?

The authors state that partnerships between the homosexual subculture and heterosexual culture enhance the creativity, range, and depth of services offered to lesbians and gays but provide no empirical evidence to substantiate their claims. In fact, they provide no compelling reason why lesbians and gays would choose to use the LGCMP other than that it offers services to those who are not heterosexual. If this is so, Ms. Craig and Ms. Nugent and their organization support and perpetuate the theoretical concept of homophily.

The authors also endorse the reality of institutionalized homophobia. The evolution of their organization within DRS confirms this reality, as does the fact that the stationery of DRS does not identify the Lesbian and Gay Community Mediation Project by name. On the Dispute Resolution Services brochure other similar projects are typed in bold face; the words "Lesbian and Gay Community Mediation Project" are printed in small letters beneath the bold face "LGCMP." Clearly this illustrates a subtle form of homophobia.

I wholeheartedly agree with Ms. Craig and Ms. Nugent that heterosexual organizers could help the homosexual subculture. However, until institutionalized homophobia is no longer a reality, homosexual acts are not considered illegal, and sexual orientation is not a political issue, gay and lesbian persons will continue to protect themselves and their communities with the cloak of invisibility. This will prevent meaningful partnerships between homosexual and heterosexual community organizers.

On the surface, such partnerships as the one between the LGCMP and DRS look like homosexuals and heterosexuals are working hand in hand to help the lesbian and gay community. Yet, once the facade is removed this coupling merely perpetuates an insidious form of institutionalized homophobia that is endorsed by the lesbian and gay community. Ms. Craig and Ms. Nugent need to be cautious in their endorsement of this dangerous liaison and not be seduced into underwriting what seems to be merely another form of institutionalized homophobia.

Is Community Organizing Dead and Is the Future Organizational Practice?

EDITOR'S NOTE: Macro practice involves the development of skills in
three areas: planning, community organization, and administration.
Much professional discussion has centered on how to join these
components into a integrated theory of macro practice. The common
theme that has the potential to weave together the three distinct, but
interrelated components is the idea of change and empowerment.
However, as the title of this debate indicates, the field is not yet ready
to embrace such an approach. While the authors of the two positions
agree that macro practice must include both organizations and communities, they differ significantly on the focus for education and training. The debate raises the following questions: Can practice that is
organizationally based adequately respond to the demands of oppressed groups for social change and justice? Does the development
of alternative organizations suggest that "traditional" organizations
have failed to meet the needs of certain groups, such as the poor and
disenfranchised? Can practice that is based in community organizing
more effectively address social problems by building on natural
community-based support systems and helping networks? Finally, the
argument that can be made is for the development of a macro practice
model that encompasses and links both organizations and communities, that recognizes their reciprocity, and that reaffirms the profession's value commitment to empowerment.

Steven L. McMurtry, Ph.D., and Peter M. Kettner, M.S.W., argue YES. Dr.
McMurtry is Associate Professor at the School of Social Work at Arizona State
University. He is Director of the child welfare specialization and also teaches

macro practice and research. His most recent writings have addressed foster care issues and decision-making processes in nonprofit management.

Dr. Kettner is Professor of Social Work at Arizona State University where he teaches macro practice, program planning, financial management, and administration. In the area of macro practice, he has coauthored, with colleagues John Daley and Ann Nichols, *Initiating Change in Organizations and Communities,* and with colleagues Ellen Netting and Stephen McMurtry, *Social Work Macro Practice.* His long-standing areas of interest and research include program planning and evaluation, purchase of service contracting, program design, and practice-oriented research.

John Michael Daley, D.S.W., and F. Ellen Netting, Ph.D., argue NO. Dr. Daley is Professor, Arizona State University School of Social Work, where he teaches organizational and community change, citizen and consumer participation strategies, proposal development and fundraising, and community practice. His research interests include evaluation of macro change episodes, intercultural practice, and the dynamics of diversity within boards of directors.

F. Ellen Netting is Associate Professor, Arizona State University School of Social Work, where she teaches in the areas of macro practice, program planning, administration, and policy. Her research interests include nonprofit organizations and gerontology, with a special recent emphasis on hospital-based long-term care services for the frail elderly. She and her colleagues Peter M. Kettner and Steven L. McMurtry have written *Social Work Macro Practice.*

YES

STEVEN L. MCMURTRY AND PETER M. KETTNER

Traditional Approaches to Community Organization

Social work has historically defined its constituency not only as individuals but also as groups of people in need of services. The "client" may be micro systems such as individuals, families, and small groups, or it may be a macro system such as a group of individuals (referred to as a *target population*). Single clients and target populations live in and interact with still larger macro systems such as neighborhoods, communities, and political systems. Social work at the macro level usually involves acting on these systems to bring resources to bear on client needs.

Traditionally, social workers have been trained in community organization as the primary means for effecting this type of intervention. Barker (1987) defines community organization as "an intervention process . . . to help individuals, groups, and collectivities of people with common interests or from the same geographic areas to deal with social problems and to enhance social well-being through planned collective action'' (p. 29).

At the center of most approaches to community organization is Rothman's well-known system of Models A, B, and C (1968). Briefly, Model A (locality development) advocates maximizing citizen participation to create consensus regarding the nature of the problem and to generate collaborative efforts for solving it. An example often used is the work of Peace Corps representatives engaged in rural community development in other countries. Model B (social planning) draws on the scientific expertise of professional planners who identify problems, devise solutions, and implement changes through already structured and sanctioned channels, such as a city planning department. Finally, Model C (social action) frames community problems in terms of oppression of disadvantaged populations by the privileged. Through organizing efforts, demands are taken into the political arena to force concessions from entrenched power holders.

Rothman notes that his models are ideal types, meaning that they are conceptual abstractions that do not exist in pure form but serve to illustrate different approaches to organizing. He and others have begun to advocate the use of these models in a more eclectic manner, in which mixing and phasing of their elements allow them to be tailored to specific circumstances (Rothman & Tropman, 1987). Still, the models remain close to the heart of most community practitioners as well as to the core of most curricula on social work macro practice.

The Realities of Macro Practice in Social Work

Our contention is that these models and the profession's traditional focus on community organization embody a number of serious problems in the way macro practice is conceptualized and taught in schools of social work. The primary reason for our concern is that this approach simply does not realistically reflect the world in which social workers find themselves. While the image of a social worker acting directly on communities to right wrongs, cure ills, and empower the oppressed is a very attractive one, it is not what most social workers do in practice, nor is it a good model to prepare students for the realities they will face.

The macro systems that are of the greatest importance to social workers are not communities but *organizations.* Some of these are informal organizations such as neighborhood groups or self-help associations, but the majority are formal, structured organizations. Most social workers are employed by these organizations, and within them they do case management; provide direct services to individuals, families, and groups; and supervise, plan, manage, and administer. If they deal with large groups of people at all, it is as a representative of an organization, not as a community organizer.

For example, results of a survey of members of the National Association of Social Workers (NASW) indicated that 88 percent worked in either a private or public agency, with only 12 percent engaged in "private practice" (NASW, 1983). In the same study, fewer than one in fifty respondents listed community organizing as their primary practice setting. Yet, community organization has remained the dominant component of education in macro practice, as though social work macro practice is restricted to the romanticized roles of grassroots organizer, community planner, or leader of a social action movement.

In fact, social workers almost never work directly on or with communities. One problem is that "community" is a notoriously ephemeral concept that is used variously to refer to shared geography, shared characteristics, or shared views. For example, even Roland Warren, in his well-known book on communities, notes that "the community as a social system is implicit in nature as compared with the explicitness of a formal organization" (1978, p. 49). Moreover, communities as geopolitical entities are themselves comprised of organizations, and it is these organizations working interdependently that carry out basic community functions. Just as the understanding of how an atom behaves is dependent on understanding its component particles, so understanding (and practicing within) a community is dependent on understanding the organizations of which it is comprised. In other words, organizations are the basic building blocks of macro systems.

Because organizations are more precisely defined than communities, there is also a vastly richer and more diverse literature on organizations and their behavior. Macro practice that is based in a primary focus on organizations provides social workers with clearer targets for intervention and with a better theoretical and practical base for undertaking such action. This is important because organizational studies also indicate that many of the problems faced by clients in interacting with macro systems are rooted in the malfunctioning of organizations that are supposed to be providing services. Too often, social workers who work with or within these organizations are unknowing participants in the oppression of clients, all the while dreaming about the wonderful things they would do if only they were powerful and influential community organizers.

In many cases, even when community organizers have been "successful," this success is measured in terms of the creation of an organization to carry out the vision of the early organizers. For example, one of the few local programs to be cited as a success from the "glory days" of community organizing in the 1960s was the movement to create community legal services (Axinn & Levin, 1992; Trattner, 1989). In every case, these developed as *organizations* created to help clients use the legal system to acquire services and benefits from *other* organizations. Unfortunately, what frequently happens after such "successes" is that the lack of knowledge and skill about running effective organizations can lead to goal displacement, loss of vision, and services that become increasingly irrelevant to the needs of the target population.

Organizational Change as the Focus of Macro Practice

Organizations carry out the basic functions of communities, including human services. To do their jobs, most social workers must work both within their own organization and with other organizations to obtain benefits and services for their clients. But organizations are by no means perfect social machines, and in many cases they provide either poor services or fail to do so entirely. Thus, we contend that the basic social work macro practice skill is the ability to effect change within organizations in such a way as to maximize the quality and quantity of services and minimize the tendency of organizations to function in an oppressive manner.

These changes are not accomplished through the use of locality development skills, social planning skills, or social action skills. Instead, they are accomplished by social workers who understand organizations and who have developed skills in bringing about planned changed from within, whether as line-level practitioners or as supervisors, managers, or administrators.

Organizations, to a much greater degree than communities, have locations within their structures and logical points of entry where change can be initiated. To be effective, however, social workers need to understand something about organizational structure; program design; job design; the workings of boards, committees, and task groups; motivation and reward systems; staff development and training; internal and external communications, including media and public relations; and other such organizational elements.

Using organizational structure as an example, it is rare to find a public servant who does not complain about the barriers to effective service that are caused by rigid and inflexible bureaucratic structures and procedures. It is equally rare, however, to find a social worker within a bureaucracy who understands alternatives to bureaucratic structure. The result is that creative and carefully conceived proposals to improve services, to address community needs, or to empower clients get buried in the system. Even more often, workers simply get burned out and no longer make serious attempts to bring about organizational change, meaning that services remain ineffective or irrelevant. Many large corporations, on the other hand, led by people who understand organizations, have recognized that a project management structure (in which decision-making authority and resources are brought down to levels closer to the client or customer) can lead to more flexible functioning, better use of creative inputs, quicker decisions, and more effective services.

There are many additional examples of elements that social workers should understand about organizations. Among those being examined in recent literature are the political economies of organizations (Hasenfeld, 1983; Austin, 1988), Deming's basic principles of "total quality management" (see, for example, Walton, 1990), and variables that Peters and Waterman (1982) found to be associated with excellent organizations.

Macro Practice for the Twenty-First Century

We do not advocate that all social workers be taught that large formal organizations are desirable venues for practice. However, whether we like it or not, the reality is that social work practice is and will continue to be primarily an organizationally based endeavor. Accordingly, it is critical that social workers understand these systems. Also, we do not promote an understanding of organizations that simply train future social workers to be mindless, acquiescent bureaucrats. To the contrary, if they are to be effective, social workers must know how organizations go astray and how they can be changed in a way that serves the interests of clients.

It is also not our position that organizational content is totally ignored or left out of the curriculum in most schools of social work, nor do we believe that traditional community organization content ought to be dropped from curriculum and practice models. Rather, it is a matter of emphasis and perspective. We take the position that the current emphasis on community organization should be replaced by a broader emphasis on macro practice, that organizational skills should be given priority in this emphasis, that these skills should be taught to all social workers, and that the teaching of community organizing skills should be placed in the proper context (perhaps even as a specialization area for practitioners who will have the opportunity to use these skills in practice).

As we move into the high-tech society of the twenty-first century, social workers will have to learn many of the same hard lessons learned by the corporate sector over the past two decades as international competition forced a comprehensive self-examination. Inertia and the temptation to continue business as usual is powerful, but the threat of extinction will eventually force changes to occur. When they do, we believe clients will be the beneficiaries.

There is also a strong temptation to continue training the dreamers and the visionaries who have the luxury of criticizing the status quo while, in fact, accomplishing comparatively little in the way of real change. Social workers must never lose their dreams of more effectively meeting client needs, but they can fulfill these dreams only through the difficult, dogged, discouraging, day-to-day work of changing organizations to make them more effective. It is unrealistic and unfair to prepare students who have only the dreams, unless we also provide them also with knowledge and skills applicable to the real world of social work practice.

References

Austin, D. M. (1988). *The political economy of human service programs.* Greenwich, CT: JAI Press.

Axinn, J., & Levin, H. (1992). *Social welfare: A history of the American response to need* (3rd ed.). New York: Longman.

Barker, R. L. (1987). *The social work dictionary.* Silver Spring, MD: National Association of Social Workers.

Hasenfeld, Y. (1983). *Human service organizations.* Englewood Cliffs, NJ: Prentice-Hall.

National Association of Social Workers (1983, November). Membership survey shows practice shifts. *NASW News, 28,* 6–7.

Peters, T. J., & Waterman, R. H. (1982). *In search of excellence: Lessons from America's best-run companies.* New York: Harper and Row.

Rothman, J. (1968). Three models of community organization practice. In National Conference on Social Welfare, *Social work practice 1968.* New York: Columbia University Press.

Rothman, J., & Tropman, J. E. (1987). Models of community organization and macro practice perspectives: Their mixing and phasing. In F. M. Cox, J. L. Erlich, J. Rothman, & J. E. Tropman (Eds.), *Strategies of community organization* (4th ed.). Itasca, IL: Peacock.

Trattner, W. I. (1989). *From poor law to welfare state: A history of social welfare in America* (4th ed.). New York: Free Press.

Walton, M. (1990). *Deming management at work.* New York: Putnam.

Warren, R. L. (1978). *The community in America* (3rd ed.). Chicago: Rand McNally.

Rejoinder to Dr. McMurtry and Mr. Kettner

JOHN MICHAEL DALEY AND F. ELLEN NETTING

We agree that understanding organizations is essential for all social workers and that macro practice must include *both* organizations and communities. Our colleagues, however, express concern that a focus on community organizing "does not realistically reflect the world in which social workers find themselves." They contend that organizations are the systems of greatest importance in carrying "out the basic functions of communities, including human services." This simplistic dismissal of the informal institutional structures and processes of society produces an extremely limited view of peoples' lives and of the social work profession. We fear that our colleagues have slipped into thinking that understanding organizations requires less emphasis on community. Why can we not emphasize *both* without assuming that one is greater or better or more important than the other?

Professions have both great and little traditions. Great traditions are the causes and commitments for which the profession developed, grounded in values, dreams, and aspirations. Little traditions comprise the day-to-day activities that professionals perform, often overlapping with what other professionals do. Whereas great traditions hold the vision, little traditions are necessary for daily practice.

Dr. McMurtry and Dr. Kettner have a realistic grasp of the little traditions of social work macro practice. They describe them as "difficult, dogged, discouraging day-to-day work." What they fail to grasp is the necessity for educating dreamers and visionaries who recognize the great traditions of social work. Are most social workers to walk away from the profession's historical commitment to use community organizing methods to pursue social justice? Is social work largely to be limited to administering service organizations that process clients? Should a small elite of organizers and perhaps administrators have sole responsibility for the remnants of social work's commitment to social justice and the great tradition of the profession? Or is the use of community organizing to pursue our profession's commitment the proper responsibility of all professional social workers?

We are appalled that our colleagues perceive a "strong temptation to continue training the dreamers and visionaries who have the luxury of criticizing the status quo." We are not in the business of training. We are educators. Training provides people with technical skills. Education is a process of empowering people to think critically and to question. We do not believe that this is a luxury. This is the essence of social work education. And contrary to the assertions of Dr. McMurtry and Dr. Kettner, a rich and growing literature exists that documents the hard-won accomplishments of community organizing professionals working with oppressed peoples. This literature provides both conceptual and empirical support for the education of macro change agents.

Social work's constituency extends far beyond individuals and "groups of people in need of services." Social work's contributions to society extend beyond the provision of organizationally based services. If one barely survives at the fringes of the job market, if one cannot secure adequate education for one's children or health care for one's family, and if one lives in fear of the youth gangs that control the neighborhood streets, even highly efficient organizationally based human services may do little to improve quality of life.

Social work has a great and proud tradition of working with oppressed and disenfranchised groups to achieve institutional change. We argue that this tradition should continue. We believe that the interests of many invisible people are not furthered by formal organizations and that there are important dimensions of life that do not fall under organizational auspices. We delight in the prospect of producing new generations of social workers who understand both organizations and communities and who are dreamers and visionaries who are offended by institutionalized injustice.

NO

JOHN MICHAEL DALEY AND F. ELLEN NETTING

Community organization is not dead, but the social work profession's passion for social change and social justice is in imminent danger of disappearance if one assumes that our future is limited to organizational practice. Passion for social change and social justice entails risk, uncertainty, conflict, and even chaos—the very elements that both organizations and legitimized professions seek to reduce. If community organization is to survive, we must inflame the smoldering embers of passion for social justice within our profession.

We live in a time of great challenges and change. Within our society, some live in a land of opportunity while others live in an era of insecurity. The American Dream is a cruel hoax for many. We suffer from gridlock on significant issues: the federal deficit, health care, education, housing, and jobs that allow individuals and families to live with dignity. Groups defined by age, gender, race/ethnicity, socioeconomic class, as so forth are pitted against each other. Traditional responses to unmet social, economic, and political needs no longer enjoy public support. Simultaneously, this is a time of great opportunities. We are emerging from the draining dynamics of the Cold War with its potential for nuclear holocaust. A rich variety of citizen groups are working to make their voices heard in civic discourse within increasingly diverse communities. Specifically we see daily evidence of renewed efforts by citizens to assume greater responsibility for community needs. After devastating riots in south central Los Angeles, citizens spontaneously appeared in the streets to clean up and to rebuild neighborhoods. Public housing tenants assume responsibility for managing their housing developments. Parents form coalitions with educators, administrators, and business and religious leaders to reform schools.

In these times of challenges and opportunities, we are not here to report or predict the demise of organizational practice. Both organizational and community practice have contributions to make in shaping a better world. We assert that community practice has unique contributions to make if we are to fulfill our moral responsibility to join with citizens and especially the poor, the oppressed, and the disenfranchised in creating a world that reflects the values of human dignity, citizen participation, and social, political, and economic justice.

Community organization is a richly diverse field of practice that includes policy analysts and developers; program planners; administrators and evaluators; resource developers and allocators; and community organizers and developers working with geographically or issue-defined interest groups and communities. Historically, many community-based social workers have worked with oppressed and disenfranchised peoples and for the cause of justice. Community practitioners work to empower and to cultivate the capacities of natural networks that are central to nurturing social, economic, and political conditions that produce strong, healthy, and just people and institutions.

To address the needs of tomorrow's citizens and especially the needs of the poor, oppressed, and disenfranchised, both organizational and community practitioners need to adopt new ways of thinking and acting. To be effective we must appreciate that organizations are units within larger community and societal systems. Social work macro practice must reject the dichotomous notion of organizational versus community practice and strive for an integration of practice that encompasses organizations *and* communities (Kettner, Daley, & Nichols, 1985). Future generations of social workers need to envision more complex practice arenas—to think intra-, inter-, and trans-organizationally. Professionals need to understand the inner workings of organizations while at the same time seeing beyond formal organizations, recognizing and valuing the importance of natural support networks that are not organizationally based but that play essential roles in the everyday lives of people.

The Limits of Organizational Practice

Two characteristics of organizational practice limit its effectiveness when working for social change and social justice: (1) a bias toward the status quo and (2) a learning disability that inhibits an understanding of and collaboration with natural support and helping networks.

First, organizations by their very nature tend toward the status quo. They are units within the sustaining system, often separate and frequently alienated from the nurturing systems of the oppressed (Norton, 1978). To empower those persons and groups that have not been part of the dominant sustaining system requires an understanding of power and a willingness to secure and use power when helping oppressed and disenfranchised groups to redress injustices (Alinsky, 1971).

Organizational practice shows a lack of political will to help the oppressed and disenfranchised to secure and use power in the cause of justice. Internally, organizations, including human service agencies, have few women, minorities, and representatives of other disenfranchised groups in leadership positions such as board members and administrators (Gutierrez & Lewis, 1992, p. 114; Middleton, 1987; and Widmer, 1987). By the end of the 1980s, even though men and women obtained the same median educational levels, " . . . executive women on the average earned 42% less than their male counterparts" (Kelly, 1991, p. 50). Organizations are strongholds for those who are part of the system. Where do women, minorities, and other oppressed and disenfranchised peoples fit in?

In their external relationships, organizations are essentially flawed as mechanisms to empower the oppressed. Why? Professional organizations have mixed motives. In addition to concern for the interests of those to be served, organizational and professional interests must be served. Although these interests are at times compatible, at other times these interests compete or are perceived to be in competition. For example, organizations and professions need to secure sanction/ legitimacy and other resources, usually given by institutions controlled by dominant elements of the community or society. Yet empowerment-focused practice often challenges the prerogatives of the privileged. This poses problems for organizational practice. Countervailing institutional arrangements are necessary.

The second characteristic that limits the ability of organizations to respond to emerging conditions, needs, and opportunities is their inability to understand and to collaborate with natural support and helping networks in developing strong, healthy, and just persons, families, neighborhoods, and institutions (Whittaker & Garbarino, 1983). This weakness is most pronounced when dealing with nondominant groups, which often suffer the most stress and injustice and are least adequately served by organizational interventions. By *learning disability* we mean the ineffectiveness of otherwise capable organizations to develop sensitive models and methods that incorporate the efforts of natural networks in their organizational services (Senge, 1990). In essence human service organizations retain significant blind spots regarding the lives, needs, problems, strengths, and aspirations of the poor and the oppressed.

All too often major social, economic, or political trends go largely unnoticed by professional organizations until the trends produce new generations of crisis, unmet needs, and problems. Examples of these unnoticed trends include the post–World War II migration of rural southern Blacks to the central cities in northern states, the recognition of the feminization of poverty, the decay of political institutions fueled by and responsive to special-interest money, and the looting of our economic base during the 1980s. Positive silent trends are equally significant—the "backyard revolution" noted by Boyte (1984) as ordinary citizens increasingly band together to pursue shared values and the emergence of the ethnic middle class and of strong new ethnic communities.

The Future of Community Organization

In this section we reflect on the implications of the challenges, opportunities, trends, and strategies that face social work as it promotes social justice. The profession is morally obligated to engage in *both* organizational and community practice. We reject the dichotomy between organizational and community practice, because organizations are interactive dancers within community systems. To choreograph organizational practice as if it could exist separately from community is inconceivable for a profession that advocates for social change and social, economic, and political justice.

First, we must address institutional change if we are committed to justice. Bellah and his colleagues (1991) call us to think about our societal institutions, defined as those patterns of interaction that enforce what people do (i.e., family, religion, polity, the market economy). Often we use *institution* interchangeably with *organization,* yet Bellah cautions against this interchangeable language:

> Organizations certainly loom large in our lives, but if we think only of organizations and not of institutions we may greatly oversimplify our problems . . . and we cannot solve [our problems] simply by improving individual organizations: we have to reform the institution itself. (p. 11)

Second, we must develop new models of practice. New models of community organizing are emerging in the social work literature. Rivera and Erlich (1992) and Daley and Wong (in press) call for new approaches to community practice with the poor, the oppressed, and the disenfranchised. These approaches are grounded in the traditions and present realities of the group to be worked with, recognize indigenous, informal networks and resources, and deal realistically with social, economic, and political power.

A recent typology of community structure and delinquency illustrates the importance of recognizing group and community networks. "Remedial intervention at the individual level cannot be a substitute for committed and continuous policy efforts to change those community circumstances" (Figueira-McDonough, 1991, p. 85). We must recognize the community as a complex field of interaction among diverse formal organizations and informal networks.

Third, we must develop new collaborative strategies involving natural support and helping systems, which are well documented as the first resources to which individuals and families turn in time of stress or need. Natural networks (i.e., family, friends, neighbors, coworkers) are best positioned to nurture healthy development, respond immediately to emerging needs, be accessible to historically underserved groups, and provide cost-effective prevention and early intervention (Berkowitz, 1982). We need to envision new roles and new relationships responsive to the life realities of citizens and especially the poor, the oppressed, and the disenfranchised. For example, as we work with natural networks, professional helping systems, and basic institutions, a unique role for community organizing emerges from intersystem dynamics—facilitating the relationships and exchanges between the citizens or the oppressed group and the other system components. The community organization practitioner facilitates efforts to pursue interests identified by citizens (or citizen groups).

Fourth and most importantly, we must reexamine and reaffirm our value commitments. If social work seeks to improve quality of life for all, we must be willing to take the heat when working with the poor and the oppressed to gain and use power. Empowerment requires that the relationships between professionals and citizens be characterized by mutual understanding and respect (Friedmann, 1973). We must be willing to work to change human service organizations and systems. Human service organizations often have limited track records when it comes to valuing, understanding, and working with the very nondominant groups so vital to the cause component of social work.

In closing, we note the arrogance of the assumption that organizational practice is the future of social work, a profession comprised primarily of women. The dominant view of society has always assumed that the "important work" occurs in organizations or is organizationally sanctioned. The invisible lives of women and women's work that occurs in the interactions of young mothers caring for children and in the mutual aid and support of older, sometimes disabled women as they age in their neighborhoods has never been valued. And since value is attached to money in our society, these efforts are considered unproductive (Waring, 1988). It comes as little surprise, then, that the efforts of nondominant groups, operating within informal helping networks, are dismissed as insignificant to the future of social work practice.

[Our world] pays no heed to the preservation of natural resources or to the labor of the majority of its inhabitants or to the unpaid work of the reproduction of human life itself—not to mention its maintenance and care. The system cannot respond to values it refuses to recognize. (Waring, 1988, pp. 3–4)

We believe that social work is a profession grounded in values, values often not embraced by the larger society nor fully lived within our own social welfare institutions. Community organizing is a necessary means to recognize and live these values.

REFERENCES

Alinsky, S. D. (1971). *Rules for radicals.* New York: Vintage/Random House.
Bellah, R. N., Madsen, R., Sullivan, W. M., Swidler, A., & Tipton, S. M. (1991). *The good society.* New York: Alfred A. Knopf.
Berkowitz, W. R. (1982). *Community impact.* Cambridge, MA: Schenkman.
Boyte, H. C. (1984). *Community is possible: Repairing America's roots.* New York: Harper Colophon.
Daley, J. M. and Wong, P. (In Press). Community Development with Emerging Ethnic Communities, Second ACOSA Annual.
Figueria-McDonough, J. (1991, March). Community structure and delinquency: A typology. *Social Service Review, 65*(1), 68–91.
Friedmann, J. (1973). *Retracking America: A theory of transactive planning.* Garden City, NY: Doubleday/Anchor.
Gutierrez, L. M., & Lewis, E. A. (1992). A feminist perspective on organizing with women of color. In F. G. Rivera, & J. L. Erlich (Eds.), *Community organizing in a diverse society* (pp. 113–132). Boston: Allyn and Bacon.

Kelly, R. M. (1991). *The gendered economy: Work, careers, and success.* Newbury Park, CA: Sage Publications.

Kettner, P., Daley, J. M., & Nichols, A. W. (1985). *Initiating change in organizations and communities.* Monterey, CA: Brooks/Cole.

Middleton, M. (1987). Nonprofit Boards of Directors: Beyond the Governance Function. In W. W. Powell (Ed.), *The nonprofit sector: A research handbook* (pp. 141–153). New Haven, CT: Yale University Press.

Norton, D. G. (1978). *The dual perspective: Inclusion of ethnic minority content in the social work curriculum.* New York: Council on Social Work Education.

Rivera, F. G., & Erlich, J. L. (Eds.) (1992). *Community organizing in a diverse society.* Boston: Allyn and Bacon.

Senge, P. M. (1990). *The fifth discipline: The art and practice of the learning organization.* New York: Doubleday Currency.

Waring, M. (1988). *If women counted.* San Francisco: Harper and Row.

Whittaker, J. K., & Garbarino, J. (1983). *Social support networks: Informal helping in the human services.* New York: Aldine.

Widmer, C. (1987). Minority participation on boards of directors of human service agencies: Some evidence and suggestions. *Journal of Voluntary Action Research, 14*(4), 8–23.

Rejoinder to Dr. Daly and Dr. Netting

STEPHEN L. McMURTRY AND PETER M. KETTNER

The points raised by Drs. Daley and Netting about the role of community practice are rich in passion but unconvincing in substance. We submit that faculty in schools of social work who advocate direct work with communities have too long been "inflaming the smoldering embers of passion for social justice" without providing the knowledge and skills that professional social workers need to help bring about this goal. Drs. Daley and Netting seem committed to continuing that approach.

At one level, they rely on the tired old tactic of questioning the ideological commitment of their opponents rather than the merit of the opponents' arguments. They also base far more of their case on an appeal to social work values than on a clear explication of why community organization as an arena of social work macro practice is worthy of the disproportionate attention it receives. Finally, though they contend that deemphasizing community organization threatens the value base of social work, they fail to explain the mechanisms by which a social worker's commitment to this value base is supposed to make a tangible difference in the lives of oppressed and underserved people.

Drs. Daley and Netting also endeavor to dismiss organizational practice by portraying all organizations as godless, merciless, and so hopelessly oppressive as to be incapable of permitting meaningful macro-level change. In our initial statement we took pains to point out that organizations may indeed act badly and may often provide poor-quality services, but we also emphasized that being within a malfunctioning organization and wishing to do something about it is neither uncommon nor a retreat from the value base of the profession. Instead, it is precisely for this reason that an understanding of organizations and an ability to change them are the most important macro practice skills a social worker needs to have.

Also, though formal organizations may be easy to demonize, they cannot so easily be dismissed. Organizations are and have long been the fundamental units of all other macro systems, including communities. Accordingly, we agree that false dichotomies should not be created between community and organizational practice. This is because, in effect, community practice *is* organizational practice.

Along these lines, a central problem we have also sought to address in our reasoning is the myth that social workers can and often do intervene with communities as a whole. This is analogous to attempting to fix a computer (or a human body, or a dysfunctional family) or any other type of system without considering its component parts. In most cases, it is not the system as a whole that is broken down, but one or more of these parts. Enabling the system to function properly requires knowing what role is played by each part and how the critical part can be fixed. Intervening in a community service system involves essentially the same process, but the "broken" parts of such a system are generally the organizations within it.

As we noted in our initial statement, survey results indicate that fewer than 2 percent of social workers are primarily involved in community organization, but virtually all social workers work both with and within complex organizations. Indeed, what most community organizers do is *create* organizations that enable a target population to advocate on its own behalf with other organizations in the community.

In summary, the goals that Drs. Daley and Netting hold out for social work are noble and vital. Nevertheless, we believe these goals are much more likely to be achieved by preparing social workers to face the realities of modern, organizationally based practice than by shaming them for lack of faith in an outmoded orthodoxy.

Should Today's Community Organizer Use the Tactics Handed Down from Earlier Generations?

EDITOR'S NOTE: Underlying this debate are issues of personal, social, and political power. All strategies undertaken by organizers deal
with the acquisition of and the redistribution of one or more types of
power to empower individuals, groups, and communities in solving
social problems and in promoting social change. Central to this debate
is the question of whether neighborhood self-help and conflict strategies or strategies that utilize a multi-level systems approach are the
most effective for organizing and empowering communities to achieve
significant social change. This debate is of particular importance given
the complexity and interrelatedness of social problems and the need
to develop partnerships to solve these problems. Continued oppression of racial, ethnic, and other disenfranchised groups, coupled with
inequalities in the distribution of societal resources, requires a critical
examination of the "old" and "new" tactics of community organization.

John L. Erlich, M.S.W., A.B.D., and Felix G. Rivera, Ph.D., argue YES.
John Erlich is a professor in the Division of Social Work at California State
University, Sacramento, where he has been Chair of the Child and Family
Services Concentration and teaches macro practice courses. He has worked as an
organizer in New York City, Michigan, and Sacramento and served as a planning
and organizing consultant to numerous community-based organizations. Professor Erlich has published extensively in the areas of community organization
and planning, social change, emerging minority communities, and burnout.
Among his coauthored or edited books are *Changing Organizations and Commu-*

nity Programs, Strategies of Community Organization: Macro Practice, and *Community Organizing in a Diverse Society.*

Felix Rivera is a professor in the Department of Social Work Education, San Francisco State University, California. He chairs the Social Development sequence and teaches in the areas of community organization and social and evaluative research. With John L. Erlich, he edited the book *Community Organizing in a Diverse Society.*

Allison Zippay, Ph.D., argues NO. She is an assistant professor at the Rutgers University School of Social Work and a Research Associate at the Center for Social and Community Development, Rutgers University. Her areas of research include community development, social networks, and economic mobility among poor and low-income populations.

YES

JOHN L. ERLICH AND FELIX G. RIVERA

"If it ain't broke, don't fix it." While there are limits to the applicability of this old adage—applied to both plumbing and community organization—it contains an extremely important truth. That is, if something has demonstrated value and utility in the past, don't throw it away just because a new or more popular replacement comes along.

The essential issue posed by the controversy question is: Should the current generation of organizers learn from, utilize, and build on the work of earlier generations of organizers? To this, the authors respond with a resounding, "Yes!" While it is clear that the history of community organization is replete with evidence of failure, so is the history of every other kind of attempt to alter the balance of power between and among the "haves" and "have-nots," ethnic and racial groups, neighborhoods and larger political entities, gender and sexual orientation groups, and nation states (and their allies). To limit current organizers to the tactics of the past would, of course, be absurd. But equally absurd would be to dispose wholesale that vast body of tactical knowledge and broad experience that they have proven successful in the past.

It is important to note that the successful tactics have drawn both extensively on consensus (community development) and more heavily on conflict (community organization or social action). The idea of neighborhood self-help and unified group action played an essential role in the emergence of community development as well as community organization (Addams, 1935). The fundamental commitment to participation of neighborhood people on their own behalf and democratic decision making, pioneered at the community level in the settlement houses, are standard elements of current development and organizing methods. It is no mistake that they have stood the test of time. This pragmatic approach to human problems, unlike the so-called scientific methods of the charity organization workers, was a precursor of the self-determining grassroots community work that exploded in the 1960s (Fisher, 1984). Another aspect of the early settlement movement that has had—and continues to have—a major impact on community practice was the strong commitment to helping people maximize their individual and group potentials.

While the field of community organization has been plagued by attacks on its ideology from its earliest days (both the left, ''too little;'' and the right, ''too much''), one continuing strength has been an emphasis on the relationship between ideology and practice. As Horwitt (1989) notes, much of this was drawn from the labor movement (brought by both those who were active in labor and students of the movement's tactics). Important and successful elements include solidarity, organizing across racial and status lines, rank-and-file participation in decision making, and fighting until victory is achieved. The value and significance of indigenous leadership was also stressed, as was the sense of people struggling not only for themselves and their families, but also for their laboring ''brothers'' and ''sisters'' as well. Not the least are tactics related to the acceptance of defeat as part of ongoing reality, the analysis of defeat, and building on defeat to sustain the organizing effort.

Techniques such as strikes, sit-ins, slow-downs, marches, and a wide variety of picketing, boycotts, and demonstrations gained currency from the experience of organized labor. The emphasis on relatively small, tight-knit organizing units that could be mobilized for joint acting was a forerunner to many of the community-level confrontations of the 1960s and early 1970s. Saul Alinsky, often regarded as the premier community organization tactician of the mid-twentieth century, paid tribute to labor leaders and the labor movement in all his major published works (Alinsky, 1946, 1971).

In large measure, because of the success of these and other similar tactics (especially in the civil rights, student, and anti-war movements of the 1960s and 1970s), community organization and community development came to be regarded as fully legitimate methods of social work practice.

The reemergence of community development as a problem-solving, community-integrating, and capacity-building process has been strongly supported by a number of authors since the mid-1950s. Murray Ross (1955) described it as:

> . . . a process by which a community identifies its needs or objectives, develops the confidence and will to work at these needs or objectives, finds the resources (internal and/or external) to deal with these needs or objectives, takes action in respect to them, and in so doing extends and develops cooperative and collaborative attitudes and practices in the community. (p. 39)

William and Loureide Biddle (1965) took Ross's conception of practice a step further by characterizing the conditions under which rapid community improvements were likely to take place:

> Progress occurs most rapidly when a collaborative effort invites the work of all institutions, agencies, class levels, and helping professions. The community approach seeks to be locally all-inclusive; focusing the efforts of many contributions upon the problem of human development, seeking no aggrandizement of any one individual or agency or fraction or association (p. 253).

The legacy of this basic perspective on community development continues to be played out in communities as diverse as Los Angeles's rebuilding in the wake of the 1992 upheavals, New York's efforts to bring services to the homeless, and Chicago's approach to drawing warring gangs into coalition efforts to reduce violence. While we may argue about the maximum effectiveness of such strategies and tactics, there is little question that they are illustrative of some modest, positive efforts that can boast of reasonable levels of success over the last decade.

Community organizing, typically because of its utilization of conflict (as well as consensual) tactics, has had an even more difficult history since the mid-1970s. There has been a marked decline (in some areas almost to extinction) of financial support for organizing efforts that bring communities (and organizers) into direct confrontations with the powers that be. Without sufficient funding, it will continue to be difficult to demonstrate the effectiveness of organizing tactics. The following "rules" for organizing, partly the legacy of the so-called Alinsky Method, seem very current in today's political and social climate (Alinsky, 1971):

1. *Power* [defined as the ability to act] *is the basis of life.* This cornerstone of Alinsky's tactics suggests that power comes from two essential sources—money and people. Without significant financial resources, the have-nots must rely on power derived from the mobilization of large numbers of people.
2. *Power is not only what you have, but what they think you have.* Related to the view of power described above is the threat of numbers and the potentials for disruption of massed groups of people.
3. *You get equality in the very act of taking it.* No individual or group can confer power on another. The "have-nots" must take a measure of power from the "haves" to gain a more equal footing.
4. *Tactics should be within the experience of the people and outside the experience of the opposition.* This means that, whenever possible,

organizers should use tactics with which people in their organization are familiar and comfortable.

5. *Make the enemy live up to their own book of rules.* The targets of change should be required to meet their own announced standards of honesty, openness, and responsibility.

6. *Do not solve problems, organize.* First it is important to organize people around a problem and then attempt to solve it.

7. *People should be organized around their own self-interest.* People should be living with the problem, an emotional "gut-level" experience.

8. *Rub raw the sores of discontent.* Consciousness raising through identification with the problem.

9. *People in positions of control often do the right things for the wrong reasons.* Those in positions of power often do what a community wishes, not because it is right but because they are reacting to political pressure.

10. *Pick the target, freeze it, personalize it, polarize it.* In modern, complex, organization-dominated society, "have-nots" must be able to focus attention on a particular issue and person(s) responsible to cause observers to take sides between the target and the "have-nots' organization."

11. *Keep a fight in the bank.* Organizers and community developers must be ready to move forward on one or more new fronts if they are victorious in their current struggle.

12. *Every negative has a positive.* It is important to believe that a negative can be turned around to provide support for organizing a group.

13. *The price of a successful attack is often a constructive alternative.* Be prepared with a plan if the opposition says, "You're right, now what do you want?"

14. *The action is in the reaction.* The change target should be goaded into a reaction anticipated by the organizer who is ready with an effective tactical response to it.

While suggestive, these rules for organizing do not exhaust the range of generations of organizers. A few other strategies demand special attention:

Coalition Building. It is clear that for disenfranchised communities to be heard, often they need to join together by identifying common concerns and issues and presenting a united front to external political forces. It is also apparent that such communities need advocates, brokers, and leaders that are able to hold together diverse interests, and change strategies—perhaps even more than in the 1960s, 1970s, and 1980s (Dluhy, 1990).

Politics and Legislative Reform. The mid-1990s present challenges at the community level that are, in many ways, comparable to the conditions that faced civil rights organizations in the 1960s. In addition, the conservatism of the Supreme Court does not auger well for less affluent communities and people. Strong, concerted organizing has resulted in some recent victories, such as the Japanese-American movement for reparations. More such efforts are needed that directly impact city, state, and federal governments (Rivera & Erlich, 1992).

Racism. The need to reinvigorate the struggle against racism seems eminently clear. No celebration of diversity can compensate for either the decline in opportunities for people of color or the increasingly overt public and private acts of racial hatred and discrimination. Indeed, racism within and among communities of color must be addressed. Murase (1992) and others have noted that we must be mindful of "exceptionalism," where the white community defines a particular community of color as being a model for others because it embraces the values of the white middle class.

Community Development. Community development during the 1960s was an integral part of the civil rights movement and the movement towards ethnic and racial pride. Community development is both process and task and can be viewed as a three-stage process. The first stage involves contract making between the worker and the community. Consent is established and goals are set. An agreement is reached to work together with a philosophy that works for all concerned. The second stage entails the development of political awareness. Action plans are prepared, outside resources are identified, an assessment and analysis of functions of the community are undertaken, and action is begun. The third stage is the implementation of the community development activities. Goals and objectives are implemented. Creation of new production and distribution ventures in cooperative modes is undertaken, community meetings are held, and the community is mobilized through multiple strategies to realize goals and objectives (Pantoja & Perry, 1992).

If community organizers and developers do not make full use of the tactics handed down from earlier generations, they will not only be doomed to repeat all the mistakes of the past but also will be unable to take advantage of new opportunities for change that our current turbulent social and political environment provides.

REFERENCES

Addams, J. (1935). *Forty years at Hull House.* New York: MacMillian.

Alinsky, S. D. (1946). *Reveille for radicals.* Chicago: University of Chicago Press.

Alinsky, S. D. (1971). *Rules for radicals.* New York: Random House.

Biddle, W., & Biddle, L. J. (1965). *The community development process: The rediscovery of local initiative.* New York: Holt, Rinehart and Winston.

Dluhy, J. M. (with the assistance of Kravitz, S. L.). (1990). *Building coalitions in the human services.* Newbury Park, CA: Sage.

Fisher, R. (1984, Summer). Community organization in historical perspective: A typology. *The Houston Review,* 8.

Horwitt, S. (1989). *Let them call me rebel: Saul Alinsky—His life and legacy.* New York: Knopf.

Murase, K. (1992). Organizing in the Japanese-American Community. In F. G. Rivera & J. L. Erlich (Eds.), *Community organizing in a diverse society.* Boston: Allyn and Bacon.

Patoja, A., & Perry, W. (1992). Community development and restoration: A perspective. In F. G. Rivera & J. L. Erlich (Eds.), *Community organizing in a diverse society.* Boston: Allyn and Bacon.

Rivera, F. G., & Erlich, J. L. (Eds.). (1992). *Community organizing in a diverse society.* Boston: Allyn and Bacon.

Ross, M. G. (1955). *Community organization: Theory and principles.* New York: Harper and Brothers.

Spergel, I. (1987). Community development. *Encyclopedia of social work* (18 ed.). Silver Springs, MD: National Association of Social Workers.

Rejoinder to Dr. Erlich and Dr. Rivera

ALLISON ZIPPAY

It is broken, and it does need to be fixed.

As Dr. Erlich and Dr. Rivera state, it would be foolish to dispose wholesale of the tactical knowledge and experiences that have been used by previous generations of community organizers. But the tactics are in need of an update. Contemporary means must be applied to contemporary conditions.

Consensus and conflict are, as the authors describe, important organizational concepts and techniques. Consensus has figured prominently in building numerous coalitions to address problems ranging from voting rights to homelessness. Conflict strategies have fueled and advanced the labor movement, civil rights, and women's movements.

But why are so many of the examples of the applications and successes of these techniques more than twenty years old? Why does most of the literature that we cite date from the 1950s and 1960s?

We have failed to keep current. Wallowing in nostalgia for the activist days of the 1960s, we have not sufficiently analyzed the strengths and weaknesses of these techniques to modify and apply them to changing populations and conditions. Dynamic social problems require a dynamic response.

For example, the work of Saul Alinsky continues to be used as a spiritual and practical guide by many community organizers. Does his work have contemporary relevance? Some aspects of it do, some do not. Without financial resources, Alinsky said, the "have-nots" must rely on the power gained from mobilizing large numbers of people. Is political influence determined by quantity or quality? Quantity or publicity or savvy? Can a few well-placed, well-connected politicians and advocates wield as much power in promoting a progressive piece of legislation as thousands of people marching in Washington? Can a clever political television ad viewed by millions prove more influential than a demonstration that isn't covered by the evening news? In the current high-tech, media-oriented world the currency of power has changed. Numbers alone do not carry the significance they did when Alinsky first wrote about them in the 1940s.

Similarly, questions arise regarding the kinds of issues or themes that can effectively mobilize and involve the disenfranchised. In citing examples of Alinsky's philosophy that have contemporary relevance, the authors note that Alinsky exhorted the have-nots to organize en masse against the "enemy" (those who have power). Who are the enemies that today's poor can be mobilized to rise en masse against? Business? The police? The schools? Federal bureaucracies? Many of the poor aspire to be teachers or police officers or postal workers. They want their children educated, their personal safety protected, and a job for themselves. Pitting the poor against the "enemy" is an oversimplistic and ineffective method for organizing heterogeneous groups of disenfranchised around complex social problems. It paternalistically assumes that the poor are not capable of a more sophisticated analysis of organizational functioning, that they will accept a blanket pronouncement that all power holders are their enemies. It thwarts rather than encourages their participation in much-needed efforts to critique and reform these organizations.

The rich experiences of earlier generations have much to lend contemporary community organizers. But it is time to look forward and expand our base of knowledge and techniques to more effectively respond to current problems and conditions.

NO

ALLISON ZIPPAY

Certain tactics used by previous generations of community organizers further isolated and fragmented poor and low-income communities rather than empowered them. Such fractious methods included elements of neighborhood self-help and conflict strategies. Often, political responses to these tactics have involved appeasement and tokenism rather than a redistribution of social and economic power. Community organization in the 1990s requires both a conceptual and tactical restructuring.

Previous Strategies and Tactics: Neighborhood Self-Help

During the 1950s and 1960s, many community organization and community development strategists within social work focused on methods of strengthening "horizontal" ties and social bonds among the residents of poor and low-income neighborhoods (Biddle & Biddle, 1965; Lippitt, Watson, & Westley, 1958; Ross, 1955). The strategy sought to increase people's psychological capacity to bring about social change by enhancing their self-image, sense of community, self-determination, and ability to work together to solve problems. Ross (1955) described community organization as "a process by which a community identifies its needs . . . develops the confidence and will to work at these needs . . . and develops cooperative and collaborative attitudes and practices in the community" (p. 40).

Within this framework, the community of focus was often defined by geography: a neighborhood locale or a group of neighborhood residents linked by a common interest or issue. The strategy stressed the development of neighborhood loyalty and community integration that was accomplished, in part, by activities aimed at improving relationships among local residents.

A key component of this strategy was the modification of individual attitudes and values: alienation, lack of motivation, and low self-esteem were to be replaced by community activism, personal responsibility, and self-respect. As a method of social change, the *process* of facilitating attitudinal adjustment and social development took primacy over the accomplishment of instrumental goals and tasks.

The tactics of this strategy were directed at encouraging and organizing citizen participation in activities such as self-help groups, neighborhood associations, skills training, social development programs, and coalition building, around any variety of issues such as youth recreation, parenting skills, substance abuse, and crime prevention.

As such, the premise of this strategy was that activities aimed at building social relationships would foster personal development, motivate greater community participation, increase problem-solving skills, spur an enhanced sense of individual and collective power and control, and ultimately lead to neighborhood-directed social change. Low-income communities were viewed as overdependent on extracommunity forces to solve social problems; this organizational method was to foster greater independence and local self-determination.

Conceptual orientations that influenced this method included the theory of a culture of poverty; assumptions linking community participation with an increased sense of personal efficacy and social integration; and organizational theories that presented social change as dependent on personal "reeducation" and attitudinal adjustment (Chin & Benne, 1976).

Conflict

A controversial approach to community organization that was used by social workers primarily during the 1960s involved conflict strategies. Conflict approaches aimed to bring about institutional change by organizing members of disadvantaged and politically disenfranchised communities to confront societal power holders and, through any number of coercive means, demand and obtain a redistribution of power and resources (Alinsky, 1946, 1972; Bailey & Brake, 1975). In its literature and practice, conflict strategists often exhorted the oppressed (members of socially or economically disadvantaged groups) to rise against the enemy (community institutions and members of the social and economic establishment). It was assumed that influence could be attained, in part, through numbers, and attention was given to mobilizing masses of people. The issues around which people were organized were to be emotionally provocative. As Saul Alinsky (1972) urged, "Pick the target, freeze it, personalize it, and polarize it" (p. 130).

The tactics in this approach were directed at organizing community residents to participate in activities that involved some level of coercion and were often disruptive. These included legal and legislative actions and confrontational events such as demonstrations, pickets, rallies, boycotts, strikes, and civil disobedience.

Conceptually, this orientation focused on imbalances of power as a precipitant of social change. Differences in social and economic power among community residents and groups were seen to arise in the course of competition for scarce goods and resources and produced disequilibrating social tensions. Moral, economic, political, and social influence could be violently or nonviolently employed to pressure individuals or groups for a redistribution of goods and services which, in turn, realigned the balance of power.

Flaws in Concept and Practice

A critical flaw in both the neighborhood self-help and conflict strategies was that their tactics often further polarized communities. While both approaches rhetorically advocated community integration, they often failed to establish, in concept and practice, viable links between disadvantaged populations and institutional sources of social and economic power.

While efforts to enhance self-esteem and increase the capacity of neighborhood residents to solve their own social problems are worthy and important, the focus of the neighborhood self-help movement on the strengthening of horizontal ties missed a critical and integral element of power brokering: the procurement and management of extracommunity resources.

Many of the problems facing low-income people—poor housing, unemployment, poverty—cannot be solved solely through local efforts; they have roots in broader structural and political forces. Effective capacity building requires promoting the concept of interconnection rather than detachment. Problem-solving skills must include methods for expanding the social networks of residents and leaders of low-income communities to include instrumental connections with the people and organizations who manage and control the distribution of resources. An example is neighborhood leaders who have the knowledge and skills to follow pending state legislation, obtain a meeting with their state representative, and deliver a constituency. To sell process-oriented personal development as a primary means to empowerment is naive (or dishonest) and incomplete; it is but one element in a complex, task-oriented, multilevel strategy needed to encourage vertical connections among disenfranchised groups.

A similar criticism can be made with regard to conflict strategies. Conflict is an important catalyst for change and has directed attention and action to issues of social and economic injustice. However, in focusing on the tactic of pitting the "oppressed" against the "enemy" to mobilize anger and action in disadvantaged communities, the approach often circumscribed and isolated low-income groups. As with the self-help approach, it assumed that the practice and concept of separation ("us" versus "them") was psychologically empowering. While the tactic was effective in mobilizing anger, its actions and resolutions were, again, often incomplete. The next phase—building the community's skills to develop and manage resources and promoting an understanding of an interdependent system in which neighborhood residents and extracommunity leaders interact in a sustained partnership to solve social problems—often received little attention and effort. Instead, the focus on disconnection and attack may have deepened alienation. Regarding institutions as the enemy, some community residents disdained and shunned efforts to engage their participation in restructuring establishments such as the schools, police, or welfare departments. Some institutional leaders likewise demonstrated their detachment and scorn through feeble attempts to develop or improve community services.

The need to facilitate vertical connections as an organizational strategy for change has been raised by some analysts (Granovetter, 1982; Khinduka, 1975).

Conceptual and Tactical Restructuring

While elements of the strategies of neighborhood self-help and conflict are important components of community organization, their separatist orientation was flawed. It can be argued that it enabled institutional leaders to more easily respond with gestures that represented tokenism and appeasement rather than a redistribution of power and resources; low-income groups were often not politically well connected or understood and were not considered integral or long-term participants in community development processes.

Conceptually, community organization strategies can be framed within a systems approach: a view of social organization that emphasizes reciprocal and mutually reinforcing relationships among individuals and organizations. Other theories such as social network analysis and social exchange can guide an understanding of the nature and function of social connections that can facilitate resource mobilization and upward mobility among disadvantaged groups.

In terms of tactics, community organization strategists need to broaden their focus beyond neighborhood residents and disadvantaged populations in a multilevel approach. In addition to organizing grassroots groups, they should simultaneously work with business, political, and other institutional leaders to systematically build *their* capacity to understand and solve social and economic problems among low-income communities, to modify negative attitudes toward disadvantaged populations, and to strengthen their ability to serve their community constituencies. Knowledge and skills development among institutional power holders can include establishing formal and informal means of exchanging information with representatives of disadvantaged groups; assessing local social problems and their causes through exchanges with community residents and leaders (and visits to low-income households, an urban high school, or a public housing project); studying the functions and dysfunctions of existing social programs; and developing and committing public and private resources to problem-solving efforts. Likewise, local residents and leaders need to develop skills in areas such as understanding the functioning of bureaucracies and political systems; fundraising from extracommunity sources; legislative lobbying; and gaining access to institutional boards, committees, and executives. This approach frames community leaders and residents as community "partners" and promotes the collective interest of efforts to increase the social and economic resources of low-income groups.

An example of a multilevel strategy, termed *parallel processing,* is currently being piloted in several urban communities in New Jersey by the Center for Social and Community Development at the Rutgers University School of Social Work (Chavis, 1992). In this approach, organizers work with both neighborhood and institutional leaders to strengthen their problem-solving capacities in strategies that include organizing city-wide committees to link neighborhood and institutional representatives in task-oriented social and community development activities.

Thus, departing from the exclusionary tactics of previous generations, contemporary community organizers should test strategies that incorporate a multilevel approach for its potential to provide a more holistic, politically viable, and effective problem-solving method.

REFERENCES

Alinsky, S. (1946). *Reveille for radicals.* Chicago: University of Chicago Press.

Alinsky, S. (1972). *Rules for radicals.* New York: Vintage Books.

Bailey, R., & Brake, M. (1975). *Radical social work.* New York: Pantheon.

Biddle, W. W., & Biddle, L. J. (1965). *The community development process: The rediscovery of local initiative.* New York: Holt, Rinehart and Winston.

Chavis, D. (1992, in press). Supporting urban community development: Renovating the social infrastructure.

Chin, E., & Benne, K. D. (1976). General strategies for effecting changes in human systems. In W. G. Bennis, K. D. Benne, R. Chin, & K. Corey (Eds.), *The planning of change.* New York: Holt, Rhinehart, and Winston.

Granovetter, M. (1982). The strength of weak ties: A network theory revisited. In P. V. Marsden & N. Lin (Eds.), *Social structure and network analysis.* Beverly Hills, CA: Sage.

Khinduka, S. (1975). Community development: Potential and limitations. In R. Kramer & H. Specht (Eds.), *Readings in community organization practice,* second edition. Englewood Cliffs, NJ: Prentice-Hall.

Lippitt, R., Watson, J., & Westley, B. (1958). *The dynamics of planned change.* New York: Harcourt Brace.

Ross, M. G. (1955). *Community organization: Theory and principles.* New York: Harper and Brothers.

Rejoinder to Dr. Zippay

JOHN L. ERLICH AND
FELIX G. RIVERA

Today's community organizers should continue to operate with the tactics and techniques handed down from earlier generations. In so doing, we must consider the reality within which the poor and disenfranchised find themselves. These communities are in situations far worse today than the 1960s. We cannot assume that part of the explanation for the present conditions may be laid at the feet of organizers who used these strategies and tactics. At the same time we cannot assume that the sudden "invention" so-called new tactics and strategies will serve as a better method by which communities in need suddenly overcome their economic, social, and political plight.

There is too much reliance on abstract social science theories. General systems theory, for example, has become so popular that it seems to serve as a panacea for explaining all of the ills of society. We do not believe that such theories will take the place of such successful approaches as neighborhood self-help (which we prefer to call *neighborhood development*), conflict strategies, and disruptive tactics. Part of the problem with the analysis of historical efforts to fully describe community organizing is that many of the analysts are writing as outsiders. There is little literature about organizing in the 1960s written by those within the communities using these methods.

As organizers and activists during the 1960s and 1970s, the authors see the old strategies and tactics as relevant for the issues of today. Part of the problem, if any, has to do with the perceptions of outside community organizers, as to what *they* think works for the communities.

Dr. Zippay argues that the neighborhood development movement focused on ''horizontal'' ties and bonds with an emphasis on psychological development of the individuals' potential to change their ''self-image.'' What is wrong with that aspect of the movement? To us it fits very nicely into what we today identify as the process of empowerment. It is over simplistic to assume that the *process* in initiating change takes precedence over the long-range goals established by the community. This was not our experience at all. There were some very healthy debates about political and economic realities and racism and how these dynamics were maintained and supported by the status quo institutions. It was also our experience that no matter what the degree of education and political leanings of the communities we were working with, these issues were always discussed with attendant sensitivity to the communities' level of understanding of the problems. If any model was antithetical to the development of self-determination within the neighborhood development movement, it is the notion of a culture of poverty. Many organizers indeed embraced that model, but those were not the organizers we worked with, they were not what we would consider progressive organizers. We were very careful about the cultural and linguistic complexities present in many communities and the implications these had for organizing (Rivera & Erlich, 1992).

We believe that one of the most efficacious strategies at the disposal of disenfranchised communities is that of disruptive tactics and other conflict strategies. The alternatives are a status quo situation that presents little tension to promote the process of change, through either negotiations or demonstrations. Dr. Zippay states that community polarization will be an outcome of neighborhood development and conflict strategies. As long as there is disagreement, there will also be the chance of community polarization. This is not a significant enough reason to not get engaged in a social change process, as long as the outcomes far outweigh the polarization.

A Reaffirmation of Organizing Principles

We agree with Dr. Zippay that a successful organizer must work toward developing extracommunity resources, institution building, as broad a power base as possible, and community leaders. But we disagree when Dr. Zippay assumes that these things were not part of the approaches taken by organizers of past generations. Of course, there were those who ignored these tenets of organizing, just like those organizers who ignore them today. It has been our experience, however, that good and effective organizers sought to strengthen communities using the same objectives that Dr. Zippay cited. We cannot believe that an effective and progressive organizer would get involved without practicing these principles.

The same may be said for systems analysis, social network analysis, and social exchange. Again, a progressive organizer has these methods in mind when working with a community, but that should not interfere with the community's needs. All issues and concerns should evolve from within the community. It has been our experience that some communities are ready for these activities, while others have yet to engage in an analysis of their condition. Woe to the organizers who come with promises and political posturing that are different from what the community sees as a need. After all, does not self-determination mean choice for the community?

Community organizing strategies employed in the 1950s and 1960s are still viable today. The ones we consider important and worth repeating were covered in our essay. Additionally, the following methods should be given special emphasis in the 1990s and beyond:

> *Culturally Sensitive Organizing.* If ever we needed to once again hear such organizing cries as "Black is beautiful," "Brown is beautiful," and so on, it is now. The civil rights gains made during the last thirty years—however meager—are being taken away from communities of color by a conservative Supreme Court and a conservative agenda by the politicians in Washington and across the United States. The rapid growth of communities of color is unparalleled in our country's history. Their needs are many and organizers working with, for example, the Vietnamese, Salvadorians, Cambodians, or Haitians, are very few. Racial pride worked as the bonding agent for mass demonstrations and social change in the 1950s and 1960s, and an aggressive reaffirmation of these principles is needed in all communities of color in the 1990s.
>
> *Conflict and Disruptive Strategies.* Clearly conflict and disruptive strategies are some of the most dramatic and controversial methods of community organization practice. When we look at the last thirty years, it is these methods of organizing that stand out in people's minds. The main advantage of conflict and disruptive strategies is that they bring issues to the fore in very dramatic ways. We cannot say enough about the viability of such strategies as strikes and boycotts. They are methods for change that continue to prove effective. They must always be at the disposal of communities as a potential threat. These methods serve to keep the opposition off balance as they try to figure out the strategies being used.

The debate over what strategies or tactics should be used is a moot one. We believe that communities should employ all methods of organizing—a mixing of strategies and tactics as dictated by the particular situation. To assume that some methods are ''outdated'' is to limit the choices available to the community.

In conclusion, we believe that the strategies and tactics utilized by earlier generations are as viable today as they were in the 1960s. While the nature of the problems change and the opposition has gotten more sophisticated, the viability of the strategies and tactics has not diminished. Is it not interesting that the conservative anti-abortion Operation Rescue is utilizing organizing strategies and tactics straight out of the civil rights struggles of the 1950s and 1960s?

REFERENCE

Rivera, F. G., & Erlich, J. L. (1992). *Community organizing in a diverse society.* Boston: Allyn and Bacon.

Should Only African-American Community Organizers Work in African-American Neighborhoods?

EDITOR'S NOTE: Within African-American communities is a long history of organizing self-help programs. These emerged primarily as a result of the systematic exclusion of African-Americans from the socio-economic resources of American society. By utilizing both the informal and formal systems of families, friends, and neighbors as well as churches, fraternal organizations, and voluntary associations, African-Americans organized to meet individual and community needs. As a result of the civil rights movement, opportunities for African-Americans greatly expanded as did guarantees of basic rights. However, in spite of the gains made, institutional racism continues to be a powerful force in American life as seen in the uneven enforcement of affirmative action and other civil rights protections. Thus, many community organizers argue that African-Americans can be the only effective organizers in their communities to empower individuals and the larger community: the focus on self-help and social change can be achieved only by African-American organizers. Others argue that white organizers can mobilize and empower African-American individuals, groups, and communities with as much effectiveness as African-American organizers. The issues raised in this debate are significant as they confront individual and collective assumptions about race and oppression.

Audrey M. Shillington, Ph.D., and William L. Dotson, M.A., say YES. Audrey M. Shillington is an N.I.M.H. Post-doctoral Fellow at Washington University School of Medicine, Department of Psychiatry. She is currently involved in research in the areas of substance abuse, its comorbidity with other psychiatric illnesses, risk factors for HIV/AIDS, and nosology.

William Dotson is currently working at St. Louis Health Department as head of Community Outreach for Risk Reduction. He is addressing problems of drug addiction and HIV prevention. Mr. Dotson is also currently working on his Ph.D. at Washington University, Department of Psychology.

Audrey Olsen Faulkner says NO. She is a professor at the Union Institute, Cincinnati, Ohio, and professor emerita from the Rutgers University School of Social Work. Her teaching, research, and practice career has focused on excluded groups—people of color, women, the poor, and the aged.

YES

AUDREY M. SHILLINGTON AND WILLIAM L. DOTSON

"Men do not build bridges for other men; they build them for themselves" (an African proverb).

That men do not build bridges for other men symbolizes an understanding, and the action, of community self-sufficiency. The concept of community self-sufficiency embodies principles and activities toward a collective purpose and will in the form of political advocacy, as well as collective commitment, ownership, control, motivation, persistence, and effort.

African-American community self-sufficiency, embodying all of the above, includes an understanding of the exploitation and plunder of the African-American community by insensitive mercenaries who called themselves community organizers, researchers, or service deliverers.

Historically, many experiences between whites and African-Americans have not been conducive to engendering trust. Slavery is a major issue that remains strong in the minds of most African-Americans and is such an obvious and well-known infringement on human liberty that it need not be elaborated on.

In more recent history another event that created distrust between African-Americans and whites: the less well-known Tuskegee Syphilis Experiment conducted by the U.S. Public Health Service (Jones, 1981). This experiment, more commonly known as the Tuskegee Study, took place in Macon County, an economically depressed area in central Alabama, which was 82 percent African-American at the Census in both 1930 and 1970. This was the longest experiment where the progress of a human disease was studied and medical treatments were withheld. The original study included 399 African-American males with syphilis and 201 controls. These syphilitic African-American males were studied for forty years to follow the progress of the disease and then to examine organ damage at autopsy. The medical professionals taking part in the study believed that syphilis was a disease of little consequences to African-Americans and, further, that as long as syphilis was dismissed as inconsequential for African-Americans, there was little chance that a health program to try fight or cure the disease would commence.

The African-Americans wanted to take part in the study because they were told they would receive free medical examinations and treatment. However, few people in this community had ever been to a doctor, and so the physicians believed their patients wouldn't understand any information they could give on the disease. Thus, the community residents were never told they had syphilis and, instead, were told they were being studied due to having "bad blood." No information was given on what caused this medical problem or how to control the spread of it. The community members underwent blood tests, x-rays, and spinal fluid testing. The goal of the investigators was to follow the subjects until the last one had died.

Not only were the community members deprived of information that would help prevent the spread of the disease or told how to recognize it, but the investigators in this study went to great lengths to ensure that no medical intervention would interfere with their data. During the physical examinations conducted for service in World War II, a number of African-American men from this community were diagnosed as having syphilis. Normally, they would have been notified of this diagnosis and ordered to obtain treatment. However, the Public Health Service (PHS) intervened, and asked the draft board to exclude the enlistees who were taking part in their study from the list of those being notified of needing treatment.

Treatment was again withheld in 1943 when the PHS started giving penicillin to patients with syphilis at treatment clinics in the United States. However, the African-American men participating in the Tuskegee Study were once again excluded from receiving treatment for their disease. In 1951, penicillin became the common treatment for syphilis. Even then, the investigators insisted on withholding treatment. They insisted the experiment should continue because "it made the experiment a never-again-to-be-repeated opportunity" (Jones, 1981, p. 179). They felt that the widespread use of antibiotics made it impossible to ever find a large group of syphilitic patients again. So, this human experiment was continued for another twenty years after a known treatment became commonly used. The experiment was finally exposed in the *Washington Star* on July 25, 1972.

This is one example in which white care givers came into African-American communities to deliver services. However, the trust of the community was abused and the members of the community were treated like guinea pigs. Many assert that, because of this history, a strong level of suspicion exists among the African-American communities in this country toward service providers. The implications of these suspicions range from the underutilization of mental health services to the suspicion of services provided to prevent and treat HIV/AIDS.

One way to restrict such exploitation in the African-American community is to require that the community organizer be African-American and that he or she work from an African-American perspective. The terms *African-American* and *African-American perspective* pertain to both the color of skin and to the state of mind of the community organizer, her or his past track record, and whether the fruit of their work will provide direct or indirect benefits to the African-American community.

An African-American community organizer is one who does not exploit the African-American community. She or he knows the African-American culture and can understand community problems and formulate strategies and solutions consistent with the needs of the African-American community. The African-American community organizer has a social change philosophy rather than a problem-solving, Band-Aid philosophy.

We can learn a lesson from an African brother, the late Tom Myboya, who pointed out the plight of the Africans, to paraphrase: when the white man went to Africa, the Africans owned the land and the white man had the Bible; now, the white man owns the land and the Africans have the Bible. Thus, it is imperative that African-American professionals and the African-American community maintain a constant vigil to prevent the perpetuation of the "benign neglect" syndrome (Moynihan, 1970) that dominates the white Americans' perceptions of the African-American experience.

Thus, there need to be bold, new strategies toward effective African-American community organizing. First, there need to be effective African-American community organizers. Ideally, and necessarily, the African-American community organizer must be African-American and competent. Second, the organizing effort in African-American communities should not address what is wrong (for we know what is wrong), but rather efforts need to address issues and strategies to help move the African-American community toward self-sufficiency. The issues of self-sufficiency include empowerment, purpose, will, advocacy, commitment, ownership, control, motivation, persistence, and effort.

Third, the African-American community organizer's focus must not be exclusively a victim's focus; the community organizer's efforts must draw attention to the victimizers. As such, the following African proverb applies: "Never let the fox into the hen house to feed the chickens."

Finally, an important issue is the AIDS crisis in the African-American community, which gives great pause and concern. The criticisms and the critics of efforts to organize the African-American community regarding this crisis are presented primarily by whites who typically are in power and decision-making positions with regard to the allocation of resources. Other critics are blacks who may think like whites but have no power in terms of the allocation of valued resources. These criticisms include the claims that African-Americans won't come to support meetings for those with the HIV infection, they won't show up for counseling appointments, and they won't volunteer to staff the AIDS hotline or to be "buddies or partners."

The critics are typically single-issue oriented (e.g., AIDS), color blind (i.e., African-Americans make too much ado about racism), or are blind to color (i.e., it doesn't matter if you are black, white, red, or polka dot). African-American community leaders, equipped with appropriate resources, may be able to address some of these criticisms due to their experiences and knowledge that color and culture are important. Therefore, it is imperative that those who desire to organize the African-American community meet the minimum criteria discussed here and also be able to distinguish clearly between what is a real problem and what is a system-induced problem. African-Americans shouldn't expect others to do that for them.

Social work programs can play a key role in aiding African-American community leaders. Schools of social work need to make extended efforts to bring African-Americans into their programs. African-Americans should be represented in social work programs because they can learn the skills and theories available to help them become better at organizing their communities. Also, there needs to be a continued effort among the social work programs to emphasize racial and cultural differences and sensitize students to issues before they go into the field. Being equipped with a social work education will provide African-Americans with the knowledge and skills to organize their communities around needs and issues that can be understood only by someone living the reality of the African-American community. Remember, "Men do not build bridges for other men. . ."

REFERENCES

Jones, J. H. (1981). *Bad blood: The Tuskegee Syphilis Experiment—A tragedy of race and medicine.* New York: The Free Press.
Moynihan, D. P. (1970, March 3). Benign neglect for issue of race? *Wall Street Journal,* p. 20.

Rejoinder to Dr. Shillington and Mr. Dotson
AUDREY OLSEN FAULKNER

The three participants in this dialogue present our views from our respective stances that reflect the reality of the world for the African-American and the white social work community.

That reality is that African-Americans are more likely to have total pessimism permeating their expectations about the commitment white community organizers bring to the African-American community, their lack of exploitative motives, and their ability to sufficiently understand and value the African-American perspective and experience. Community memory and personal history of actual and perceived betrayal makes even considering trust and a positive outcome seem dangerous and futile. This leads to the political position that the only choice available to the African-American community is to choose an organizer of the same color and community. Further, it leads to a belief that he or she will have a point of view that encompasses all African-American perspectives, understands all community needs, and can be expected to put community purpose ahead of personal gain, and, therefore, will be able to lead the community to empowerment. This view of reality ignores the imperfections and the drives for status and gain, which are probably randomly distributed in the population, African-American and white, as well as divisions of opinion in the African-American community. Dr. Shillington and Mr. Dotson allude to this when they refer to "blacks who may think like whites." Skill and special African-American knowledge may bring a successful outcome, but betrayal, or at least less than optimum commitment and effort, can come from within as well as without.

White community organizers who want to work with the African-American community approach the task with relative optimism, expecting that their training and their skill will make it possible to bring about change. No matter how excellent their social work education, when they enter the African-American community for the first time, in no way can they have adequate knowledge about the grinding effect of centuries of exploitation on that community. Nor can they have complete understanding of their own vulnerability to the personal pain and professional disappointment that is certain to occur even if they are able to help the community empower itself. The more aware community organizers know they are not likely to be trusted by African-Americans, expect that they must demonstrate they are worthy of trust, and perhaps accept that total trust may never occur. Still, since a belief that individuals and communities can change is a requirement for continuing community organization practice, they are prone to be over optimistic about the possibility that enough trust can be established to make it possible to work effectively and in ways that are personally satisfying.

Dr. Shillington and Mr. Dotson give the AIDS crisis in the African-American community as an example of why white community organizers should not work in the African-American community. The issues they raise here reflect the African-American pessimism; they also reflect the reality of the refusal of those in power to engage in cross-cultural understanding or an equitable distribution of resources—the original source of the pessimism. This refusal to share is recognized by the African-American community for what it is—at best, a morally irresponsible disregard for the basic welfare of people of color and the poor and, at its worst, an evil manifestation of raw power.

The AIDS issue, however, serves as an example of the kind of intractable social problem where the mutual self-interest requires joint action by both communities. It is a systemwide problem that cannot be solved by African-Americans alone or by whites alone, but by both working on their unique configuration of a common agenda. Color cannot be the primary criterion for choosing the community organizer who can mobilize and support concerned and talented leadership in either community.

NO

AUDREY OLSEN FAULKNER

The United States is rapidly taking on many of the characteristics of a Third World nation. Increasingly there are only two economic strata, the very rich and the very poor. A huge pool of surplus labor exists—educated and uneducated—for whom there are no current jobs and no apparent future jobs that guarantee an income above the poverty level. This shortage of jobs is accompanied by an absence of capital for domestic economic development. Corruption plagues major institutions. Expenditures for military programs and the hardware to support them dominate the national budget.

The physical and social infrastructures are crumbling. Sanitation and water works are unsafe, highways go without maintenance, and public buildings are not being repaired. Public health services have sustained crippling cutbacks. There is an upsurge in tuberculosis, children of the poor are not receiving measles vaccine or polio inoculations, and infant mortality rates are startling. Public schools are unable to provide an education for many of the children who attend them (Kozel, 1991).

There is an abdication of public responsibility for using tax dollars to support the general health and welfare and an increasing expectation that the voluntary sector will provide for these needs. Individuals who are poor or homeless are the targets of citizen anger, and "compassion fatigue" is considered an acceptable response to poverty and homelessness.

Abuse of civil rights is accepted with little public outcry about the racial incidents occurring daily in our neighborhoods and on our campuses. All of these are intimidating and many of them are violent.

These developments have had a disproportionate impact on the urban poor, large numbers of whom are African-American (Jackson, 1991). The recent riots in Los Angeles were a tragic consequence. Once again this country treated its citizens of color with unequal justice, and the results were cataclysmic. The Los

Angeles disturbances differed from those in past decades, however, for this time the shield of affluence did not protect white neighborhoods from destruction. They, too, experienced arson, looting, and fear.

The Los Angeles events demonstrated the absence of commitment to a moral imperative to include people of color as full participants in our society. The damage to white life and property suggests that enlightened self-interest and the desire for self-preservation, born of fear, may make the white majority more willing to support more equitable African-American–white relations. Social work values have always supported the moral imperative; it is time now to add the more pragmatic imperative of white self-interest as leverage for change.

If the social work community is to exploit the opportunity the current situation presents, the question, "Should only African-American organizers operate in African-American neighborhoods?" has to be answered "No." (This assumes that non-African-Americans who are going to work in those neighborhoods should be chosen or choose themselves carefully, need to continuously engage in learning about the African-American community, and recognize that there may be tasks they cannot perform in certain situations at certain times). Several arguments can be made for community work that does not restrict the job location to the racial identification of the organizer.

The White Community Organizer and the African-American Community Need Each Other

White American community organizers also have issues of self-interest and self-preservation. They belong to the professional middle class, which can be viewed as an endangered species. Powerlessness also affects them. Automation threatens the profession, without improving the quality of service to clients. Declassification of civil service positions undermines the delivery of professional services. Social services are being privatized, which gives social workers less power and less control. Pressures for accountability, often focused inappropriately on narrow quantitative measures of outcome, interfere with work with social welfare clients. Clients, especially those who are African-American, are blamed for their problems, welfare budgets are being cut, and professional jobs are being lost.

Under these conditions, neither white community organizers nor African-American communities can afford to put racial constraints on good community development practice. They need each other as allies. They cannot be allies if they do not understand their partners in the enterprise. Association from a stance of goodwill leads to the possibility of trust, and trust can lead to mutual endeavor and mutual power.

White Community Organizers' Roles with the White Community Are Essential to Change Efforts

White community organizers have two vital roles with the white community that are essential to an improvement in the situation of both white Americans and African-Americans. They are: (1) catalyzing and energizing the white community of goodwill to ally more substantially with the African-American community and (2) serving as educator and change agent with the more racist white community, making the self-interest and self-preservation imperative convincingly evident.

As social work practitioners generally deal with the individual as she or he interfaces with her or his environment, so to must the white community organizer has the opportunity to be a broker between the African-American and the white community by interpreting the needs and the point of view of the excluded community to the majority community of power.

The white organizer has access to ''people of goodwill'' in the white community who can contribute to the effort and who have resources that may be made available to African-American neighborhoods. There is a tradition of whites of goodwill helping African-Americans that is as old as the tradition of white betrayal of the African-American community (Levy, 1968). White community organizers can revitalize the white community for continuation of that tradition.

For example, concern with the environment has tended to crowd out concern for racial reform. The surroundings in which African-Americans in poor neighborhoods find themselves are polluted surroundings with disintegrating housing, poor schools, drug dealing, and random violence. White community organizers can bring to the predominantly white environmental movement the perspective that the social environment of poor neighborhoods needs to be included in the list of environmental hazards. They can interpret to the white community that the African-American community's problems are structural and racial, and not of its own making. They can teach whites about the African-American community and make it more troubling and less rewarding for the white community to absolve itself of any responsibility for the African-American community.

White Community Organizers Have Essential Roles with the African-American Community

Here there are three roles: (1) the technical expert in catalyzing and supporting existing African-American leadership; (2) connecting the African-American community with resources in the white community of goodwill and the more racist white community; and (3) encouraging and supporting neighborhood leaders to teach an excluded generation of poor, young African-Americans desirable norms that are a necessary although not a sufficient condition for success. Not all African-American communities are poor or underdeveloped, and none is without indigenous leadership, but those that most need a community organizer's skills are those where experienced leadership is limited and where economics and racism have excluded ordinary citizens from the expected benefits of the society. The competent community organizer has a broad repertoire of skills and knowledge at her or his command. This includes a technology for leadership development and social change that can be transferred to neighborhood people to help them make their voices heard and regain control over their lives.

It is not that white American organizers can do this more successfully than African-American organizers. But there are fewer organizers of color, and not all of them wish to work in the African-American community, which needs an array of skills and talents.

The white organizer is more likely than neighborhood leadership to have contacts with and access to the white power structure. The white organizer knows the "codes" and may be more able to secure the ear of individuals and groups with significant resources—both people of goodwill and people whose interests are self-serving. Knowing the impacts of racism on white Americans (Bowser & Hunt, 1981) will allow her or him to press the issue of our common good.

Finally, if a huge generation of young African-Americans is going to be successful, as defined by getting an education, holding a job, achieving a good measure of self-potential, being an adequate parent, and having personal safety from violence, it will have to adopt more desirable norms for behavior. Whether African-American or white American, one has to have an education, has to work for a living, has to neither abuse nor neglect one's children, and cannot settle personal affairs with guns and knives. Organizers, in alliance with neighborhood leadership who already support these norms, can help to find resources, especially in the white community, to support the creation of a climate for community acceptance.

But personal behavior is only half the equation. One also needs to have access to education in a setting that conveys respect, a job that is available and that permits support of self and family, resources for help with parenting problems beyond one's skill to solve, and protection from others with guns and knives, including the police.

The second half of the equation has to be forcefully interpreted to the white community, utilizing both the moral imperative and the imperative of enlightened self-interest. Interpretation across the two cultures is the organizer's job.

There Is a Special Role for White Female Community Organizers

The feminist movement has borrowed from the civil rights movement many of its tactics for seeking change, and white American women community organizers have a special role to play with the African-American community. African-American women have historically played a strong leadership role in their communities, often in spite of poverty and lack of formal education.

White feminists tend to invite African-American women to white endeavors focused on white agendas, without understanding how the two groups' agendas differ; they are less likely to seek alliances with African-American women on African-American terms in their settings around their agendas. This has weakened the women's movement and made African-American women feel that it is irrelevant to them (Kopacsi & Faulkner, 1988). A significant opportunity exists for white female community organizers to engage in coleadership endeavors with women of color in locating, developing, and nurturing neighborhood leaders.

Working in African-American Communities Will Increase White Organizers' Social Change Skills

White community organizers cannot fulfill these roles unless they work with the African-American community. If they work only with people like themselves, they are less able to serve as a bridge between the races; they are not forced to confront their own feelings and behaviors in relation to people of color; and they are not able to do those things they need to do to combat structural and individual racism in the white community.

Working closely with African-Americans in their neighborhoods is the quickest and most effective way to understand the daily assault on the souls and the psyches of the people who live there (Terkel, 1992). This is true regardless of the socioeconomic class of the members of that community.

If community organizers do not work with communities of color, they do not hear the response of those communities to local or national policies that affect them. This limits the white organizer's ability to analyze national or local policies for their unstated consequences for people of color.

It is frightening for whites to be in some African-American neighborhoods. It is frightening for African-Americans to be there, but they *live* there. It is their home. If that is not understood, in an affective as well as an intellectual way, it is difficult to aid in the empowerment process or to convey knowledge of the dynamics of racism to the white society.

The racial complexion of this country is changing; survival of the white community will depend on adopting new perspectives and new approaches to national unity. White community organizers can help the society see that neighborhoods can be recreated where people care for and about each other, if the opportunity for life with health and decency exists (Rivera & Erlich, 1992).

Public leaders, the media, and a substantial number of white Americans see the crises in which many individual African-Americans live their lives as a matter of choice. White community organizers can bring a perspective to public consciousness that views African-Americans from the standpoint of their strengths, instead of seeing them as self-destructive, vulnerable, and powerless. The self-preservation of one group depends on self-preservation of the other. As Cornell West writes, "Either we [whites] learn a new language of empathy and compassion, or the fire this time will consume us all." This is the message the white majority community must hear in its own self-interest. The white social work community organizer can send that message.

REFERENCES

Bowser, B., & Hunt, R. G. (Eds.). (1981). *Impacts of racism on white Americans.* Beverly Hills, CA: Sage Publications.

Jackson, J. S. (Eds.). (1991). *Life in Black America.* Newbury Park, CA: Sage Publications.

Kopacsi, R., & Faulkner, A. O. (1988, Fall). The powers that might be: The unity of black and white feminists. *Affilia, 3*(3), 33–50.

Kozol, J. (1991). *Savage inequalities.* New York: Crown Publishers.

Levy, C. J. (1968). *Voluntary servitude: Whites in the Negro movement.* New York: Meridith.

Rivera, F. G. and Erlich, J. L. (1992). *Community organizing in a diverse society.* Boston: Allyn and Bacon.

Terkel, S. (1992). *Race: How blacks and whites think and feel about the American obsession.* New York: The New Press.

West, C. (1992, August 2). Learning to talk of race. *New York Times Magazine,* 25–26.

Rejoinder to Professor Faulkner   AUDREY M. SHILLINGTON AND
WILLIAM L. DOTSON

One theme of Professor Faulkner's argument states that white community organizers should be working in African-American communities so that whites can take the perspective of the African-Americans back to the white community. An underlying assumption seems to be that African-Americans cannot do this for themselves. Another assumption may be that whites can communicate the needs of the African-American community better than the African-Americans who live there.

The word "perspective" is used throughout this paper. The social interaction theorists use this word to describe one's view of reality. This theory states that one can never know another's perspective because each has a different history and different experiences.

Based on this theory one would have to argue that it is not truly possible for someone from one diverse and different cultural experiences, such as whites, to assess the needs of another very diverse cultural group, such as African-Americans. It is assumed in Professor Faulkner's essay that someone can go into a very different community, learn the essence of their needs, and be able to address them in ways that are satisfactory and efficient as well as acceptable to the community. Given the greatest of intent, it is improbable that the white community organizer in today's very strong ethnic/culturally specific climate can lead the way toward decisions that will often be both in contrast to and in conflict with the white "power holding" community.

Continuing to have white Americans go into the African-American communities and organize them is a fraud designed to prolong false dependencies of these communities on outside help. If anything, the white community organizer should be unconditionally supporting efforts to educate and guide African-Americans to organize their own communities. A people should be taught how to help themselves rather than expecting that someone else should accept that responsibility for them.

African-Americans need and must lead their own communities. Only they can accurately interpret their needs. Only African-Americans can get true information from their communities on the basis of understanding and trust. Because of the suspicion and mistrust among the African-American communities of white service deliverers, it is not possible for them to obtain the cooperation or the information they need to address basic issues.

It is implied that in "serving as a bridge between the races" we build on a white bridge. That sentiment is not the solution but rather part of the race relation problem. If anything, the bridge builders should be black and white. Persons should trust and allow that blacks can build in their own communities.

It is true that people should be forced to confront their own feelings and behaviors in relation to people of color. However, can someone of the same culture force this within their own culture? Would it not be more effective if African-Americans were a truly contributing part of that bridge? a part of that force? The stance of these authors is that whites alone cannot effectively organize African-American communities based on the reasons discussed above and, further, that African-Americans are essential to effective community organizing in African-American communities.

Finally, if there is to be effective communication between the races and effective organizing of African-American communities, then the white community must accept and try to understand that the African-American community cares less about how much one knows and more about how much one cares.

Why is there never any discussion of African-Americans organizing white American communities? When one thinks of this, there seems to be something perpetuatingly racist about this nonquestion.

Are Quick and Dirty Community Needs Assessments Better Than No Needs Assessments?

EDITOR'S NOTE: Many different approaches are used in conducting needs assessments such as social surveys, social and health indicators, and community group forums. The methodology chosen depends on how the information is to be used, the time and resources to be allocated to it, and the perspectives being sought. Needs assessment is a critical component in planning human services. However, needs are variable, subject to different definitions within the same community, and consequently often difficult to measure. Yet based on needs assessment, programs are developed and resources allocated to meet the identified needs of a community. The central focus of this debate is whether a quick and dirty needs assessment can provide useful information in the identification of community problems and the planning of solutions for these. Several questions emerge: Are quick and dirty needs assessments synonymous with "careless work" or with an approach taken when resources or time are limited? Do needs assessments always need to be undertaken in a systematic, scientific, and comprehensive manner to be credible? Is it better to know nothing of the needs of the community than to have some limited knowledge based on a quick assessment? Debating these questions is important because so much of what is taught to social work students and subsequently undertaken by practitioners in the field involves a process that includes conducting community needs assessments to plan and develop human services.

Evelyn F. Slaght, Ph.D., answers YES. She is Professor of Social Work at George Mason University in Northern Virginia. In addition to teaching, she has done research in domestic violence, child welfare, and substance abuse. She worked for twenty years as an administrator and consultant in the juvenile justice and social service fields.

Janice H. Schopler, Ph.D., argues NO. She is a professor and the Associate Dean, responsible for the master's program at the University of North Carolina at Chapel Hill School of Social Work. She currently teaches courses related to macro practice and focuses on the development and testing of practice theory, with a particular interest in conceptualizing and evaluating interorganizational systems.

YES

Evelyn F. Slaght

The purpose of a needs assessment is to document the extent of a social problem and the gap between need and response. It is an essential part of planning that administrators should undertake routinely (Anderson, Frieden, & Murphy, 1977; Kettner, Moroney, & Martin, 1990). Given that most administrative and budgetary decisions are incremental, the decisions that proceed from the needs assessment usually have a longstanding impact, whether or not the assumptions that guided the assessment were accurate. Improvement of service delivery or alteration of priorities often depends on forcing a reevaluation of the assumptions associated with ongoing programs. Sometimes the only way to challenge the system is through needs assessments carried out by volunteer staff in nontraditional organizations, that is, use of the "quick and dirty" method. The alternative of scientific longitudinal studies conducted by highly trained research consultants is sometimes too costly and lengthy, especially with problems that require an immediate response.

This argument suggests ways in which community groups and coalitions can undertake needs assessment responsibilities without sacrificing credibility or validity. The process must begin with problem identification, including establishing the size of the potential target population and the nature and severity of the problem to be addressed (Lewis, Lewis, & Souflee, 1991). In tight budget times, it is not realistic to expect agencies with limited means or motivation to undertake problem identification when they are struggling to justify maintaining the services they are already delivering. They are hardly in a position to initiate new ones. Consistent with Siegel, Atchison, and Carson's advice (1987), they ought not undertake needs assessments unless there is a commitment to respond to the needs identified.

Politically, coalitions, advocacy, and other community groups are in a better position than the agencies to conduct needs assessments since part of their mission is to focus attention on problems that are not being addressed. Coalitions are preferable to advocacy and other special-interest groups because they tend to involve a greater range of organizations and agencies and to be broader in the issues they address.

Coalitions have the potential for generating viable planning data that is preferable to decisions based only on personal judgment or managerial bias. Even if the data are incomplete or not based on the strictest scientific methodology, they can stimulate program change. An example of a coalition-driven needs assessment is a project undertaken by the author as a part of a B.S.W. community organization senior elective course. Bachelor's level social work students, working in conjunction with a coalition of local agency leaders, conducted a needs assessment of domestic violence in the county surrounding the university.

Assessing Domestic Violence

Determining the extent and need for services to victims of domestic violence was a two-part process. First the extent of the problem had to be documented. Coalition members believed that the problem was getting more severe, but had no data to support requests for additional resources. Second, as with any needs assessment, the response of the community to the problem had to be assessed along with the community's willingness to commit to a solution (Kettner et. al, 1990).

The involvement of the Social Work Department was in response to the request of the Interagency Coalition on Domestic Violence that an impartial party undertake a needs assessment of domestic violence in the county. The coalition had no funding for this project. The research expertise was provided by the course instructor pro bono and the labor by the student volunteers.

The coalition was comprised primarily of county agencies, although there were several private nonprofit service organizations represented (e.g., shelters). It included the police, hospitals, social services, shelters, court services, and mental health. Services to domestic violence victims are fragmented in the county, and the coalition is the only link between them. The members of the coalition believed that a needs assessment would stimulate a reevaluation of community agency priorities and provide a basis on which to request additional resources for the services they were rendering.

As the first step in data collection began, it became clear that there were serious gaps in service statistics. For example, the police were not routinely maintaining records on the number of domestic violence calls they were handling; instead, they were being merged with other simple-assault cases. Similarly, hospitals had no method of identifying or recording information on injuries they treated that were domestically related. And the magistrates indicated that there were *no* domestic violence cases coming before the courts, and therefore they had nothing to contribute.

Four strategies were used to respond to these problems. First, a team of students was assigned to work with the police, who agreed to conduct a survey of all domestically related calls for a one-month period in two of the six precincts in the county. Applying a "social indicators" approach to these data (Warheit, Bell, & Schwab, 1984), students were able to arrive at a rate of domestic violence (number of assaults per 1,000 households) that was used to estimate the number of cases in the unsurveyed precincts and to provide an overall estimate for the county of domestic violence cases handled by police. While there were obvious reliability questions in generalizing in this way from one precinct to the next, the product provided a reasonable estimate of the number of cases and demonstrated to the police the advantage of collecting the data. For example, the police became aware not only of the variance across precincts in the number of domestically related calls, but also of the amount of time officers spent at the scene. (The wide variance in time spent suggested dramatically different handling of these calls.) This led to a reexamination of distribution of personnel at peak times to high-risk communities as well as a recognition of the need for updated policies so that officers could be clear about their responsibilities in these cases. Shortly after the coalition-motivated survey, the police began maintaining data separately on domestic dispute complaints.

Second, a student team worked with the hospitals to design a survey form that could be completed in a matter of minutes by emergency room (ER) staff. This field survey had secondary benefits for victims using the hospitals since ER staff became more sensitive to family violence cases and began referring more to community resources. Currently the Commission for Women is intervening with the hospitals to urge them to adopt a standardized form (Figure 8.1) as part of their ongoing data collection system.

A third group of students was assigned to observe the court process and record any and all domestic violence cases coming before the magistrates. Observations of the magistrates over the next month revealed that, when victims attempted to secure warrants for their spouses' arrest, they were usually turned away. When the chief magistrate was questioned about this, he admitted to the students that magistrates are reluctant to issue warrants because they "get tired of victims requesting warrants and then dropping charges." In this instance, the absence of data was very revealing and brought to light biases and barriers to service delivery. The fact that it was students collecting this data probably improved the reliability of the information secured from this key informant since the chief magistrate was probably less threatened by students than he would have been by coalition members or professional consultants.

Last, a group of students worked with social services to analyze the geographic distribution of child abuse cases, on the belief that child abuse is a reasonable surrogate measure of the spatial distribution of spousal abuse and other domestic violence. Students discovered that the county was not inputting data geographically, requiring that students break down cases by ZIP code by

FIGURE 8.1 DOMESTIC VIOLENCE SURVEY

Hospital: _____

Zip Code	Age	Sex	Patient's First Visit?	Police Involved?	Relationship of Suspected Abuser?	Referral or Information Provided?
		M/F	Y/N	Y/N		Y/N

Using available information and your best judgment, please complete the above for patients you suspect have been physically abused. Created by Evelyn F. Slaght for Fairfax County Interagency Coalition on Domestic Violence (1990).

hand. These results were crosschecked with recently generated police data, and the areas of high child abuse were found to coincide with areas of high police complaints of domestic disputes. It was found that the agencies in the coalition by and large are not located in the high-risk areas, although social services and mental health have decentralized offices nearby. The geographic data have since been used to justify maintaining these decentralized offices in the face of threatened budget cuts.

No community survey was undertaken for several reasons. First, because so much domestic violence is hidden, it is extremely difficult to identify a representative sample. One way the project had of gaining some idea of the characteristics of victims of domestic violence was to examine the characteristics of the areas that were found to be at greatest risk. Additionally, some information was obtained through the rates-under-treatment approach (Warheit et al., 1984), although, not surprisingly, few minorities went for treatment, and Hispanics in particular were underrepresented in the treatment programs. The clinics, shelters, and victim assistance hotline served few minorities and attributed this under-representation to the absence of staff and volunteers with the necessary language skills. The needs assessment increased their sensitivity to the need to expand their staff recruitment and public information to include a wider range of cultural backgrounds.

Usefulness of the Approach

No single agency is responsible for the problem of domestic violence, as is the case with many problems that have gained attention recently, including home-lessness, AIDS, and substance abuse. The need for interagency/interdisciplinary approaches is generally recognized, but staffing for planning across agencies is seldom forthcoming, requiring dependence on volunteers, students, interns, and other less professionally trained personnel.

The success of the needs assessment may also vary depending on the type of problem being addressed. Domestic violence proved to be an appropriate problem for the quick and dirty approach, partly because it is a newly surfacing issue that doesn't challenge norms in the same way that homelessness or AIDS does. But there can be no doubt that surveys of the homeless and AIDS victims are warranted, if for no other reason than the attention that would be directed at the problem. The latest tactic of the unemployed to panhandle cars at stop lights offers an opportunity to survey a portion of the population of homeless that has made itself visible. The methodological problems presented, such as sample representativeness and appropriate interviewing approaches, could be addressed through a quick and dirty approach in lieu of funding or other professional help.

A quick and dirty assessment requires input from the target population. Sometimes surveys are useful; other times a community forum may be more appropriate. The difficulty with community forums is that those who come to speak do not necessarily represent the targeted population, and, as Hobbs (1987) points out, "Some segments of any populations are typically more assertive and active than others" (p. 30), and some spokespersons are more articulate than others. But recent efforts that have involved persons with disabilities in their own advocacy have altered our thinking about who is and is not a good spokesperson for a cause. In spite of language difficulties, the presence of persons with mental retardation at public hearings has had an impact, and this needs to be taken into consideration when orchestrating a community forum.

In spite of our best effort, some problems will remain at least partially hidden, but when persons in need do utilize the entry points into the system (police, hospitals, courts, shelters, schools), we need to be sure that the problems they bring are properly identified and reliable data maintained. The social work profession's recent interest in single-subject design in research suggests that sampling is not always essential to understanding social problems. Quick and dirty needs assessment, even with its sampling errors and dependence on esti-mates, can provide insight into emerging issues and enable the profession to establish documentation of unmet needs that can be used to influence policy makers and local agencies. Studies by professionally staffed consulting firms or professional planners are appropriate in many cases, but quick and dirty assess-ments are a viable alternative.

REFERENCES

Anderson, W. F., Frieden, B. J., & Murphy, M. J. (1977). *Managing human services.* Washington, DC: International City Management Association.

Hobbs, D. (1987). Strategy for needs assessment. In E. E. Johnson, L. R. Meiller, L. C. Miller, & G. F. Summers (Eds.), *Needs assessment: Theory and methods.* Ames, IA: Iowa State University Press.

Kettner, P. M., Moroney, R. M., & Martin, L. L. (1990). *Designing and managing programs.* Newbury Park, CA: Sage.

Lewis, J. A., Lewis, M. D., & Souflee, J. F. (1991). *Management of human services programs,* 2nd ed. Pacific Grove, CA: Brooks/Cole.

Ott, J. S. (1991). A comparison of two methodologies for assessing human service needs and an assessment of the impacts of methodological choices on identified needs. *Journal of Health and Human Resources Administration, 14,* 132–155.

Siegel, L. M., Atchinson, C. C., & Carson, L. G. (1987). Need identification and program planning in the community context. In F. M. Cox, J. L. Erlich, J. Rothman, & J. E. Tropman (Eds.), *Strategies of community organization,* 4th edition. Itasca, IL: F. E. Peacock.

Slaght, E. F. (1991). Focusing on domestic violence to teach community intervention strategies. *Arete Education Digest, 16,* 39–44.

Warheit, G. J., Bell, R. A., & Schwab, J. J. (1984). In F. M. Cox, J. B. Erlich, J. Rothman, & J. E. Tropman (Eds.), *Tactics and techniques of community practice.* Itasca, IL: F. E. Peacock.

Rejoinder to Dr. Slaght JANICE H. SCHOPLER

Dr. Slaght's statement has a great deal of merit. She suggests ways that community groups can carry out needs assessments ''without sacrificing credibility and validity,'' illustrates her approach, and discusses its usefulness. She does not, however, make a convincing case for a ''quick and dirty'' community needs assessment, nor does she deal with the issues that result from this type of approach.

Throughout her discussion, Dr. Slaght's statement supports exemplary practice. She makes some sound observations about the important role community groups and coalitions can play in drawing attention to unmet needs. Further, the needs assessment Dr. Slaght conducted with her students at the request of the Interagency Coalition on Domestic Violence illustrates a creative and challenging approach to professional social work education. The ''hands-on'' process of determining the extent and need for services to victims of domestic violence provided the community with valuable information. In addition, students were involved in a memorable learning experience—one that gave them an opportunity to explore an important social problem, gain technical skill in applying classroom knowledge, and test their values as they struggled with real-world issues.

Based on Dr. Slaght's description of how the assessment was carried out, I have no quarrel with the usefulness of the approach she advocates, but I wouldn't describe it as "quick and dirty." She and her students worked with key groups in the community to ensure the assessment was relevant to their needs, used multiple methods, identified sources of bias, clearly conveyed the limits of their conclusions, were sensitive to political implications, and laid the groundwork for ongoing data collection. Essentially, Dr. Slaght and I are in agreement on the criteria that should be followed for a credible community needs assessment. Our basic disagreement centers on our definitions.

I define quick and dirty as "careless work" in keeping with the commonly accepted, pejorative sense of this slang expression. Dr. Slaght equates quick and dirty methods with "needs assessments carried out by volunteer staff in nontraditional organizations." She sees the alternative as "scientific, longitudinal studies conducted by highly trained research consultants," which she describes as costly and lengthy. Dr. Slaght's definition focuses on who does the needs assessment and how much it costs; my definition addresses how the assessment is conducted.

Dr. Slaght makes faulty assumptions in defining a quick and dirty approach and, consequently, ignores some of the critical implications of this approach. She assumes that contracting with a professional planner or consulting firm to conduct a needs assessment assures greater validity, but takes more time and costs more than arranging to have an assessment carried out by volunteers with professional expertise. Then, through her illustration, Dr. Slaght affirms that the volunteer approach can produce a very credible product and concludes that both approaches are appropriate. Obviously, when professionals are paid, the cost to the community is greater than when services are donated. It does not necessarily follow, however, that paying professionals to carry out a needs assessment will increase the time required for study or the quality of the product. In fact, a professional firm that routinely conducts community needs assessments may be able to produce results faster than volunteers who have to spend time getting organized and developing methods for data collection and analysis. Further, engaging a professional planner does not guarantee that a needs assessment will be of higher quality than a volunteer effort. A slick report prepared by an outside consultant without community involvement can be as shoddy as one hastily compiled by local volunteers advocating for a special interest.

Following Dr. Slaght's logic is of little use in determining whether a quick and dirty needs assessment is preferable to no needs assessment at all. Her position implies a continuum of choices from paying a professional and taking more time to obtain quality information about needs to relying on volunteer efforts to produce quick and adequate information. Casting the issue in these terms implies that the decision is pragmatic, based primarily on the time and money available, and ignores the repercussions of making decisions based on incomplete, biased information. As Dr. Slaght points out, decisions based on community needs assessments "usually have a longstanding impact." The danger of a quick and dirty approach is that the final report takes on the appearance of credibility, and shortcomings may not surface for a long time (especially when the needs of the underserved or unserved are overlooked). Unfortunately, inappropriate or unresponsive services that stem from a carelessly conducted needs assessment may linger as long as, or longer than, the positive programs that grow out of a credible assessment. Even if some constituencies reject the information provided by a quick and dirty needs assessment, the report is likely to attract attention in the community and generate political pressures that influence community planning. Quick and dirty doesn't mean cheap, it means careless. The potential costs of this approach to needs assessment are never worth the risk to the community.

NO

JANICE H. SCHOPLER

Conducting a quick and dirty community needs assessment is not an acceptable course of action under any circumstances, even if the only alternative is no needs assessment at all. Granted, the quick and dirty approach may appear tempting and seem expedient when attractive funding opportunities appear and the time and resources available for developing a proposal are limited. This position becomes untenable, however, when the implications of justifying needs based on a quick and dirty assessment are examined. According to Green (1985, 1986), in the popular vernacular the term "quick and dirty" is synonymous with careless work. He also equates this slang term with a "quick fix," which refers to an instant, simplistic remedy with derogatory overtones. Given this definition of terms, the argument against a quick and dirty community needs assessment is based on the premises that this approach threatens credibility and that the potential costs of carelessness are always unacceptable.

Threats to Credibility

Community needs assessments provide information essential for responsible planning and program change, but their value depends on a credible process and a credible product. What qualities should decision makers and participants expect before they are willing to trust and act on a needs assessment? An overview of the literature and practice experience suggests that a needs assessment should be understandable, relevant and useful, acceptably accurate, representative, politically sensitive, and future oriented.

These criteria have been gleaned from the work of authorities on assessment, evaluation, and community change (Gilmore, Campbell, & Becker, 1989; Kettner, Daley, & Nichols, 1985; Rossi & Freeman, 1985; Royse, 1992; Warheit, Bell, & Schwab, 1977) and are supported by reports of effective community needs assessments (Bowen, 1987; Orthner, Smith, & Wright, 1986; Orthner & Zimmerman, 1991; Randolph, Lindenberg, & Menn, 1986), discussions with colleagues at the Human Services Research and Design Laboratory at the University of North Carolina School of Social Work, and the author's own involvement in assessing human service needs at the state and local level over the past two decades. A brief description of the way each of these qualities influences the overall credibility of a needs assessment highlights their critical importance:

> *Understandable.* Can the procedures, methods, and results be easily understood by all involved? Unless the statement of purpose, explanation of the process, framing of questions, and presentation of results are in clear, straightforward, objective language, they can be misunderstood and lead to mistrust. Unless written material and verbal presentations reflect sensitivity to the way community differences relate to race, culture, ethnicity, and class influence perceptions and responses, pejorative language can cloud interpretation. Inability to comprehend and misinterpretation plant seeds of doubt and can lead to discord. The risk of a careless assessment is that there may be no attempt to develop mutual understanding, and decision makers may spend their money for a slick report that provides little direction and ends up gathering dust on a shelf or, worse, creates ill will in the community.
>
> *Relevant and Useful.* Do the findings answer the questions that prompted the study, and do they provide direction for change? To ensure relevance, decision makers and other key participants should be involved from the beginning of the assessment (Chambers, 1986). The evaluators and decision makers need to be in agreement about what information is needed and why it is required (Royse, 1992). Unless agreement is reached on the purpose of the study, the methods selected, the questions that are asked, and the approach to analysis, the study may not yield results that address the concerns that led to the assessment. Further, to ensure that the assessment will be useful in addressing community concerns, the evaluators and decision makers need to agree on the scope of the assessment and how it will be used. Unless the evaluator takes care to make clear the nature of the results that can be obtained given the available time and resources, decision makers may have false hopes about what they can learn from the assessment. The superficial scan characteristic of a quick

and dirty approach may appear sufficient to satisfy funding requirements or marketing needs, but is not likely to produce the commitment and information necessary to guide decision making.

Acceptably Accurate. Do the findings provide a trustworthy base for making decisions about how to structure change and allocate resources? While all community needs assessments are prone to bias, the threats to validity need to be recognized and care needs to be taken to achieve a reasonable level of accuracy. Validity can be enhanced by clearly conceptualizing the change process, by selecting instruments that have proven effective in the past and have known reliability and validity, by using multiple methods to verify findings, and by applying accepted analytic techniques to establish the nature of the identified relationships (Orthner & Zimmerman, 1991; Rossi & Freeman, 1985). Unless decision makers are aware of how much confidence they can place in the results, they can make costly errors. One of the dangers of a careless assessment is that the sources and extent of bias are unknown and decision makers may act on inaccurate information.

Representative. Are the findings broadly representative of all community interests? Community conditions have a differential impact on different groups and concerns vary. Because it is usually impossible to survey everyone, the evaluators should use sampling techniques that poll a broad cross-section of those affected. To ensure that no significant concerns are overlooked, methods should be responsive to differences related to culture, ethnicity, race, gender, and class. With a quick and dirty approach, the convenience of sampling is likely to be of more concern than representation of all affected parties. Thus, community needs may be misconstrued and planning may be based on flawed conclusions.

Politically Sensitive. Is the process of responsive to all of the relevant stakeholders? Community change occurs in a political context and the process should include representatives of all of the relevant constituencies, not just special interests or those currently in power. Decision makers and evaluators also need to be aware of the potential for uncovering negative, unexpected findings as well as gaining the information desired. Unless there is widespread understanding and acceptance of the purpose of the assessment and politically sensitive reporting, there may not be sufficient support for change when unpopular findings surface. A quick and dirty approach can result in long-term political costs as factions argue over the misinformation produced by polling only special-interest groups.

Future Orientation. Does the needs assessment take into account the dynamic nature of change? A needs assessment should do more than reflect the transient needs of the current moment. The findings of a credible needs assessment provide guidance for future planning. The process should not be geared to producing a report that will soon fade from public attention. Evaluators and decision makers need to be aware of the dynamic nature of today's communities. Community change is ongoing and needs can shift quickly. Unless needs assessment is regarded as a critical part of an ongoing planning process, the findings may well be outdated by the time the ink is dry. Obtaining a clear picture of current conditions is easiest when needs are assessed with regularity and results for any time period are produced promptly. Establishing a reliable system for ongoing data collection, analysis, and reporting makes it possible to continually refine procedures. When a needs assessment is regarded as a one-shot deal, there are always start-up costs. A more efficient approach to assessment not only reveals current needs but also provides a template for assessing future needs.

The Potential Costs of Carelessness

A needs assessment that is completed in a hurried, careless manner provides no assurance that the criteria for credibility have been met. Producing a needs assessment that is credible requires an interactive planning process that involves decision makers and key participants in coming to agreement on why an assessment is necessary and what they want to accomplish. The evaluator should also adhere to acceptable standards for data collection, analysis, and reporting and ensure that all parties involved are clear about the limits and advantages of the assessment approach that is selected.

A skilled evaluator certainly can produce a report that has the *appearance of quality* using a quick and dirty approach, but when care is not taken to involve the community in a systematic planning process, evaluation is likely to be based largely on fragmentary information and intuition (Kettner et al., 1985). In either case, there is a risk that conclusions about the nature and scope of need will be misguided. Fragmentary information is likely to distort the true situation, and intuition is subject to both conscious and unknown sources of bias. Thus, while the needs assessment may satisfy immediate requirements for information, there is no guarantee that results will stand the test of time and provide future direction. In the long run, a quick and dirty approach can potentially result in professional costs, political costs, and consumer costs.

Professional Costs

The professional costs incurred stem from the unethical practice of doing careless work. While the National Association of Social Workers Code of Ethics (1987) does not speak to many macro issues (Loewenberg & Dolgoff, 1992), carelessness is identified as a clear violation of professional ethics. Section II.F.1 of the code, which addresses the social worker's ethical responsibility to clients, states: "The social worker should serve clients with devotion, loyalty, determination, and the *maximum application of skill and competence*" [emphasis added]. The integrity of a social worker who purposefully offers services in a careless manner is impugned. Further, because of the high visibility of practitioners involved in macro activities such as community needs assessment, the image of the profession is tarnished by implication and the credibility of other social workers in the community is likely to be questioned.

Political Costs

On a practical level, a quick and dirty needs assessment can result in a loss of legitimacy for human services and for human service planning in the community. Taxpayers may well be outraged about dollars spent on a community needs assessment when remedies based on the assessment do not improve conditions. Decision makers who have been burned by the backlash from their misguided actions, which were based on the flawed conclusions of a careless report, may decide needs assessments are an unnecessary expense in the future. Support for human services may decline when responses to community needs prove ineffective.

Consumer Costs

One of the most unfortunate outcomes of a quick and dirty approach to assessing needs is that the potential cost of any inadequacies that result will inevitably be borne by consumers, those who are directly and indirectly affected by community needs and problems. If the true nature and scope of community needs are not correctly assessed, there is little likelihood of an effective response. A careless approach is not replicable and provides no credible standard for program evaluation. The long-run costs are higher because the process of assessing needs never becomes routinized and refined. Each time a problem or change opportunity arises, assessment must begin anew. The community as a whole suffers opportunity costs if resources are misallocated based on the assessment and the resulting actions do not improve conditions. Thus, a quick and dirty approach results in a loss of faith in the process of needs assessment and undermines a community planning process that could lead to more responsive services.

A More Credible Approach

Clearly, the potential long-run costs outweigh the expected short-run gains of doing a quick and dirty community needs assessment. If the choice is between a quick and careless assessment or no assessment at all, the wiser decision would be to opt for no assessment. No funding opportunity is worth risking credibility, professional integrity, and community support for human services.

There is a better choice: quick does not have to be careless. No matter what the time pressure, the purpose needs to be clearly defined. Decision makers and other participants should be involved and committed to the purpose and process. The methods do not have to be sophisticated to be effective, but potential sources of bias and the limitations of study conclusions should be clearly defined. When time and resources are in short supply, a frequent occurrence in human service communities, everyone involved needs to be clear about what can be accomplished and what is beyond the scope of the study. If a quick but credible needs assessment is not a possibility, decision makers should be advised to act on their best judgment rather than risk community resources and their own credibility on a quick and dirty approach.

REFERENCES

Bowen, G. L. (1987). Community needs assessment: A strategy and case example. *Evaluating Practice, 8*(3), 5–21.

Chambers, D. E. (1986). *Social policy and social programs: A method for the practical public policy analyst.* New York: Macmillan Publishing.

Gilmore, G. D., Campbell, M. D., & Becker, B. L. (1989). *Needs assessment strategies.* Indianapolis, IN: Benchmark Press.

Green, J. (1985). *The dictionary of contemporary slang* (p. 225). New York: Stein and Day.

Green, J. (1986). *The slang thesaurus* (p. 46; p. 144). London: Elm Tree Books.

Kettner, P., Daley, J. M., & Nichols, A. W. (1985). *Initiating change in organizations and communities* (pp. 72–76). Monterey, CA: Brooks/Cole Publishing.

Loewenberg, F. M., & Dolgoff, R. (1992). *Ethical issues for social work practice* (4th ed.) Itasca, IL: F.E. Peacock Publishers.

National Association of Social Workers (1987). *Code of ethics.* Silver Spring, MD: NASW.

Orthner, D. K., Smith, S., and Wright, D. (1986). Measuring program needs: A strategic design. *Evaluation and Program Planning, 9,* 199–207.

Orthner, D. K., & Zimmerman, L. (1991, February 15). Proposal: Community needs assessment for Wake County, NC. (Unpublished manuscript.)

Randolph, F. L., Lindenberg, R. E., & Menn, A. Z. (1986, Summer). Residential facilities for the mentally ill: Needs assessment and community planning. *Community Mental Health Journal, 22* (2), 77–89.

Rossi, P. H., & Freeman, H. W. (1985). *Evaluation: A systematic approach* (4th ed.). Newbury Park, CA: Sage.

Royse, D. (1992). *Program evaluation: An introduction* (pp. 15–35; 159–171) Chicago: Nelson-Hall.

Warheit, G. J., Bell, R. A., & Schwab, J. T. (1977). *Planning for change: Needs assessment approaches.* Washington DC: National Institute of Mental Health.

Rejoinder to Dr. Schopler   EVELYN F. SLAGHT

Dr. Schopler provides excellent guidelines to follow when conducting needs assessments. She rightly identifies the process as a political one and cautions us to be sensitive to representativeness, involving constituents and decision makers in determining purpose, methodology, analytical approach, and intended use. But politics and the process of change are controversial and do not always lend themselves to consensus or mutuality. The conduct of research or data collection cannot depend on the anticipated reaction of decision makers, who often are resistive to change. The sources of vital data are not ultimately responsible for how information will be used, and decisions regarding data use are rightfully left to the political process.

If, as Dr. Schopler suggests, the quick and dirty approach leads to carelessness and results in misinformation, then it is both intolerable and unethical. But whether this occurs depends on how skillful the researcher is in narrowing the scope of the assessment so that the data can be collected and key informants involved within the available time constraints. Credibility problems with quick and dirty approaches can be overcome if early planning is rigid in setting limits on the scope of the study so that it is manageable (i.e., it can be quick without necessarily being dirty).

It is not necessary or even desirable in many cases for the needs assessment to include an interpretation of the data. While facts rarely speak for themselves, it is not up to the researchers, but rather the decision makers, with input from consumers, to decide what to do with the facts.

Bias and inaccuracies have occurred with traditional needs assessment; they are not problems unique to the quick and dirty approach. Neither the possibility of error nor presence or absence of funds should be the determinant of whether to proceed. Rather, evidence of a growing problem should stimulate investigation, whether or not there is a commitment to respond.

The changing nature of societal needs argues for the use of quick and dirty approaches. Lengthy planning can delay data collection and create its own kind of bias. More often than not, the demands for data preclude lengthy studies, and the question is whether some data are better than no data at all. If the information provided is misleading, there is no question that no information is better; but when data enables decision makers to question their present approach or their system for measuring service needs, it can be useful. Reexamining and streamlining the amount and type of information that an agency collects can be a valuable by-product of a quick and dirty assessment.

Dr. Schopler contends that careless assessments lead to bias, misinformation, and reliance on intuition. More often it is the absence of data that promotes guesswork in planning. Even limited information may be better than no information at all when it represents a beginning effort to bring objective evaluation to decision making.

The criteria used to select key informants must be scrutinized before passing judgment on quick and dirty assessments to be sure that their selection was based on their knowledge and credibility rather than their influence or persuasiveness. Likewise, scientific methodology allows for margins of error, and as with any research, as long as these rules are respected, quick and dirty assessments should be considered a valid approach.

Will Privatization Destroy the Traditional Nonprofit Human Services Sector?

EDITOR'S NOTE: Privatization of social and health services has been increasing rapidly during the past decade. Nonprofit human service agencies have had to focus on competing with for-profit agencies as well as with other nonprofit agencies for limited public dollars and on developing a marketing strategy to secure fee-for-service dollars, grants, and private donations. Considerable difference of opinion exists within the professional social work community as to whether this trend has or will destroy the voluntary social service system. Several key issues are involved in this debate: Does privatization ensure that social services are delivered more effectively and efficiently? Does privatization mean that the needs of the poor and disenfranchised are being ignored or going unmet? What role should the competitive market model play in the delivery of social welfare services? This debate is timely and is likely to remain an issue in the coming years as both government and nonprofit agencies are asked to do more with less.

F. Ellen Netting, Ph.D., and Steven L. McMurtry, Ph.D., argue YES. Dr. Netting is Associate Professor, Arizona State University School of Social Work, where she teaches in the areas of macro practice, program planning, administration, and policy. Her research interests include nonprofit organizations and gerontology, with a special emphasis on hospital-based long-term care services for the frail elderly. She and her colleagues, Peter M. Kettner and Steven L. McMurtry, have written *Social Work Macro Practice.*

Dr. McMurtry is Associate Professor at the School of Social Work at Arizona State University. He is director of the child welfare specialization in the school and also teaches macro practice and research. His most recent writings have addressed foster care issues and decision-making processes in nonprofit management.

Peter M. Kettner, D.S.W., and Lawrence L. Martin, Ph.D., M.S.W., argue NO. Dr. Kettner is Professor of Social Work at Arizona State University, where he teaches macro practice, program planning, financial management, and administration. In the area of macro practice, he has coauthored, with colleagues J. Michael Daley and Ann Nichols, *Initiating Change in Organizations and Communities* and, with colleagues F. Ellen Netting and Steven L. McMurtry, *Social Work Macro Practice.* His longstanding areas of interest and research include program planning and evaluation, purchase of service contracting, program design, and practice-oriented research.

Dr. Martin is an associate professor of Public Administration at Florida Atlantic University in Boca Raton. His research interest are in public–private sector relations, state and local government, and human services administration.

YES

F. Ellen Netting and Steven L. McMurtry

Privatization in the human services refers to the reduction of direct service delivery by governmental organizations in favor of increased reliance on services provided by private agencies. It is an idea that appeals to persons from diverse political persuasions, since it suggests benefits such as avoidance of bureaucracy, enhanced local control of services, and increased personal choice of service providers. However, we argue that what is actually taking place is a form of "ad hoc privatization" (Wolf, 1986) that accomplishes little in the way of service improvement and seductively masks the real issues of a welfare state adrift (Gilbert, 1983).

In particular, we focus on the consequences of privatization for nonprofit human service agencies. Contrary to its promised benefits, privatization is threatening the very existence of agencies in this sector. First, privatization increases competition both among nonprofit agencies and between nonprofit and for-profit organizations. Second, nonprofit providers have been forced to think and function much more like their for-profit counterparts, thus risking the loss of their voluntary identity and their legitimacy as community-based agencies. Finally, as nonprofit organizations compete for limited dollars, they are becoming more entrepreneurial and focusing ever more exclusively on consumers who can pay for services or who are attached to reimbursement streams. Legally, this challenges their tax-exempt status, and morally it undermines their basic charitable mission.

Privatization within a Political Economy

One way of understanding the impact of privatization on the human services system is to view this system as part of a *political economy*. Conceived by Adam Smith in 1776 and viewed as a basis of modern economic thought, political economy essentially means managing the public household. It also implies that the rules governing the economic system reflect the moral imperatives of individuals who make up the polity. "Political economy is thus a moral and institutional, as well as a technical term" (Bellah, Madden, Sullivan, Swidler, & Tipton, 1991, p. 84).

Though it has been defined in a bewildering diversity of ways, privatization can be viewed as the introduction of market mechanisms into government. Its adherents often assume that it is purely an economic process, but in a political economy it is neither possible nor meaningful to separate the economic from the political. Therefore, privatization, like political economy, is a moral as well as a technical term.

Palumbo and Maupin (1987) delineate three aspects of privatization: (1) deciding, (2) funding, and (3) providing. Deciding implies intent on the part of government to address an issue or concern. It is often manifested in the development of policy and in the regulation and oversight of policy intent. Funding involves the allocation of financial resources to program development. Finally, providing is the function of carrying out the intent of policy and funding through program implementation. Privatization, then, may be formally defined as the process of delegating public responsibility for deciding, funding, and providing to the private sector. It is a technical process with enormous political and moral implications for the larger society.

Increasing Competition

The contemporary push toward privatization is actually a call for reprivatization. Local, state, and federal governments were providing grants, contracts, subsidies, and tax incentives to nonprofit and for-profit agencies as early as the colonial era (Abramovitz, 1986). Only when the Great Depression forced the nation to respond to urgent need did the public sector reluctantly move toward assuming a greater role in direct service provision. Privatization, therefore, is not new.

What is new is rapidly intensifying competition among nonprofit and for-profit agencies to obtain limited public dollars, and their use of market strategies to obtain private dollars from persons who can afford to pay for services. In a system driven by reimbursement from government agencies or other third-party payers, the nonprofit sector's traditional attention toward the needs of the disadvantaged is turned away, except when these individuals qualify for contracted services.

The market-economy mentality also thrusts nonprofit agencies into competitive rather than collaborative roles with other agencies at a time when coalition building and interorganizational relationships are essential in advocating for human needs. The sense of community among voluntary sector agencies is in grave danger of being lost. Moreover, small, undiversified, community-based nonprofit agencies will find it ever more difficult to compete for limited funds. They will not have advertising budgets, full-time fund raisers, or the ability to shift services rapidly to attract remunerative clients or contracts. Many eventually will be swallowed up by larger agencies or simply cease to exist, with the likely result that the specialized services they brought the community will be lost.

The predominance of market mechanisms contrasts starkly with the traditions of nonprofit organizations. As Abramovitz (1986) notes, this sector was founded ''on the principle of service provision, outside the market, on the basis of need and regardless of ability to pay'' (p. 258). If market mechanisms worked for everyone, we would have no need for a voluntary human service system in this country. The system did emerge, however, because free market forces do not meet the needs of all the members of society. It is thus not surprising to learn that gaps also arise when nonprofit organizations are required to respond to these forces alone.

Finally, those who contend that commercializing services will enhance efficiency and save taxpayers' money need look only as far as the nation's health care system to find a major flaw in their arguments. In health care, the orientation toward private, fee-for-service care has clearly not produced an affordable and available system. Instead, many people lack basic coverage, and ''health care costs are far higher in the U.S., which relies heavily upon the commercial sector, than they are in Canada'' (Parry, 1990, p. 111). Moreover, these costs are common to both nonprofit and for-profit hospitals, and, indeed, the distinctions separating the two have almost entirely disappeared. Poor people are just as likely to be denied health care at nonprofit hospitals as at for-profit ones, and overburdened governmental facilities are now their only option.

Identity Erosion

Nonprofit-sector organizations have traditionally defined special missions and service roles for themselves that set them apart from governmental agencies and commercial firms. Though these distinctions are sometimes blurred, and though they also vary by service area and community, they have nonetheless helped to ensure that a continuum of services is present. In general, each sector has had a niche to fill, and a particular trademark of nonprofit organizations has been their capacity for flexibility and innovation. Privatization jeopardizes these traditional advantages by eliminating the distinctive character of these organizations (Ferris & Graddy, 1989).

Hodgkinson (1989) identifies five factors that have attributed to the changing role, functions, and missions of nonprofit organizations. These are: (1) federal funding cuts during the 1980s, (2) the increasing focus by nonprofit agencies on fees for service and commercial venturing, (3) growing for-profit competition in a changing service economy, (4) complaints by small business organizations that nonprofit agencies are competing with them, and (5) the development of adversarial relationships between the public, nonprofit, and for-profit sectors.

In other words, as nonprofit agencies have become more dependent on government dollars, they have grown more like government organizations. As they have moved to attracting paying clients, they have also had to become more like the for-profit organizations with which they must compete for these clients. Yet, their legitimacy as service providers has historically centered around values such as community representation, diversity, participation, charity, and philanthropy. The conflicts inherent in attempting to maintain these values while becoming more like other types of organizations has thus led to a developing identity crisis among agencies in this sector. A very real danger is that the nonprofit organizations that survive this crisis will be solely resource driven. For some, the focus will be on public contracts, which do not reflect the needs of the helpless but the values of those in power. For others, concerns for attracting profitable clients will overwhelm charitable goals.

Those Who Cannot Pay

A principal argument for privatization is that the influx of government contracts monies, funds from third-party payers, and direct fees for service will provide the resources needed to revive struggling nonprofit agencies. What is not addressed in this argument is what the availability of these services will mean for agencies' involvement with clients who cannot pay for services and do not qualify for reimbursement under government contracts or private insurance. Evidence indicates that the policy underlying government funds and the mechanisms with which they are provided have more to do with the nature of services than the ideology of the provider organization.

For example, Gronbjerg (1990) studied nonprofit agencies' commitment to serving the poor in response to changing governmental funding policies in the 1980s. Her findings suggested that ''the nonprofit sector mirrors government and the private sector in devoting most of its concern to middle and upper-middle income groups'' (p. 226). Later, she also notes that:

> Nonprofit organizations are not as responsive to the poor as public stereotypes might suggest, probably because they have enough to do without focusing on the poor and their difficult problems . . . [Government

policies] falsely assumed that nonprofit organizations have a strong commitment to the poor that is independent of the incentives provided by government funding (pp. 228–229).

In other words, nonprofit agencies base their actions in large part on the directions set (implicitly or explicitly) by government funds. Just because agencies in the nonprofit sector have a traditional orientation toward the poor, government cannot assume that undirected purchase of service from these agencies will ensure that the poor will continue to be served.

Sosin (1990) reviewed consequences of the decentralization of government programs in the 1980s, which was one aspect of the privatization movement. His findings also indicate that more funding to private agencies from governmental sources does not necessarily lead to service improvements. He notes that "increased governmental financial support of private agencies is not fully used to expand the total number of individuals served. Rather, it may encourage substitution, that is, the replacement of private resources by government revenue" (p. 625–626). Thus, services to the most needy are not expanded by privatization-related efforts; the status quo is merely maintained by a different mix of funds.

Conclusion

Some observers have predicted that by the year 2000 the existing nonprofit sector will split into two distinct types of organizations—commercial and donative. Commercial nonprofits will focus exclusively on earning income from the sale of service to individuals, insurers, or the government, while the relatively few donative nonprofits remaining will struggle to serve the poor and distressed (Hansmann, 1989). Others propose a picture of the welfare state adrift in a sea of uncertainty, not knowing to what government is truly committed and for what it is responsible (Gilbert, 1983). This latter vision represents a continuation of ad hoc privatization, in which the private sector must assume responsibility for public policy regarding human services.

In such a situation, the feeding frenzy among nonprofit agencies and between nonprofit and for-profit organizations will continue unabated, and the persons who suffer will be the persons for whom no one will take responsibility—those without value because they do not come with dollars attached. The nonprofit human service sector will move further and further away from its voluntary roots, and the agencies that once represented the values of community participation, charity, and philanthropy will no longer be recognizable. The voices of revenue-seeking and zero-sum games will drown out all others in the boardrooms and offices of agencies that were once considered the best hope of the downtrodden.

REFERENCES

Abramovitz, M. (1986). The privatization of the welfare state: A review. *Social Work, 31*(4), 257–264.

Bellah, R. N., Madden, R., Sullivan, W. M., Swidler, A., & Tipton, S. M. (1991). *The good society.* New York: Knopf.

Ferris, J. M., & Graddy, E. (1989). Fading distinctions among the nonprofit, government, and for-profit sectors. In V. A. Hodgkinson & R. W. Lyman (Eds.), *The future of the nonprofit sector* (pp. 123–139). San Francisco: Jossey-Bass.

Gilbert, N. (1983). *Capitalism and the welfare state.* New Haven, CT: Yale University Press.

Gronbjerg, K. A. (1990). Poverty and nonprofit organizational behavior. *Social Service Review, 64*(2), 208–243.

Hansmann, H. (1989). The two nonprofit sectors: Fee for service versus donative organizations. In V. A. Hodgkinson & R. W. Lyman (Eds.), *The future of the nonprofit sector* (pp. 92–102). San Francisco: Jossey-Bass.

Hodgkinson, V. A. (1989). Changing roles and responsibilities of the non-profit sector. In V. A. Hodgkinson and R. W. Lyman, (Eds.), *The Future of the Non-Profit Sector* (pp. 123–139). San Francisco: Jossey-Bass.

Palumbo, D. J., & Maupin, J. (1987). The political side of privatization. Paper presented at the annual meeting of the American Political Science Association, Chicago, IL.

Parry, R. (1990). *Privatisation.* London: Jessica Kingsley Publishers.

Sosin, M. R. (1990). Decentralizing the social service system: A reassessment. *Social Service Review, 64*(4), 617–636.

Wolf, J. (1986). Can voluntary nonprofits survive privatization? Changing the social contract. *Business Quarterly, 51*(3), 62–69.

Rejoinder to Dr. Netting and Dr. McMurtry

PETER M. KETTNER AND
LAWRENCE L. MARTIN

We must confess we have difficulty understanding the Netting/McMurtry arguments against privatization. If one believes that something will "destroy" the traditional nonprofit sector, presumably one is against it. If one opposes privatization, what, then, is the alternative? The only alternative we know of is direct delivery by government and a withdrawal of government funding from private, nonprofit, and for-profit agencies. We have several problems with deprivatization.

First, if anything would destabilize and destroy the private not-for-profit agency, it would be the withdrawal of government funding. By most accounts, private agencies are dependent on government funding for upward of 50 percent of their budgets. Second, Dr. Netting and Dr. McMurtry are highly critical of the government's role in serving the poor. How, then, will the poor be better served if all publicly funded services are delivered only by government agencies?

If the issue, as defined by Dr. Netting and Dr. McMurtry, is that government has not done a very good job of comprehensive planning or defining the roles and relationships of not-for-profit, for-profit, and government-delivered services, we would, in many cases, agree. However, if this is a basis for arguing for deprivatization and delivery of all services by government, we would have to disagree.

Privatization, we believe, has little to do with the changes Dr. Netting and Dr. McMurtry see occurring in the American social welfare system. Privatization is an international trend that transcends the social welfare arena and is based in a belief that the private sector can do some things better, more efficiently, and more flexibly than government. Privatization is not the cause of cutbacks in federal and state funding for human services. Cutbacks are the result of declining revenues in combination with changing federal and state priorities over the last decade. Neither is privatization the cause of increasing competition. In a healthy economy, most government contracting agencies would welcome increasing competition and the opportunity to select from a range of potential providers. In fact, whatever competition exists is among established providers for a share of a shrinking pie. Again, limited resources, not privatization, are the culprit.

All the evidence points to an increasing use of the partnership model of contracting between government and private agencies and a decline of the competitive market model. In those cases where the competitive market model is abused, such as those cited by Dr. Netting and Dr. McMurtry, it is within the power of government contracting agencies to correct those abuses. However, having government terminate its relationships with all private not-for-profit and for-profit agencies and take over direct delivery of all services where such abuses occur is clearly a drastic and inappropriate response that destroys the many benefits of a partnership relationship for the sake of correcting a single flaw. There are better ways to correct that and other flaws in the system.

A dominant theme running through the Netting/McMurtry essay is that of serving those who cannot pay. Again, we ask what is the issue being raised? If government withdraws all contracting dollars, will private not-for-profit agencies somehow be better able to serve the poor? We think not. Furthermore, when one looks closely at what organizations are currently running the homeless shelters, the soup kitchens, and the board and care homes for the seriously mentally ill, it invariably turns out to be the private not-for-profit agencies with the help of government funding.

In summary, we submit that Dr. Netting and Dr. McMurtry make the mistake of many who accuse privatization of destroying the American welfare system. Making privatization the "enemy" is a disservice to the private not-for-profit agency, government contracting agencies, clients, and communities. The "enemy," we submit, is a general lack of commitment to poor individuals, families, and communities; failure to plan for comprehensive services to communities; inadequate funding; lack of knowledge about how to use contracting mechanisms to achieve community, state, and federal goals; and other such factors. Taking public funds away from private, not-for-profit agencies is not the solution. It has been said that for every problem there is a simple, neat, and incorrect solution. Blaming privatization for the changes being experienced in the American welfare system is simple, neat, and incorrect.

NO

PETER M. KETTNER AND LAWRENCE L. MARTIN

Concerns about the Impact of Privatization on Social Services

A number of authors over the years have raised concerns about the threats to traditional social services posed by the trend toward privatization (Abramovitz, 1986; Gilbert, 1986; Hurl, 1986). The major argument seems to be that the diminished role of government leaves social services at the mercy of a potentially unscrupulous marketplace. Organizations in the private sector then become a part of a local community's social service system without the best interest of client and·community at heart. Their interests revolve around profit or some sort of fiscal advantage through tax benefits, vouchers, contracts, or profit-making ventures. Incentives are to serve the highest paying clients, while the needs of the most severely deprived go unserved.

Without question, privatization of social services holds the potential for becoming a marketplace where entrepreneurs look for ways to increase their income at the expense of clients and communities. Using defense contracting and health care as models, it is not difficult to imagine skyrocketing, out of control unit costs. Without controls, such services as counseling, day care, meals, and other goods and services provided by states and communities to people in need can deteriorate into a gold rush on state and local treasuries. Without controls, intense competition can be focused on the highest paying clients, while the most needy receive only token attention. However, no one seriously proposes that privatization operate without controls, and experiences to date simply do not support the development of an exploitive type of a social service system.

Experiences to date demonstrate that: (1) private, not-for-profit and for-profit organizations have an important role to play in the provision of services at the local level and (2) a collaborative relationship between government and the private sector strengthens, not destroys, the social service system.

Privatization Is Here to Stay

The term *privatization* means a lot of different things to different people. Originally coined by Peter Drucker as "reprivatization" in his book *The Age of Discontinuity* (Drucker, 1969), the term has come to refer to varying types of public–private relationships designed to fulfill the obligations of government.

Having various organizations in the private sector carry out responsibilities of government is not a new idea. In colonial America, orphaned children were cared for by local families and paid from community tax resources. From colonial times to the New Deal, public subsidization of the private sector was the norm. The Social Security Act of 1935 ushered in an era of government dominance in funding and direct provision of services. From the 1960s on, privatization, primarily in the form of purchase of service contracting, has grown steadily, with a major boost coming from Title XX of the Social Security Act.

Privatization generally refers to a shifting of government responsibilities to nongovernment entities with the expectation that market forces will improve productivity, efficiency, and effectiveness in the provision of services. Privatization in human services can include assigning responsibility to nonpublic entities for anything from needs assessment to funding, policy making, program development, service provision, monitoring, evaluation, or any combination of these activities. In most states, 50 percent or more of their service dollars are contracted to private, not-for-profit and for-profit organizations.

Dependence on private agencies to provide services such as residential treatment, long-term nursing care, day care, home health care, transportation, and other services is so great that it is unlikely that these activities will ever again be provided exclusively by government. Furthermore, there is little indication that this type of working relationship is unsatisfactory. All indications are that a sharing of public responsibility and public funding between the government and the private sector has become the new status quo.

Returning to the defense and health care industries as examples, although the market mechanisms hoped for by advocates of privatization have not worked as well as they might have to drive down costs and improve products and services, there is little serious discussion of direct government ownership of these industries, direct government employment of a work force to produce the necessary goods and services, or termination of the contracting relationship with the private sector. Far from destroying the defense and health care industries, privatization has greatly strengthened their role in economic and political arenas. The challenge is to find ways to bring these industries under control and to make marketplace mechanisms work to the advantage of the purchaser of goods and services—namely, units of government and the clients they serve.

The Important Role of the Private Sector

Drucker and other advocates of privatization could certainly be accused of having overoptimistic expectations of private sector involvement in the delivery of services for which government is responsible. Drucker, for example, identifies the following as some of the advantages of privatization (authors' paraphrasing, not Drucker's words): (1) results are expected of private-sector organizations; they are not expected of government; (2) government organizations are subject to political influence; private-sector organizations are not; (3) government programs are perpetuated regardless of whether or not they continue to meet a need; private-sector organizations go out of business when they no longer meet a need; (4) government values loyalty; private-sector organizations value performance; (5) government employment bloats the bureaucracy; private sector employs only the necessary work force to get the job done; (6) privatization allows for greater flexibility in matching resources to need; government provision makes change cumbersome; and (7) government is not good at innovation; the private sector is.

In human services, not all of these high hopes for privatization have been realized, but some have. One example is a growing trend in some programs toward performance contracting, a mechanism that focuses on results achieved with clients. The same emphasis on results is not as readily found in direct-delivered government services.

As a second example, contracting has provided greater flexibility in targeting resources to areas of highest need. When funding is increased or decreased, contracts can be modified to match resources to need, whereas government reductions in force tend to follow rather strict rules of seniority. Another area of success is innovation. In some programs such as residential treatment, drug and alcohol, services to the homeless and others, provider agencies have demonstrated an ability to innovate and to respond quickly in terms of startup and shutdown, as needed. Finally, total dollars have been stretched by combining public dollars with privately generated dollars to increase the total pool of resources available to provide services to clients. Furthermore, private organizations often provide services to government clients at less than break-even cost when units of government do not have the resources to provide full reimbursement.

The disappointing aspects of contracting with private-sector agencies, to advocates of privatization, have been, first, that decisions about funding and

service provision continue to be highly politicized. The private-sector participants have demonstrated that they are every bit as capable as government
providers of participating actively in the political arena and of basing decisions
on factors other than client and community need. Second, serious competition
has rarely emerged in contracting for human services. Market forces have not
come into play to drive down prices to any significant extent. Finally, the type of
bureaucratic red tape than tends to clog the system and acts as a barrier to good,
efficient provision of services has, in many cases, been carried over to the private
sector. On balance, however, in spite of some of the drawbacks, most human
service professionals today recognize that the private sector has important contributions to make to every local human services system.

Toward a Mutually Beneficial Model of Privatization

Part of the problem with the controversial issue of privatization is that expectations differ, depending on one's perspective. Some expect competition and lower
costs, some expect higher quality services and improved outcomes, some expect
a lean and streamlined government organization focused on contracting with
delivery in the hands of private-sector providers. Any or all of the above are
possible, depending on the particular unit of government understanding what it
wants from its privatization efforts and knowing how to make it happen.

The authors have, in earlier work, developed and described a framework
within which all of the above can be achieved (Kettner & Martin, 1991). We refer
to this framework as the *market and partnership models* of purchase of service
contracting. What that means is that, handled correctly and with a sound understanding of all the relevant variables, contracting can operate either in a "market" context or in a "partnership" context.

A market approach to privatization focuses on generating competition and
contracting with the lowest qualified bidder in the interest of stretching the
dollars as far as possible. A partnership approach focuses on strengthening the
working relationship between government and provider in the interest of stabiliz-
ing the service system and providing the best service possible to the client.

One of the more important considerations in selecting an approach to
contracting is that of the impact on the client. In some types of service, such
considerations as stability and continuity of care override cost cutting. For
example, in purchasing residential treatment for adolescents, it is theoretically
possible to create a market environment and generate competitive bidding for
clients on an annual basis. This approach, however, totally undercuts the objective of providing a stable, predictable environment and building trusting relationships with staff for a population that, in most cases, has a long history of
instability in home life. Contrast this type of service with transportation, for
example. If a particular client population (take, for example, the physically

disabled) needs to be transported around the community, there are several considerations: wheelchair-adapted vehicles and safe, courteous drivers, among others. As long as these important considerations are addressed by a provider, it may not really matter if the provider changes every year. In this instance, a market approach can be used with contract specifications established and the contract going to the lowest bidder. This can, and often does, happen in transportation contracts as well as with the provision of meals, job placement, training, and other such services that can be clearly defined and the conditions of delivery specified and evaluated.

The "failures" of privatization surface when individuals or groups of people with a particular set of expectations attempt to impose these expectations on the entire system and don't really understand where to look for "successes." If a partnership relationship between government and child care agency provides stable, predictable, high-quality services and achieves good results, then privatization in that instance can be said to be successful regardless of whether or not the services were provided at a cost lower than what it would cost the government to provide the service. If transportation is provided to more people at a lower unit cost as a result of competitive bidding, then privatization in that instance can be said to be successful regardless of the number of times the service provider changes.

A final concern often raised by opponents of privatization is that private agencies "cream" clients—that is, they serve the least needy, most self-sufficient who offer the best chances of success, and they ignore the most needy. Again, we take the position that the population served is defined by the government unit that pays for the service. Government contracting agencies have the prerogative to define eligibility standards, to specify demographic characteristics, problem type, level of severity, or any variables deemed important. It should be recognized and acknowledged, however, that the more severe the problem, the more costly it is to treat. Higher unit costs often must be paid for treatment of people with chronic conditions than for services to people with mild conditions. Outcome expectations also need to be adjusted accordingly.

Will Privatization Destroy the Social Service System?

In summary, our response to those who fear that privatization will destroy the stability of the social service system is that their concerns are focused on the wrong target. The focus of concern need not be so much on private providers exploiting the system, on what is perceived to be conservative political philosophies "winning the day," or on the system ignoring the problems of those most in need. Instead, the focus of concern should be on ensuring that the government contracting agency understands how to make contracting work in the best interest of clients and communities.

The loosely connected infrastructure that we call the social services system within our states and local communities can be destroyed or rendered ineffective in two ways: inadequate funding and the failure of the government contracting agency to perform effectively either in direct delivery or in achieving its contracting objectives. The control, stability, and predictability of any community's social service system is in the hands of the government contracting agency and not in the hands of the private-agency providers. The attentions of concerned people, therefore, ought to be focused on the philosophy, policies, and procedures of the government contracting agency. If a state, county, or city's objective in privatization of services is to save money, then quality of service and client outcomes should be made the issue. If the objective is to improve client outcomes, then adequate funding and other necessary resources should be made the issue. Blanket criticism of either public or private sectors serves no effective purpose.

In the end, the quality and effectiveness of service, whether delivered by government or by the private sector, are issues of adequacy of resources, of achieving a better understanding of problems and interventions, and of cooperation and collaboration in the interest of building an effective system. A movement toward deprivatization is clearly no panacea.

REFERENCES

Abramovitz, M. (1986). The privatization of the welfare state: A review. *Social Work 31*(4), 257–264.

Drucker, P. (1969). The sickness of government. In P. Drucker (Ed.), *The age of discontinuity.* New York: Harper & Row.

Gidron, B., Kramer, R., & Salamon, L. (1992). *Government and the third sector.* San Francisco: Jossey-Bass.

Gilbert, N. (1986). The welfare state adrift. *Social Work 31*(4), 251–256.

Hurl, L. H. (1986). Keeping on top of government contracting: The challenge to social work educators. *Journal of Social Work Education 22*(2), 6–18.

Kammerman, S., & Kahn, A. (1989). *Privatization and the welfare state.* Princeton, NJ: Princeton University Press.

Kettner, P., & Martin, L. (1991). Purchase of service contracting: Two models. *Administration in Social Work 14*(1), 15–30.

Martin, L. (1991). Privatization and federal budget reform. In T. Lynch (Ed.), *Federal budget & financial management reform* (pp. 185–205). New York: Quorum Books.

Salamon, L. (1987). Of market failure, voluntary failure, and third-party government: Toward a theory of government-nonprofit relations in the modern welfare state. *Journal of Voluntary Action Research 16*(1 & 2), 29–49.

Terrell, P. (1987). Purchasing social services. *Encyclopedia of social work* (18th edition) (pp. 434–442). Silver Springs, MD: National Association of Social Workers.

Rejoinder to Professor Kettner and Dr. Martin

F. ELLEN NETTING AND
STEVEN L. MCMURTRY

Professor Kettner and Dr. Martin's arguments, which can be summarized as "just give privatization a little more time," are reminiscent of those of Herbert Hoover, who clung to an unshakable belief in the power of market forces even as the nation plunged into the Great Depression. The question remains, how much time is enough for a flawed policy? How long should ad hoc privatization be allowed to undermine the foundations of the nonprofit sector before there is a change? Our argument is that the time is now.

Professor Kettner and Dr. Martin argue that "there is little indication that [privatization] is unsatisfactory," but they fail to address the research cited in our initial statement that suggests precisely the contrary. They also contend that "sharing of public responsibility and public funding between the government and the private sector has become the new status quo," but they offer no specific support for this claim. They use this argument to support their position, reminding us of the phrase "everyone's doing it." Obviously everyone is engaged in privatization, but shared responsibility is deceptive. Shared responsibility often means that no one takes responsibility for what is happening.

Professor Kettner and Dr. Martin challenge us "to bring [the defense and health care] industries under control." They indicate that they have developed a way to fix these problems through a market or a partnership model of contracting. There is some relief in reading this until one realizes that unless policy decision makers as well as implementers understand policy intent, these policies will fail. Studies indicate repeatedly that unless a basic understanding of policy intent exists, grounded in a sound philosophy, the implementation of that policy will be altered beyond recognition.

A critical problem in Professor Kettner and Dr. Martin's points is that they do not distinguish between nonprofit and for-profit organizations in discussing the impact of privatization. For example, they cite services such as "residential treatment, long-term nursing care, and day care" as examples of arenas where privatization has worked. However, they fail to note that these and other examples are precisely the service arenas that are becoming increasingly dominated by for-profit providers. Not coincidentally, none of these arenas has a noteworthy track record for serving very poor clients.

Marketplace forces do work with great effectiveness in certain circumstances, but the age-old problem of an unrestrained market is that some are enriched at the expense of others. The welfare state is specifically intended to deal with this problem, but the paradox of privatization is that the work of the human services system is given over to the very market forces whose effects the system is designed to ameliorate. Though the model may work well in specific services arenas, by its very nature it is destined to fail in others. In particular, it runs the risk of turning traditional nonprofit agencies into traditional for-profit organizations. The losers in this transition will also be traditional ones—those whose need for services is greatest.

Current political realities dictate that privatization itself is not at stake. What is at stake is the maintenance of a healthy division of labor between the nonprofit, for-profit, and governmental sectors. This division is endangered by current privatization practices. A new approach is needed that will ensure the autonomy of nonprofit providers and enable them to act on their historical strength in providing services to the most needy.

Is Coordinating Social Service Organizations to Improve Client Services a Waste of Staff Effort?

EDITOR'S NOTE: As the social service system has grown, programs have become increasingly specialized and often targeted to narrowly defined populations. For example, a client who is pregnant, homeless, and disabled may find herself involved with three or four different organizations, each seeking to provide her with appropriate services to meet *one* of her identified needs. How well her needs are met depends not only on her willingness and ability to negotiate and use services, but also on the ability of the providers to work together on her behalf. Recognizing both the complexity of client needs and the fragmentation and duplication often inherent in service delivery systems, many professionals suggest that organizations need to coordinate and integrate their services. The growing use of case management in all areas of social services suggests that coordination of services is a critical and evolving issue for the profession. This debate focuses on whether service coordination will make better use of resources, provide more effective services to clients, and overall promote the self-sufficiency of clients and the satisfaction of workers.

Thomas P. Holland, Ph.D., and Charlene Flagg, M.A., say YES. Dr. Holland is Professor and Director of the Doctoral Program at the University of Georgia School of Social Work, Athens, Georgia. His specialty areas are Ethics, Management, and Evaluation Research. He is currently engaged in national studies of nonprofit organization boards.

Ms. Flagg is currently a doctoral student in Sociology at the University of Michigan, Ann Arbor, Michigan. Her specialty areas are poverty and women.

Ray H. MacNair, Ph.D., says NO. Dr. MacNair is Associate Professor in the School of Social Work and Public Service Consultant in the Institute of Community and Area Development both at the University of Georgia, Athens, Georgia. He is active in the National Association of Community Organization and Social Administration, the Georgia Network for Rural Human Services, and the National Rural Caucus. His writing interests emphasize theory and research methods for community organization practice.

YES

Thomas P. Holland and Charlene Flagg

The Limits of Service Coordination

Efforts to coordinate social services on behalf of clients have already been repeatedly shown to be wasteful of staff time and effort. The evidence for this conclusion is clear and extensive, since such activities have regularly led to unresponsive, unaccountable bureaucracies. What is less evident is why this approach is so persistently trumpeted by professionals in the human services industry, despite its repeated failures there and elsewhere.

People are interested in self-direction and in the availability of an array of goods and services tailored for and responsive to their individual needs. The advocates of more coordination, on the other hand, talk of clients' interests but act in ways that operate rather to diminish client options while increasing the professionals' own control over programs and services.

Accountability follows from control over resources. When I have the money and can spend it on what I want, I will choose the uses of it that I deem best. Like any consumer, if clients have opportunities to choose among services, they will choose the ones that meet their needs most satisfactorily, leaving the less desired organizations with fewer resources. Responsiveness to the aggregation of individual consumer choices serves to guide organizations into those activities that are desired and away from those that are not. Effective coordination is done by the consumer, whose expectations prompt voluntary actions from providers seeking to maximize the responsiveness of their services to the consumer's demands. Why these simple customs operate everywhere except in social services is never explained by the advocates of professional control over human services.

Control by professionals is given the more benign name of coordination on behalf of clients. Sometimes it is called a case management system. Sometimes it involves elaborate, computer-based information systems intended to link service providers into a vast, centrally planned network. Regardless of the disguise, essentially the plan involves expansions of the decision-making power of providers over the allocation of services and access to resources on behalf of clients, who presumably are incapable of identifying and pursuing their own needs and interests.

If clients must comply with the directives of a service coordinator or case manager, the clients' own capacities for self-direction and responsibility are undermined by the power of the professionals. In such circumstances, clients have little power to hold providers accountable, and clients' interests are addressed only to the extent that providers' interests are not jeopardized. The risks from dissatisfied consumers are minimized and can easily go ignored. Self-serving bureaucracies are the result.

It should be no mystery why greater centralization of control over social services has many negative effects. The supply of social services is far smaller than what is needed by clients. Certainly there is little oversupply or duplication requiring reduction or elimination. Diversity and individualization of services are limited, forcing clients to conform their needs to the few categories preferred by the bureaucracies. Diverting more resources from an already scarce supply of services into more "coordination" has never produced a single new service. Rather, increasing centralized coordination typically results in greater control and standardization, based on the lowest common denominator of service types and units that the providers design. Fewer services and less individualized responses are the actual results of increased coordination. More and more resources are diverted away from clients and into maintaining and extending the providers' system.

The assumptions underlying such moves are clearly paternalistic. Individual choice and self-direction on the part of clients are undermined as they are cast in the role of dependent receivers of directives, which reduces their capabilities for deciding what is really needed. There is perpetuated a self-fulfilling prophecy that clients are incapable of autonomy and responsibility for themselves. They lack judgment and are inept in identifying and seeking services to meet their own needs. They require supervision in obtaining information and making use of services. Rather than empowering persons who need services, clients are made even more vulnerable to the decisions and manipulations of experts.

Truly autonomous client choice and increased self-direction would suggest that coordination of services be carried out by the one person most immediately familiar with the needs—the client. What would truly serve that person's interests would be structures of service delivery that maximize, not reduce, self-direction and opportunities to make choices that will support responsibility for one's own needs.

Why do human service professionals avoid conclusions that most others have reached and, instead, continue to seek greater control for themselves? The calls for greater coordination by providers serve to disguise a common and familiar human tendency among individuals in any marketplace of services or products for sale. After a period of competition in which a variety of providers survive, some of the stronger participants begin to see how their competitive position in this arena could be enhanced even further by reducing the access of others to the resources on which they all depend. These efforts to constrain some segment of the marketplace to gain control over it are widely known as trying to create a monopoly, no matter how carefully disguised as being in the public interest.

In the human services sector, the resources that providers want include access to other organizations and to private sponsors and public sources of financial support, as well as control over how choices are made by clients. The issue then becomes one of how an organization can find ways to increase its control over these resources and reduce others' access to them, all without jeopardizing its own credibility or status. A favorite cover for such efforts is to label them as steps to serve the public or some segment of it more efficiently by eliminating wasteful duplication of efforts. In any other industry, this process would be seen as efforts to create a monopoly and then challenged publicly through the courts. Restraint of trade has been accepted as harmful to consumers and detrimental to the economy.

Popular distrust of the poor fuels a desire to minimize services and choices for them. Advocates for greater coordination pander to such views with promises to increase efficiency and reduce an imaginary "wasteful duplication" of services. Claiming to be the real experts regarding client needs, they promise to set up an intricately coordinated system where information about their private sufferings is available to the providers, who are to be trusted to make those important personal decisions for clients that they cannot do for themselves ("Trust us, we're the professionals.")

A thoughtful public would not forget the many important and relevant lessons from its shared history. The closer any industry comes to monopolistic control by a few corporations, the more self-serving and unresponsive to consumer interests it becomes. For example, our nation's automobile manufacturers enjoyed years of great profits and immense salaries for those at the top, made by producing huge, inefficient, poorly constructed cars. They fought Japanese imports with calls for trade barriers, government bail-outs, and ideological attacks that those who wanted the smaller, more efficient, better built cars were somehow unpatriotic. Efforts to constrain consumer choices would thus "guide" Americans into those decisions that would serve the interests of the big domestic corporations. But consumer choices were enhanced by the availability of numerous competitors offering a variety of cars in the marketplace, and such variety served to bring pressure on domestic manufacturers to pay more careful attention to consumer desires.

Another example may be seen in the recently ended monopoly over the nation's telephone communications system, which was dominated by one corporation until competing groups fought to break it into smaller parts. Soon there followed a dramatic surge of innovations that expanded the communications choices for all consumers. Yet another example may be seen in the current public elementary and secondary schools, which have long resisted efforts to allow consumers free choice through such means as vouchers to families instead of direct public funding of schools. Failure rates that exceed graduation rates in many cities' public school systems are increasingly pointing to the conclusion that this monopoly, like others, is not meeting the consumers' needs.

Closer to home for social work professionals may be Lipsky's (1980) analysis of one form of service coordination, the street-level bureaucrats. These front-line gatekeepers of public service agencies serve to structure and limit people's choices and opportunities under the guise of ''helping'' them. Coordinators' activities were found to be distorted by bias and favoritism despite official regulations to the contrary. The system of central coordination fosters such behavior, he concluded. ''They believe themselves to be doing the best they can under adverse circumstances . . . but the poorer people are, the greater the influence street-level bureaucrats tend to have over them. Indeed these public workers are so situated that they may well be taken to be part of the problems of the poor'' (Lipsky, 1980, p. 11).

Such sad examples could be listed extensively. Examples of the advantages of centrally controlled industries are few, chiefly drawn from wartime circumstances when responsiveness to individual needs was not a major concern. Clearly, the evidence leads one to the conclusion that there is considerable doubt about the claims of benefits for clients from greater central coordination of services. The evidence points in quite the opposite direction.

Enhancing the responsiveness of services to clients and accountabiliṭy to their interests is indeed a laudable goal. It would be better met through the direct empowerment of consumers by allowing them control over the most important resource that agencies want and need—money. Making that resource available directly to consumers through negative income taxes, vouchers, or other means would allow clients to vote with their feet, just as everyone does when he or she decides to shop at one store and not at another. Social service organizations would quickly find that individually tailored services, with appropriate adaptations to the services of other providers that the client desired, is the best way to survive in this marketplace.

Virtually everyone else except perhaps a few holdout, old-guard apparatchik in Moscow and Havana has already come to the recognition that people are better served and organizations are more accountable to them when they are linked through the marketplace, instead of through central planners and coordinators. It's long past time that social workers caught up with the nearly universal conclusions of the late twentieth century, relinquished efforts to disguise this atavistic impulse toward monopolistic central control as a more benign coordination, and directed their well-intentioned energies to the development of service delivery systems that are directly responsive to the intended consumers.

REFERENCE

Lipsky, M. (1980). *Street-level Bureaucracy: Dilemmas of the individual in public services.* New York: Russell Sage Foundation.

Rejoinder to Holland and Flagg RAY H. MACNAIR

The authors' suggestion that a free enterprise model can be employed in the human services is intriguing but simply not applicable. It overlooks the central mandate of public human services: to be effective in the use of public resources to achieve positive client social functioning and self-sufficiency. Individuals suffering from chronic distress ought not be left to fend for themselves in a complex, malintegrated system that is often biased against them. I feel sure the free enterprise model is a comfortable one for the entrepreneurial upper-middle classes because it allows them to ignore the profound problems experienced by increasing numbers of people within our current uncoordinated arrangements.

Contrary to their assertion, their critique of the coordination experience is totally unsubstantiated and undocumented. The fact is that coordination has failed largely because of a quasi-entrepreneurial spirit among both public and private human service managers. What is needed is a team spirit, the kind of mutual and collective mindedness that makes Japanese industry as effective as it is.

I do not argue their point that bureaucratic controls can be stifling. It is less clear to me that the current system is preferable to an integrated approach that enhances communication among various alternative sources of assistance. An effective case manager is one who is aware of various alternatives and provides the client with a point of reference for discovering the opportunities and avenues that are available. I am unaware of any evidence that modern case managers are despots who stifle initiative and serve only to protect an entrenched bureaucracy. They are employed to open doors for their clients and hold bureaucracies accountable for following through with their services when needed. The human service teams I have seen are dedicated to encouraging initiative on the part of their clients.

There is evidence that a voucher system leads to abuses when the bureaucracy does not pursue its requirement for accountability. A case in point is the technical and trade schools that have cheated the public and their students with fraudulent claims and inadequate educational programs.

It is an open question whether the European model can be emulated in the United States. In the typical European system, opportunity, client initiative, accountability, and integration of services are seen as compatible qualities of their bureaucracies. Given the fact that chronically dependent clients do not always respond spontaneously to the suggestion of opportunity, a careful assessment of the readiness of each client is needed, along with features of service that offer encouragement and information at each step along the way.

Further, if bureaucracies are likely to become entrenched and self-protective, a program of community initiatives is needed to watch, analyze, stimulate, and support change in each local situation. This is what the Atlanta Project and others like it have proposed and demonstrated. It is the American way.

NO

Ray H. MacNair

News item: "Former President Jimmy Carter asked President Bush on Wednesday for his help in getting federal agencies to pool their efforts on behalf of Atlanta's poor. . . . In laying the groundwork for his Atlanta Project to focus government and private efforts on the city's poor, Mr. Carter has found that federal agencies often do not, or cannot, cooperate with one another on programs. Impoverished, often illiterate parents face tedious and duplicative forms when they apply for food, housing, and education aid.

"Federal agencies, the former president said, 'have been divided from one another over generations of specific legislation that comes out of the Congress, so they really can't cooperate' . . . Mr. Carter emphasized that he thinks there is enough federal money available to treat social ills. What is missing, he said, is coordination and a stronger sense of purpose" (*Atlanta Constitution,* 1992, p. A10).

What Jimmy Carter has discovered, of course, is what many federal, state, and local officials have known for decades. Our disconnected system in the community human services is inefficient and wasteful. Special efforts are required to overcome the hurdles that have been placed in the way of integrated service for families and populations that suffer from multiple problems.

History

The issue of integrated services has been recognized ever since the Charity Organization Societies (COS) were established in the 1880s to overcome the separation between churches and other charities for the poor. The efforts of the

COS did not, however, endure through the World Wars. Throughout the 1900s, human services have been a growth industry, but they have grown in specialized pieces, one by one, in the context of the political and economic philosophy of limited government. Each movement has produced a limited, specialized bureaucratic domain.

After the major south-north migrations of the 1940s, Bradley Buell (1952) documented the problem in definitive fashion. In a tracking study of more than one hundred multiple problem families in Minneapolis, he cited six problems in the delivery of human services:

1. *Duplication.* Numerous agencies provide the same service. That means clients can hustle among them; it also means that legitimate claims that are inadequately addressed by one agency result in duplicated efforts by the client with other agencies to obtain an adequate response.
2. *Gaps in service.* Multiple agencies, each addressing a narrow field of interest and small sector of the population, are unable to cope with each of the problems that need to be addressed.
3. *Contradiction.* Related agencies, such as a child welfare program and a family service agency, often give contradictory advice such as (a) give up your child to foster care and (b) keep your child and learn to care for the child. Workers become inefficient and unproductive when this happens because they inadvertently work against each other.
4. *Fragmentation.* Specialized agencies, each with its elaborate forms of knowledge and practice, view the client's problems as though they were entirely within their purview, ignoring the need for alternative forms of specialized knowledge. The practitioner's sense of self-importance becomes a barrier to effective service, and efforts are wasted, as many problems that remain unresolved impinge on those receiving attention.
5. *Bias.* Lower class and culturally diverse clients are either ignored or discouraged from following through with service because they are not well understood. They are considered difficult or unmotivated clients; therefore, it is not efficient or productive to continue working with them. In fact, such clients become alienated and unmotivated.
6. *Barriers to access.* Distances, transportation, illiteracy, long forms, records requirements, language barriers, waiting lists, long waits during working hours, distrust of bureaucrats, or lack of day care may impede access to services. Again, unresolved problems reverberate back on problems receiving attention, and efforts may be wasted.

Behind many of these problems, of course, stands a complex of separate administrative hierarchies with proud administrators who are, in many instances, fearful of close contact and recognized dependency on other administrations. Each is aware that he or she does not solve the most intractable problems.

Consequently, they do not want to risk the close scrutiny of practices and budgets that integration of services implies.

In the 1960s, the Economic Opportunity Act mandated coordination of services for poor people. This effort failed because of the hasty presumptions of the organizers, diminishing resources, and the absence of structured expectations for coordination among established agencies. In the 1970s, a much more reasoned and cautious attempt was made through Services Integration Targets of Opportunity (SITO) demonstration programs. Much was learned through these experimental programs, but this knowledge was lost when the Reagan administration removed its funding and created budgetary panic among many of the participating agencies. Surviving SITO demonstrations can also be found (e.g., the Louisville Alliance for Human Services).

Currently, the Department of Housing and Urban Development (HUD) is attempting to revive the services integration movement through the Community Development Block Grants and related housing programs. This effort and Jimmy Carter's localized Atlanta Project are sufficient basis for the statement that a resurgence of professional interest is called for.

Justification: Is It Worth the Effort?

There are some distinctive reasons for saying that the investments in integration of services are too expensive and the political will supporting it is too tenuous to justify a protracted campaign. Clearly, administrative careers have been established within the context of specialized agencies and professions. Few careers have been built in the context of integrated services. Hence, special efforts are required to generate administrative commitments to the goals, procedures, and organizing processes of integration.

There are few constituencies for integration outside the machinery of government. A few human service and public administration professionals have championed the cause. A scattering of state and federal agencies personnel can be found who favor the concept, especially now in HUD. There is no clamor for integration of services among citizens outside these spheres, nor is there likely to be. Citizens at large have little basis for understanding the issue. For this reason, traditional legislators are unlikely to take up the cause.

A Superordinate Vision: The Community Human Services System

The motivation to launch such a campaign must come from the desire to achieve the goals of self-sufficiency and optimal functioning among the nation's underclass. Jimmy Carter's vision is:

. . . ambitious, an effort to make this a city where social service organizations effectively coordinate and target resources to fight poverty, homelessness, drugs, crime, illiteracy, unemployment and teenage pregnancy. The focus [will] be on Atlanta's poorest neighborhoods (Shumate, 1992).

Resources must be provided for integrated services; the "middle mandate" (Schumacher, 1975) must be provided. And community interagency networks (COINS) must be organized on a sound social work basis, with open communications and sensitivity to the barriers, so that a crippling resistance is not created.

These efforts can be focused incrementally on mechanisms of integration, such as integrated intake or case coordination, or they can be generated by a superordinate sea change. Such a sea change might be conceived as "the community human services system." This would be a system in which specialties are seen simply as cogs in a wheel. Agencies as they now exist would be closely bound up with the larger system which serves to rally resources toward the goals of optimal client functioning, achieved through rehabilitation and social care.

The system would be problem focused, so that resources of a variety of specialty agencies are readily shifted to priority goals, such as:

- addiction rehabilitation and prevention
- social support for the chronically mentally ill
- housing for the homeless
- delinquency prevention
- correction for criminal offenders
- child and adult protection; family preservation
- rehabilitation of physically challenged (already an integrated system)
- treatment of emotionally disturbed children (troubled youth)
- employability of the chronically unemployed

Such a system would begin with public–private partnerships in COINS, each held together in a unified system as shown in Figure 12.1.

Numerous linkages will be needed between the COINS because of the contributions to be made by agencies whose services have multiple utility. For example, adult technical schools are pertinent to the physically challenged, criminal offenders, the chronically unemployed, addicts, the homeless, and the chronically mentally ill. Some boundaries may be needed, but it is not necessary to duplicate adult technical education within each of those spheres.

Community practitioners are needed who are skillful in opening up communication among human service administrators, state officials, and local governmental administrators and legislators. Past experience demonstrates that communication in structuring and carrying out mutual planning activities has been a key flaw in failed demonstration projects (Project Share, 1979). Community

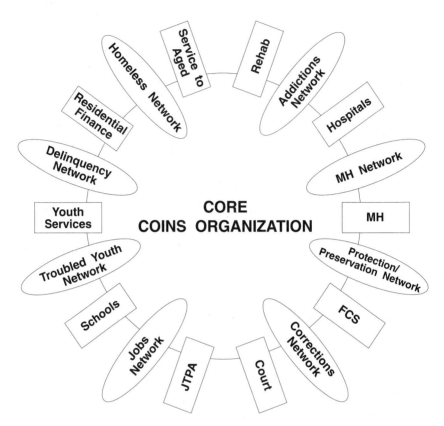

FIGURE 12.1 COMMUNITY HUMAN SERVICES SYSTEM

social work skills are essential to the development of service integration programs. Indeed, the "mission" orientation of community practitioners is necessary if these programs are not to deteriorate into minimalist bureaucratic exercises.

Conclusion

Jimmy Carter is right. Much can be done with the resources we have if the inefficiency of fragmented services is eliminated. Higher levels of funding in the human services is feasible, once their effectiveness in solving problems is demonstrated. This will require more than a few "protocols" between social agencies. It will require a social movement. It may also be that the Atlanta Project will be a successful demonstration project that may provide the needed stimulus to initiate a community networking movement across the country. A national administration committed to these goals and to integrated services can do much to provide the atmosphere for a major sea change. It can be done, interestingly, with either a conservative or a liberal political leader as President, but this person must be an activist, such as Jimmy Carter was or Jack Kemp might be.

With each part of the orchestra playing its part, it will then be up to the professional associations, the schools, the professionals, and the bureaucrats to get on board. We are challenged to demonstrate that we are truly dedicated to our mission of alleviating suffering and resolving problems of dependency, to open ourselves to the scrutiny that integration implies, and to drop the bureaucratic barriers that we may find convenient. We are capable of much greater effectiveness than we currently think.

REFERENCES

Aiken, M., & Hage, J. (1975). *Coordinating human services.* San Francisco: Jossey-Bass.

Congress welcomes Atlanta project. *Atlanta Constitution,* (1992, April 2) page A10.

Beatrice, D. (1990). Inter-agency coordination: A practitioner's guide to a strategy for effective social policy. *Administration in Social Work 14*(4), 45–60.

Benson, J. (1973). *Coordinating human services: A sociological study of an interorganizational network.* Washington, DC: Project SHARE.

Buell, B. (1952). *Planning for community human services.* New York: Columbia University Press.

Curtis, R. (1981). *Managing human services with less: New strategies for local leaders.* Project SHARE Monograph Series, Number 26.

DeWitt, J. (1977). Managing the human service system: What have we learned from services integration? Washington DC: HEW, Project SHARE.

Gardner, S. (1976). Roles for general purpose governments in services integration. Washington DC: HEW, Project SHARE.

Gibelman, M., & Demone, H. (1990). Negotiating: A tool for inter-organizational coordination. *Administration in Social Work 14*(4), 29–44.

Gummer, B. (1990). Current perspectives on inter-organizational coordination. *Administration in Social work 14*(4), 117–128.

Horton, G., Carr, V., Corcoran, G., Aspen Systems Corporation, & Project SHARE. (1976). Illustrating services integration from categorical bases. Washington, DC: HEW.

Lauffer, A. (1978). *Social planning at the community level.* Englewood Cliffs, NJ: Prentice-Hall.

Merritt, J., & Neugeboren, B. (1990). Factors affecting agency capacity for inter-organizational coordination. *Administration in Social Work 14*(4), 73–88.

Neugeboren, B. (1990). Introduction: Coordinating human services delivery. *Administration in Social Work 14*(4), 1–10.

Northern Illinois University Center for Governmental Studies. (1979). Dimensions of services integration: Service, delivery, program linkage, policy management, organizational structure. Rockville, MD: Project SHARE, HEW.

Project SHARE. (1976). Evaluation of services integration demonstration projects. Washington, DC: HEW.

Project SHARE. (1977). Multi-service centers: Co-location and services integration. Washington, DC: HEW.

Project SHARE. (1979). Services integration methodology. Rockville, MD: HEW.

Schumacher, E. (1975). *Small is beautiful: Economics as if people mattered.* New York: Harper and Row.

Shumate, R. (1992, April). Citizen sweat. *Atlanta Magazine,* pp. 60–63; 127–128.

Taylor, S., & Roberts, R. (1985). *Theory and practice for community social work.* New York: Columbia University Press.

Walden, T., Hammer, K., & Kurland, C. (1990). Case management: Planning and coordinating strategies. *Administration in Social Work 14*(4), 61–72.

Warren, R., Rose, S., & Bergrunder, A. (1974). *The structure of urban reform.* Lexington, MA: D.C. Heath.

Weiner, M. (1990). Trans-organizational management: The new frontier for social work administrators. *Administration in Social Work 14*(4), 11–28.

Weissman, H. (1978). *Integrating service for troubled families.* San Francisco: Jossey-Bass.

Weissman, H. (1970). *Community councils and community control: The workings of democratic mythology.*

Wimpfheimer, R., Bloom, M., & Kramer, M. (1990). Interagency collaboration: Some Working Principles. *Administration in Social Work 14*(4), 89–102.

Rejoinder to MacNair

Thomas P. Holland and Charlene Flagg

We heartily agree with Professor MacNair's diagnosis. Many human service programs are indeed fragmented and biased, uncooperative with one another, and unresponsive to clients. They impose multiple barriers for clients through such characteristics as repetitive forms, long waiting lists, insensitive staff, and inaccessible locations. Propping up such obstacles are rigid administrative hierarchies and arcane bureaucratic regulations. The needs of clients are forced into the rules and procedures that serve the convenience of the organizations. Decades of well-meaning efforts by planners and policy makers have resulted in a virtually impenetrable maze, which serves to diminish, not to enhance, client self-sufficiency and optimal functioning.

What is incredible is the prescribed treatment for this sickness. Certainly no client who has tried to wade through the existing morass would conclude that what we all need is *more* incremental tinkering by the planners and organizers, however they may dress up their efforts with words about "integration" or "coordination" on behalf of clients.

What is needed is a treatment that gets at the real illness. That illness is located in the paternalistic arrangement of provider controls over services. It's time to acknowledge that providers cannot give clients greater autonomy or independence through any form of services that the providers themselves control or coordinate. Pretensions otherwise are self-serving illusions.

The existing, paternalistic system of services has taught clients well that they are indeed dependent on the largesse of the providers and must jump through the providers' hoops, no matter how arbitrarily they may be set. Tightening up the parts of this system by whatever means will serve only to drive that demeaning lesson home more strongly.

If human services are to be truly responsive to their consumers, they cannot avoid the mechanisms that have been demonstrated elsewhere for the accomplishment of that objective. Organizations that are directly dependent on their customers for their income are the ones that are the most responsive to their customers needs and interests. Indeed, if these organizations are to survive, they must adapt their procedures and products to those configurations that are preferred by consumers. Anything that impedes such responsiveness must be jettisoned, regardless of its charm to the bureaucrats or planners. Biased and unresponsive behavior will not last long under conditions where the staff depends on the customer for their income. If the organization is to attract and retain its paying customers, program accessibility must be optimized by convenient locations and hours as well as by quick and courteous service.

The development of consumer control is the way to stimulate responsiveness and coordination among programs. Changes that move the field in that direction will result in better services to the client, however awkward they may be for comfortable professionals. Changes toward more efficient provider control will make the existing mess worse for clients, not better.

To pick up on Professor MacNair's concluding metaphor, musicians will be much more highly motivated to play together when they know that their survival as an orchestra depends on ticket sales to audiences than they will when some musicians union steward tells them that it would be nice if each of them would look at the same musical score. Real integration of services will occur when programs are dependent on clients, rather than when they are structured into more elaborate systems of control by providers.

Should Clients Have Control over the Policies of the Agency?

EDITOR'S NOTE: Many would trace the debate about how much control clients should have over the policies of the agency to the 1960s. During this time, the concepts of maximum feasible participation and community control became guiding principles in the development of service delivery models. However, changes in the political, social, and economic environments of the next decades led to a deemphasis on client control and participation in the policies of agencies. As social service agencies have struggled to manage these environmental changes, increasing attention has been given to new management approaches that focus on accountability and effectiveness of service delivery. If social services are to be client-centered, what role should clients play in the development and control of agency policies and procedures? How does the practice of client empowerment affect service delivery and the agency-client relationship? Is there a distinction between client control and client participation in agency policies? As clients are described more often as consumers of services, these questions take on added importance to social work managers in developing their approach to agency administration.

Yeheskel Hasenfeld, Ph.D., argues YES. He is a professor of social welfare at the School of Social Welfare, University of California, Los Angeles. His main research focus has been on the organization of human services with special emphasis on client-organization relations. He is currently conducting research on welfare to work programs. His most recent publications include *The Moral Construction of Poverty: Welfare Reform in America* (with J. Handler) and *Human Services as Complex Organizations.*

Alfreda P. Iglehart, Ph.D. says NO. She is Assistant Professor of Social Welfare at the University of California, Los Angeles. She has conducted research and written in the areas of women and work, female offenders, organizational systems, and child welfare. Before joining the UCLA faculty, she worked as a child protective services worker, an ombudsman for senior citizens, and a case manager for juvenile delinquents. This hiatus from the academic setting enabled her to further separate rhetoric from realism in social work education and practice.

YES

Yeheskel Hasenfeld

Responsibility of a caseworker to an organized group which is at once her board of directors and her clientele is, in part, a responsibility of knowing what the members want in the way of help. Being close to their daily lives, in an association with their own organization so that they feel free to say what they think, is an immense advantage (Reynolds, 1951).

Bertha Reynolds' insightful principle is particularly appropriate to the management of personal social services in which workers are vested with a great deal of discretion. In contrast to public assistance programs, where benefits can be allocated on the basis of some universalistic and standardized principles, personal social service agencies must tailor the care giving process to the specific needs of each client. Consequently, their workers wield a considerable amount of power through their discretionary decision-making processes. Moreover, in such agencies, the quality of the services hinges on a trusting relationship between the clients and the workers. It is in such agencies that clients should have control over agency policies, because in doing so they gain some measure of power, are confident that their trust will not be abused, and most importantly, they can contribute immeasurably to the effectiveness of the services.

Social service agencies buffeted by diminishing fiscal resources, increased service demands, external pressures for accountability, and restless and frustrated staff often fail to recognize that their greatest asset is their clients. Clients are an untapped source of legitimacy; they possess knowledge and experiences that are indispensable to effective management, and they have potential personal and collective resources that can be harnessed to strengthen the service delivery process. Paradoxically, the professional care giving perspective tends to reinforce a conception of the client as maladaptive, irrational, passive, and dependent. With the notable exception of self-help groups, clients are viewed as atomistic individuals rather than as actual or potential members of a collectivity. As a result, their participation in the organization is highly circumscribed and mostly confined to the worker-client dyad. Even when clients are given an active voice in the design and implementation of their own care or treatment, their voices are seldom heard beyond the boundaries of the worker-client relationship. Indeed, the inevitable discretion that workers possess and the professional demand for autonomy and confidentiality are formidable barriers to the transmission of client voices throughout the agency.

Yet, as Hirschman (1970) so aptly points out, the voice of the client is a fundamental vehicle to improve organizational effectiveness, and it is the only avenue available to clients lacking the exit option, namely, the vulnerable and the powerless. Indeed, the voice option is a powerful early warning system in sensitizing the agency to the need to improve its services. For once the clients exit, if they can, or if remain silent because their voices are not heard, it may be too late.

What does *voice* mean in this context? It certainly does not connote having a complaint box in which clients can drop letters of protest, nor does it signify clients' resistance to their workers. To be effective, voice must be collective and heard at the policy-making level of the agency. This can happen only when clients are active participants in the policy decision-making processes of the agency. These decisions, first and foremost, determine the allocation of resources in the agency, particularly who will be served, what services will be provided, and who will provide them. Hence, they ultimately define the experiences of clients in the agency and the quality of care they will receive.

Active clients participation and control of agency policies encompasses important structural changes. Clients become organized as a collectivity when interacting with agency executives and managers. Their role in the agency changes dramatically. No longer are they only clients; they, or their representatives, are bona fide members of the organization and have a stake in how services are organized and delivered. Most importantly, their perspectives and views must be incorporated in the policy decisions of the agency. Hence, they assume greater responsibility for the outcomes of policies and can no longer ascribe success or blame exclusively to the staff.

The participation and ultimate control of agency policies by clients has several specific advantages to improving organizational effectiveness. First, when clients have a stake in the agency they become not part of the problem but rather part of the solution. This is the inherent rationale behind client empowerment. When clients feel that they can effectively shape agency policies, they become motivated and committed to the very success of these policies. Such a commitment invariably touches the worker-client relationship; clients can trust their workers, knowing that their voices will be heard, and it reinforces the client's motivation to change. Trust and commitment to change are the two ingredients that have been shown, time and again, to be paramount to service effectiveness. Moreover, there is an incentive for other clients to become collaborators in the service or care giving process, because as a collectivity they have a stake in the success of the agency, and they can see a direct benefit to themselves. Studies, for example, of parent-controlled schools show that parents become committed and involved in the educational process itself, greatly enhancing the achievements of their children. Similarly, when residents of a nursing home are mobilized to assert their rights, not only do they influence agency policies but also they improve their own level of functioning. Put differently, when clients can influence and control agency policies they also contribute their own untapped resources to the service delivery process itself, and in doing so enhance their own well-being. In this context, Gutierrez (1992) has shown that when oppressed ethnic minorities gain control over agency policies, they are able to restructure its services so that they become ethno-conscious, resulting in far greater service effectiveness.

Second, when clients control agency policies, they provide a powerful feedback loop that is indispensable to effective management. One of the Achilles heels of social services management is the inherent disjuncture between policies and procedures and the actual experiences of clients. That is, the intended policies are only partially reflected in the actual service delivery process because the former can seldom anticipate fully the exigencies of the latter. Moreover, policies almost invariably produce unanticipated consequences at the service delivery level. Without a close feedback loop between the two, policy makers are deprived of crucial information and cannot readily adjust their policies to improve effectiveness, correct mistakes, or respond to developments and changes at the service delivery level. Yet, it is the actual delivery of services that is the driving engine for the entire agency. While "front line" workers are an important source of information, their own perceptions are colored by the very policies and procedures they are asked to implement as well as by their own personal and professional interests. In contrast, when clients participate and control agency policies, they add the experiences of the clients themselves as a crucial test of the relationship between policy and practice. There is no substitute to client experiences as data to assess the processes by which services are delivered and their effectiveness. There is a significant difference in the validity and reliability of client data when it is generated by clients or elicited by the staff. When clients know that they have the power to shape agency policies and are less dependent on the workers for their well-being, they are far more likely to be candid and forthcoming. Workers, too, have a greater incentive to carefully listen to the clients' voices.

It has been often argued that giving clients control over agency policies results in the devaluation of professional expertise and thus deprives clients, in the long run, of the benefits accrued from professional knowledge, training, and experience. Such a danger does exist when the professionals are preoccupied with the protection of their status, feel threatened when they need to share their knowledge with their clients, and perceive clients' participation as a zero-sum game. In fact, once professionals respect the experiential knowledge of their clients as highly valuable to the effectiveness of their own practice, the clients reciprocate by recognizing the value of professional expertise.

Finally, some will point to the apparent failure of "maximum feasible participation" of local residents in the policy making of community action agencies during the War on Poverty as evidence of the infeasibility of giving clients control over agency policies. It is true that clients, like professionals, have diverse interests and are not immune to power struggles which grant some elite status while excluding others from meaningful participation. This is particularly the case when other interest groups—funders, administrators, and professionals—exploit the potential divisions among clients. Ultimately, however, the failure of clients' participation in agency policy making rests in the unwillingness of political and professional elites to share power with those who they claim to serve.

REFERENCES

Gutierrez, L. (1992). Empowering ethnic minorities in the twenty-first century: The role of human service organizations. In Y. Hasenfeld (Ed.), *Human services as complex organizations.* Newbury Park, CA: Sage Publications.

Hasenfeld, Y. (1987). Power in social work practice. *Social Service Review, 61,* 469–483.

Handler, J. F. (1992). Dependency and discretion. In Y. Hasenfeld (Ed.), *Human services as complex organizations.* Newbury Park, CA: Sage.

Hirschman, A. O. (1970). *Exit, voice and loyalty.* Cambridge, MA: Harvard University Press.

Rapp, C. A., & Poertner, J. (1992). *Social administration: A client-centered approach.* New York: Longman.

Reynolds, B. C. (1951). *Social work and social living.* New York: Citadel Press.

Rejoinder to Dr. Hasenfeld
ALFREDA P. IGLEHART

When did administrative decision making turn into administrative dictatorship? When did worker discretion become worker domination? When did professionalization turn into professional elitism? One of the legacies from the tumultuous 1960s is the apparent disdain of anything that might hint at a status differential between people. The politically correct position today entails creating the illusion of egalitarianism and, in "personal service agencies," this means using smoke and mirrors to make the lines separating staff and clients vanish.

The debate here seems to be over the *extent* of client involvement in agency decision making. Professor Hasenfeld has indicated that clients should be "active participants in the policy making processes of the agency." Client participation, however, is not synonymous with client control.

Client control is predicated on clients having equal or greater status than agency administrators and staff. In reality, there is generally an asymmetry of power between the agency and the client and, therefore, between the worker and the client (Hasenfeld, 1992, p. 266). An agency is made more humane when the needs of the clients are integrated in its operative goals (Hasenfeld, 1992, p. 262). Client control leads to the domination of client goals over agency goals, rather than the integration of the two.

Worker discretion is inevitable in the modern welfare state (Handler, 1992, p. 293), and this discretion reflects the worker's power over the client. However, the worker is socialized to a set of professional norms and ethics that ensure such power will not be abused (Hasenfeld, 1992, p. 264). Consequently, the client's dependency status and the worker's power advantage are not synonymous with client disempowerment.

It has been argued that client control leads to commitment to agency policies, trust of workers, and motivation to change. Why would a client group not be committed to policies that reflect its vested self-interests? Since voices vary from a whisper to a shout, some clients will undoubtedly be more committed than others. Why would clients not trust workers hired according to guidelines they established? Surely these workers pose no threat to clients and endorse the clients' agenda. Why would clients not be motivated to change, particularly if they determined the delineation, direction, and degree of the change desired.

The idea of client control is both seductive and engaging. Unfortunately, it oversimplifies and obfuscates some rather complex social service issues. It is like fool's gold—it offers the promise of riches that are worth very little. The real challenge confronting social service delivery is the altering of professionalization, technology, and organizational structure to routinely and formally incorporate realistic and meaningful client participation in agency decision making.

REFERENCES

Handler, J. F. (1992). Dependency and discretion. In Y. Hasenfeld (Ed.), *Human services as complex organizations.* Newbury Park, CA: Sage Publications.
Hasenfeld, Y. (1992). Power in social work practice. In Y. Hasenfeld (Ed.), *Human services as complex organizations.* Newbury Park, CA: Sage Publications.

NO

ALFREDA P. IGLEHART

As new social problems emerge and old ones become more complex, criticisms of the social work profession are rampant. The effectiveness of the profession in eradicating or alleviating social ills is the target of a barrage of indictments. Indeed, charges of "throwing money at the problem" are often levied against social programs that seem to simply soak up countless dollars while squeezing out little or nothing in return. In addition, attempts at greater effectiveness appear to be tied to pleas for more and more funding. The situation is further compounded by a climate of fiscal austerity, and human service organizations are being forced to do more and more with less and less. The scramble for answers has placed social service delivery systems under intense scrutiny for the sources of this purported failure of effectiveness.

The quest for solutions has reached a number of different arenas that include posing the promise of privatization, berating bureaucracy, maligning human service management, wrestling with worker burnout, illuminating public ignorance of social work, and, to some extent, deifying the downtrodden. The path toward increased human service effectiveness includes some consideration of all these areas; however, one or two may overshadow the others. For example, the repositioning of clients in the service delivery equation has been gaining momentum.

The debate over client control of agency policy and practice is far from new. Proponents of client control argue that it leads to client-responsive services, increased client commitment to program participation, enhanced client motivation, genuine client advocacy, and serious social change efforts. In addition, some maintain that client experiences can infuse agency policies with a much-needed realism that serves as the basis for effective interventions. It thus seems that the client becomes an expert in defining his or her problems and in identifying appropriate solutions. The client's indisputable insight into his or her situation is a critical factor in the client's elevation to expert. Unfortunately, this quest to redefine the client role may generate more problems than solutions.

Several observations highlighting these problems are presented here: (1) the fallacy of the "client as insider" and the "worker as outsider" position; (2) consequences of client self-interest; (3) the disregard for professionalization; and (4) the unfair expansion of client responsibility to include problem-solving expectations.

Merton (1972, p. 15) provides a discussion on the insiders and the outsiders. According to him, the *insider doctrine* can be put in the vernacular with no great loss in meaning: you have to be one to understand one. The argument for client control of agency policies seems lodged in this insider doctrine. Certainly client backgrounds and experiences often differ markedly from those of the social worker. This difference, however, has often been construed as a deficit on the part of the worker because it appears to provide the client with "credentials" that are not available to the worker.

Social workers generally know that intervention with service populations is not predicated on membership in those populations. Social work values and social worker qualities have been the cornerstones of effective service delivery.

Because the worker may not have "walked a mile" in the client's shoes, empathy has been regarded as a crucial aspect of the worker-client relationship. Empathy has connected individuals of disparate backgrounds, classes, ethnic groups, and life-styles. Clients do bring insight into their circumstances that are beneficial to the intervention process and, through empathy, trust, support, and rapport, those insights are shared with workers and incorporated into the intervention process.

Historically, social work has not been guilty of ignoring the client's input about his or her situation. In fact, social work as a profession is growing even more attentive to client voices and needs as the tenets of multicultural practice are currently undergoing further refinement. Social work interfaces with such an array of diverse and unique groups that there has never been one way or "the right way" to define or conduct service.

While the insider doctrine may hold limited validity, client input is, nonetheless, circumscribed by *self-interest* that promotes what the client sees as good and beneficial for him or her. Clearly, client experiences are a valuable component of the service delivery process because they provide a necessary context for framing delivery strategies. These experiences and insights represent a view of the world and a picture of how the individual fits into this world. Such a world view, however, either dismisses the value of other, and often competing, interest groups or places them in a peripheral position.

One major disadvantage to granting clients control over agency policies lies in the fact that clients do not form a homogeneous group with one world view, one ideology, or one set of agreed on self-interests. Just as social workers may not always agree on the problem definition or problem solution, the same is true for clients and client groups. A consensus is the result of a political process that frequently has opposing groups vying for dominance. Cliques, claques, and factions emerge among client populations that compete for their fair share of service resources. Since each group is committed to its self-interests and may have little insight into the position of opposing groups, some battles can become so heated that the conflict may never be fully resolved. Tensions may continue to exist to the detriment of service delivery. The goal then shifts from equity in services to each group wanting to win and soundly trounce the opponent.

Administrator-staff control of agency policies serves to minimize and neutralize conflict and competition between client groups. The agency often represents the neutral third party that seeks to maneuver cautiously and fairly through potentially volatile client-group eruptions. With the agency in command, all client groups have an opportunity to be heard, and all interests can be considered in the intervention process. Less dominant groups with less forceful voices are more than just whispers in the political process.

Managing the interests of client groups is a significant role of the professional social worker. Social work expertise and *professionalization* form a solid base for agency policy decisions. Client insight and input alone are a fragile foundation for granting control over policies that extend beyond the definition of problems and the identification of solutions. Numerous agency policies focus on management and include operationalization and implementation of designated social policies; allocation of fiscal resources; the distribution of all other resources; identification of needed staff; deployment of staff; identification of client groups to be served; definition of the most appropriate agency structure for discharging services; selection of intervention technologies; and determination of criteria for success (Patti, 1987).

In recent years it seems that "professionalization" has become a distasteful word connoting an arrogant, know-it-all, client-blaming attitude. The term has also been linked to the predominance of clinical practice because a client-blaming ideology requires reliance on *professional* diagnostic skills (Powell, 1986). Some, no doubt, would consider professionalization and client control to be a rather unique oxymoron. While the path to professionalization may have been paved with potholes and detrimental detours, the value of professionalization itself should not be sacrificed at the altar of client control. In actuality, professionalization covers a range of knowledge and skills that are prerequisites for quality service delivery and agency management. To deny this is to deny social work's historical quest for education, training, standards, and certification/ licensing.

Clients are service beneficiaries with experiential input that can be integrated into the service delivery process. They are not, however, social work professionals with the technical know-how of defining, planning, implementing, and evaluating the intervention process. In the best of cases, clients are committed to participating in the process and improving the quality of service. In the worst of cases, they are resistant, hostile, and apathetic. In some cases, physical or mental limitations render clients incapable of contributing to policy decisions. As the human service dollar shrinks, those clients who receive services are more likely to be society-identified rather than self-identified. These may be individuals who are deemed dangerous to themselves or others. In this case, clients are often involuntary service recipients who have no commitment whatsoever to agency policies.

Finally, advocacy for client control seems to imply that the client should be responsible for *articulating problem causes and coming up with the solutions* to these problems. Two decades ago, Ryan (1971) called attention to a pattern in social policy of "blaming the victim." For social work, this meant that clients were, in some cases, held responsible for "causing" whatever misfortune that befell them. Social structures and institutions were exonerated from any exacerbating contribution they may have made to these misfortunes. This tendency to look to clients for causes truly reflected a bias against the client.

Even though the situation has shifted and the client is now seen in a much more favorable manner, the client is still held responsible. In this case, the client is responsible for pointing out solutions to problems that have puzzled the public for years. Again, societal structures and institutions (also responsible for problem solving) are off the hook from which the client now dangles. While the quest for client power may seem to be politically correct, this quest may inadvertently place the greatest expectations for problem solving at the feet of those least equipped to adequately respond. The view of client as expert further penalizes the client.

The answer lies in client *input* rather than client control over agency policies. Client control would turn every agency into a self-help group. While self-help groups are desirable and effective, not all clients and not all services can be accommodated in this arrangement. The public's mandate for the provision of social services is embodied in professionally guided human service organizations that are capable of negotiating constituency demands while remaining responsive to client needs.

REFERENCES

Merton, R. K. (1972, July). Insiders and outsiders: A chapter in the sociology of knowledge. *American Journal of Sociology, 78,* 9–47.

Patti, R. J. (1987). Managing for service effectiveness in social welfare organizations. *Social Work, 32*(5), 377–381.

Powell, D. M. (1986). Managing organizational problems in alternative service organizations. *Administration in Social Work, 10*(3), 57–69.

Ryan, W. (1971). *Blaming the victim.* New York: Vintage Books.

Rejoinder to Professor Iglehart   YEHESKEL HASENFELD

There is a peculiar twist to the way social workers morally construct their clients. Despite professional values espousing the clients' self-worth and their right to self-determination, they are nonetheless seen as "deficient," "outsiders," or "deviants." Some say, for example, that clients are driven by narrow self-interests, cannot reach a common consensus, lack the capacity to comprehend their own predicament, and cannot possibly be relied on to know what is best for them. It is perhaps the need to establish and rationalize professional hegemony that drives many helping professions to assume a moral superiority over their clients.

There is absolutely no evidence to suggest that clients are somehow more driven by narrow self-interests than are agency executives, middle managers, or staff. True, agency staff are guided by organizational norms and policies that buffer against self-interests, but there is no reason to assume that clients could not be similarly guided once they are members of the organization. Nor is there any evidence to support the notion that clients are less capable of reaching consensus about agency objectives than are professionals, if an appropriate decision-making structure is instituted. Most troubling, however, is the assumption that clients could not possibly control agency policies because they lack the necessary wisdom and skills. Why do we not make a similar assumption about the lay members of thousands of boards of directors of voluntary social service agencies who control agency policies yet have no specific professional expertise or training? Is it merely because they are recruited from "respected" social strata and have not been labeled as "clients"?

What is confused in this debate is the distinction between technical knowledge and expertise and political acumen. Control over agency policies that determine who gets what and when requires political wisdom, not technical expertise. What is necessary are the ability to listen to the wishes and aspirations of potential and actual clients; the capacity to sense, appreciate, and articulate the needs of various constituencies; and the wisdom to make choices among competing normative objectives. Technical expertise and skills, in contrast, refer to the ability to *implement* normative choices effectively and efficiently. They enable policy makers to understand the consequences of alternative choices, and they become paramount in the development and administration of the service technologies. Professionals have no particular advantage over clients in political wisdom. When clients control agency policies they exercise political judgment. They do not usurp the technical skills of the staff, but rather accord them their rightful role. Weber, (1947) in articulating the theory of bureaucracy, cautioned against the tyranny of the bureaucrats who use their technical expertise to control the policy decision-making processes, thus isolating the organization from public opinion and political influence.

REFERENCE

Weber, M. (1947), *The theory of social and economic organization.* New York: Oxford University Press.

Will the Quality of Work Life in Public Human Service Organizations Be Significantly Improved by Using Quality Management Techniques?

EDITOR'S NOTE: Social workers spend a significant portion of their lives working in organizations, directing their expertise toward the attainment of the organization's goals. The quality of work life in the organization affects the individual's social and psychological well-being by the way the workplace is structured and by how the skills of its workers are utilized. Employee satisfaction with the work environment also affects how services are delivered to clients. Public human service organizations have been under pressure to do more with less and to manage more complex social problems. As a result, the quality of work life often has deteriorated. An approach being adopted by many social service agencies to improve the workplace is quality management. This approach to management seeks to redesign the work environment, increase worker participation in decision making, and focus on the clients (customers) and their needs. Quality management recognizes the relationship among worklife, employee satisfaction, and effective service delivery. This timely and significant debate explores the pros and cons of adopting total quality management as a way to improve the work life of human service organizations.

Kenneth L. Robey, Ph.D., and Steven Ramsland, Ed.D., argue YES. Dr. Robey is Director of Research and Evaluation for SERV Centers of New Jersey, Inc., a specialty provider of mental health services. His research interests include work-life issues in mental health organizations and the study of the social role of "psychiatric patient." He also lectures in research methods at the School of Social Work, Rutgers University.

Dr. Ramsland is Executive Director of SERV Centers of New Jersey, Inc. He has served on numerous state advisory committees and presently serves as President of the Board of Directors of the New Jersey Association of Mental Health Agencies.

Burton J. Cohen, Ph.D., says NO. Burton J. Cohen is Adjunct Assistant Professor at the School of Social Work of the University of Pennsylvania, where he directs a Quality of Working Life Project in child welfare. His other research interests include the creation of "negotiated orders" and action research as a vehicle for social learning and change.

YES

KENNETH L. ROBEY AND STEVEN E. RAMSLAND

"Quality" has become a corporate buzzword in recent years and is now making its way into the human services domain as well. Such terms as "total quality management" (TQM), "total quality improvement" (TQI), and "continuous quality improvement" (CQI) are now within the vocabularies of human services administrators in both the public and private sectors, particularly in health-related areas. These terms denote management philosophies that emphasize organizational attention to quality to ensure the organization's success. From these philosophies have sprung a variety of strategies and interventions aimed at organizational structure, process, and outcomes, with a commitment on the part of all personnel toward continuous organizational improvement.

Industry has instituted quality management techniques with the objective of meeting or exceeding certain productivity, service, and customer satisfaction standards to increase profit. Beyond the traditional "bottom line," however, American companies are under tremendous pressure merely to survive and compete successfully in today's global economy. TQM has enabled scores of corporations to pick themselves up from their doldrums and move toward productivity and prosperity.

But what happens to the employees of companies that successfully institute TQM in their drive to compete effectively? The bottom line may improve, but what about employee quality of work life? And what about human service agencies? Can TQM techniques taken from the corporate sector improve the quality of work life for their employees?

Yes, when effectively implemented, TQM techniques can and should be used in human service agencies both to improve the ability of the organization to effectively meet its mission and to improve the quality of work life of its employees. TQM works to the extent that its techniques empower employees to be invested in their work in a positive, productive way. Let us explore a few key concepts utilized in TQM that may bring about improvements in quality of work life.

Constancy of Purpose

The successful quality management program conveys to employees the importance of sharing the organization's commitment to quality and provides staff with the skills and resources necessary to meet those objectives. According to Deming (1986), it promotes a "constancy of purpose" toward the improvement of products or services. It helps employees recognize the importance of meeting the organization's commitment to quality *not only for the organization's sake but also for the sake of realizing the employee's own personal goals,* however defined.

In one application of TQM concepts to the human services setting, we instituted a brief quality management intervention within a subset of our own agency, a large and geographically distributed community mental health corporation. In a one-day retreat format, employees were given an opportunity to think about and privately articulate their own personal missions. Then they were helped to understand the organization's goal of providing the highest quality services possible to best enhance the lives of their mentally ill clients. Finally, they were given an opportunity to assess the alignment of the organizational mission and their own; that is, to determine the degree to which meeting the organization's goal of quality services did or did not move them toward meeting their own individually defined goals.

Relative to those units that did not attend a retreat, those that did attend a retreat showed considerable improvements in staff job satisfaction and in perceptions of a variety of aspects of the workplace (Robey, Ramsland, & Castelbaum, 1991). The perceived well-being of these staff benefited from a management approach intended in part to impress on them the organization's commitment to quality services and in part to tap into their own personal interest in doing quality work.

Focus on the System

Another principle valued by proponents of the quality management movement is that problems are typically not the result of lack of effort or lack of skill on the part of individual employees, but rather are inherent in the processes and environments in which they work.

In TQM, an emphasis on examining aspects of the work process and the work situation that might introduce problems replaces an emphasis on individual responsibility for problems. The approach allows opportunity for both management and line staff to "seek out" aspects of the workplace and process that make employees' jobs difficult. Not only is blame for error moved away from the individual and toward work systems and procedures (where it typically belongs), but also the employee is empowered in the process. He or she becomes the "expert" in the work process and is encouraged to identify and recommend areas for possible change.

System-oriented change may take place in areas such as administrative procedure, program structure, evaluation and training, facilities, equipment, and so on. Efforts are made to maximize all components of the organization in TQM. In taking this approach, TQM addresses change in the areas of work life described by Herzberg (1966) as "maintenance factors" (dissatisfiers), as well as the upper-level needs he refers to as "motivators" (satisfiers). Herzberg's research has demonstrated that deficiencies in maintenance factors (such as policy and administration, supervision, working conditions, interpersonal relations, salary, status, job security, personal life) lead to job dissatisfaction. The presence of motivating factors (achievement, recognition, interesting work, responsibility, advancement opportunity, growth) in the workplace leads to job satisfaction and effective performance. Both areas should be maximized; to the extent that TQM focuses on system change in these areas, the quality of employee work life will improve.

Focus on the Customer

Fundamental to TQM is its insistence that everything focus on the needs of the customer and not the limitations or values of the organization. What could be more natural and appealing to the typical human services employee? After all, it was the desire to meet the needs of clients (customers) that motivated most social workers and other human service professionals to enter the field in the first place. And then they discovered that organizational needs took precedence over client needs. TQM, in contrast, orients the attention back to the needs of the client/customer.

Focus on Outcomes

By the same token, TQM's focus on outcomes data is also directly in line with what has drawn human services professionals to enter the field—the desire to have a positive impact on the lives of others. With outcomes data, we can demonstrate in certain terms the positive influences that our efforts are having on individuals and on institutions. Outcomes information is critical in helping staff derive a sense of purpose and satisfaction in their work.

TQM and other emerging approaches to maintaining quality are oriented toward the identification of problems, not the identification of problem individuals; the outcomes of processes, not of people. Traditional quality assurance approaches are based almost solely on client by client (and hence, staffperson by staffperson) review. This emphasis notoriously leads to staff who are defensive, anxious, and afraid.

While recognizing that it may not be possible (or desirable) in the human services to totally eliminate review of individual staffperson's contacts with clients, it is possible, as prescribed in quality management approaches, to emphasize the view of the individual staff member as contributor to a larger process. If given the choice between working where the primary purpose of quality assurance is to examine the work of individual employees in search of deficits versus working where the focus is on outcomes for a functional unit of the organization and using those outcomes to guide staff in identifying and remedying deficits in the work process, where would you be more comfortable?

Potential for Tangible Benefits

Returning to the notion of a bottom-line motive as being responsible for bringing quality management techniques to the forefront in major corporations, it should be recognized that nonprofit human service agencies are equally motivated not only to survive but also to prosper financially. There is no mission without a bottom line. Performance for human service agencies must be measured in terms of both client and financial outcomes. Quality of work life cannot be enhanced in a threadbare agency that is constantly struggling merely to survive.

Nonprofit organizations operate in a competitive environment. We compete with other nonprofit agencies for funding and clients and we compete with for-profit organizations for the best workers. The best workers typically have high expectations for performance and greater commitment to working in environments that foster participation. TQM-oriented agencies are more likely to attract and retain better employees and, therefore, compete more effectively in today's marketplace. They will survive long after others close down because they stretch their employees continually, encouraging them to learn and expand their abilities.

Conclusion

In summary, quality management techniques popular today in American industry hold great promise for human service agencies. In particular, they can help (and are currently helping) human service organizations to offer their employees a more satisfying and rewarding work life. These strategies enhance the quality of work life by: (1) helping employees to feel a sense of connectedness with their work; (2) empowering them to change the environment and systems in which they work; (3) focusing on client needs and on feedback regarding how well those needs are being met; and (4) providing the organization with an opportunity to share with the employee the tangible rewards of concentration on quality.

REFERENCES

Deming, W. E. (1986). *Out of crisis.* Cambridge, MA: MIT Press.
Herzberg, F. (1966). *Work and the nature of man.* Cleveland, OH: World Publishing Company.
Robey, K. L., Ramsland, S. E., & Castelbaum, K. (1991). Alignment of agency and personal mission: An evaluation. *Administration and Policy in Mental Health, 19,* 39–45.

Rejoinder to Drs. Robey and Ramsland

BURTON J. COHEN

As much as I would like to share Drs. Robey and Ramsland's enthusiasm for the future of TQM in public human service organizations, I'm unable to do so for two basic reasons. The first is my concern with whether TQM as developed in the corporate context can simply be transferred to human services. They argue that "quality management techniques popular today in American industry hold great promise for human service agencies." Most proponents of TQM have likewise proclaimed its general applicability in other settings without modification. I believe it is unwise to expect TQM to be so easily transferred, and doing so will likely lead to frustration and failure. One of the fundamental principles of TQM is to "focus on the customer." However, this is much more difficult in public human services than in corporate settings. First, of all, in many program areas, as noted by Swiss (1992), "defining the customer is a difficult and politically controversial issue." In child welfare agencies, is the customer the child who has been abused or neglected, or the family whose preservation is desired? Furthermore, in public human services, there is a distinction between the immediate customers or clients and the less immediate customers such as the general public and other service systems or providers of service. Orthodox TQM provides little guidance in addressing these issues, and an overemphasis on its importance is likely to lead to frustration. It also focuses too much on the customer and too little on the workers. In human service organizations, where more discretion ought to reside with the workers, the focus should first be on them. Only when the workers feel more empowered will they be able to focus fully on the needs of their clients.

A second tenet of TQM that will be difficult to transfer is the call for "constancy of purpose" supported by strong executive leadership, a major shift in organizational culture, and an unending commitment to quality. Drs. Robey and Ramsland's example of a "brief quality management intervention" consisting of a single one-day retreat, while well-intentioned, points out the difficulty in making this a reality in public human service settings. TQM can't be viewed as an "event," and yet the conflicting demands and changing circumstances imposed on most human service agencies make it extremely difficult to manage a long-term cultural change. The likelihood of long-term, sustained support from top management is also much less than in the corporate sector, because of frequent changes in top management positions and competing pressures exerted by outside forces.

My far greater concern about relying on TQM techniques to improve the quality of work life in public human service organizations is a fear that those with the responsibility for managing these organizations won't really take it seriously, that they will continue to blame individual workers for the system's deficiencies and to be frustrated when the changes that they seek don't occur quickly and painlessly. Drs. Robey and Ramsland state that TQM techniques can be useful "when effectively implemented," but implementation is the Achilles heel of most change efforts, and they say nothing about what effective implementation would entail.

As long as quality management is seen as a new set of techniques that can be picked up and unleashed inside an organization with the hope of producing improvements, I fear it will meet the same fate as its predecessors. Real improvements in the quality of work life will come about where those in leadership positions, and this can be anywhere in the organization, are prepared to display the courage and creativity to challenge the status quo and to actively manage the processes of change. Successful efforts may then become contagious and spread to other areas where learning can take place. When this occurs, the specific techniques that are utilized become less important.

REFERENCE

Swiss, J. (1992). Adapting total quality management to government. *Public Administration Review, (52)*4, 356–362.

NO

BURTON J. COHEN

Ever since Robert McNamara's "whiz kids" promised to bring rationality and increased efficiency to the Defense Department in the early 1960s, we have had a fascination with one generation after another of management techniques that were supposed to improve the management and delivery of public services. Human service organizations have been visited by all of these techniques, and the general conclusion in human services, as elsewhere in the public service, has been that the techniques seldom manage to live up to expectations. As much as I might like to think that "quality management techniques" will succeed where others have failed, I can see no basis for making such a prediction. In fact, the evidence is more persuasive that the same obstacles to planning, programming, budgeting systems (PPBS), management by objectives (MBO), zero-based budgeting (ZBB), and management information systems (MIS) will also prevent total quality management (TQM) from having a fundamental impact on how public human service organizations treat their employees and their clients.

The sad part of this is that I strongly believe that the quality of work life in public human service organizations does need to be significantly improved. Recent studies on recruitment and retention of social work staff (Ewalt, 1991) and job satisfaction (Arches, 1991) indicate that workplace conditions have a significant impact on how social workers view their jobs and on their desire and motivation to remain with their organizations. Arches (1991) has described how increasing bureaucratization in the social services workplace has led to isolation, fragmentation, and deskilling. My own research in the field of public child welfare (Cohen, 1992) indicates how these conditions can lead to a sense of powerlessness and cynicism and a "culture of blaming" in which no one is willing to take responsibility for improving any aspects of the system of service delivery.

According to Camman (1984), the quality of work life (QWL) movement is concerned with creating organizations that more effectively deliver services and products valued by society, while simultaneously being rewarding, stimulating places for employees to work. QWL programs generally aim to redesign the work environment, the manner in which work is performed, and manner in which decisions are made. It is indeed ironic that the field of human services, with its concerns for client self-determination and empowerment, has not applied the same values to its own work force and has not embraced the QWL movement more strongly.

So the issue is not whether QWL should be improved, but whether the techniques of "quality management" provide the answer. Quality management has been popularized in the business world over the past few years to the point where it has attracted a huge following of true believers, an enormous amount of publicity, and even a national competition as companies vie for the prestigious Malcolm Baldridge National Quality Award. The essence of quality management seems to be that all parts of an organization should be enlisted in a crusade aimed at continuously improving the organization's capacity to meet or exceed the expectations of its customers or clients. Indeed, "quality" is generally defined as meeting or exceeding the needs and expectations of the customers.

Quality management (also known as total quality management, or TQM) is closely associated with the work of W. Edwards Deming who has articulated fourteen points or principles for continuously improving the organization's performance (Walton, 1986). Some of the basic ideas are:

- Stay focused on the long-term purpose of the organization.
- Focus on the customers and their needs.

- Involve all employees in the process of continuous improvement.
- Utilize teamwork to break down barriers among staff.
- Use data to make decisions.

Much of what is contained in TQM is not new and much of it is "good advice." The problem is that "good advice" doesn't produce significant organizational change, and techniques themselves don't lead to improvements in the quality of work life. Lynn (1981) has reviewed the efforts to improve public management in the 1960s and 1970s through the introduction of techniques such as planning-programming-budgeting system (PPBS), management by objectives (MBO), zero-based budgeting (ZBB), and others. All were shortlived, and he concludes that "the system is not the solution," that is, management systems and techniques are not the solution to incompetent organizations and poor performance. While numerous reasons can be cited for their failures, Lynn believes that the major reason is that in each case, there was a desire to see improvements in the management of public services without anyone having to spend too much time actually managing. Without the commitment of organizational leaders, all management techniques fall victim to a variety of "enemies."

I believe that in the long run, quality management will fare no better than its predecessors. Among those public human services agencies that embrace TQM, it will likely be seen as a "quick fix" and will be discarded when it fails to live up to its promises or when its supporters get tired of the battle against those who would maintain the status quo. I see five basic obstacles to the quality of work life in public human service organizations being significantly improved by quality management techniques:

1. *The tendency to think short term.* The pressure for quick results is even greater in the public sector than in the private sector. Those who are appointed to manage public human service organizations are expected to demonstrate results if they wish to maintain the support of elected officials. Government regulatory agencies and funding sources also tend to look at short-term results. TQM, on the other hand, promotes slow and steady improvement and tends to begin with small pilot efforts rather than trying to change the whole organization at once.

2. *The techniques may fail to deal with the issues that the human services executive really cares about.* Those who initiate TQM efforts, in the interests of generating some activity, often leave the decision of which issues to undertake to the members of the TQM teams. While this may be successful in motivating team members, it often ignores the issues that are of most interest to the top executives, who may see TQM as not addressing their agendas. The issues that are of interest to top management, on the other hand, may be controversial and subject to political dispute.

3. *Unwillingness to promote leadership throughout the organization.* According to Walton (1986), Deming says that organizations should promote leadership at all levels; that everyone can and should become a champion for the projects that they care about. This notion will be threatening to many human services executives who are used to tight hierarchical control and the notion that there is always "one best way."

4. *Too little patience for process.* I recently heard a union official lament that too many executives think that changing an organization is an event rather than a process. They think that change can be brought about by simply announcing that a new order will come into being on a certain date. This belief goes along with the tendency to see improvement as occurring through one-time large step increases in productivity or effectiveness, rather than continuous smaller increments which TQM promotes. They also fail to recognize the importance of including others (e.g., subordinates, line workers, unions) in the decision-making process.

5. *The tendency to blame the staff for the problems of the system.* When something goes wrong, the tendency in large public bureaucracies is to blame it on individuals and their deficiencies. The proposed solution is often to give them training, without attempting to discover what it is in the operating system itself that is producing poor results. This solution is also well-received by many academics and consultants who are more accustomed to offering training programs aimed at changing individual behavior. TQM, on the other hand, tends to change the focus from individual to systemic causes.

For the above reasons, I believe that public human service organizations will tend to avoid giving quality management a real chance to succeed, or they will pull the plug if the initiatives threaten the ways in which business is normally conducted. Let me give a couple of examples of the problems that I have observed in TQM initiatives, and that other efforts are likely to face. In one instance, the leaders of the effort failed to include middle managers in the process. TQM teams were composed primarily of line workers who were selected by top management. Middle managers were understandably threatened by this and were resistant to any of the changes proposed by the teams. In this case, top management failed to recognize that leadership roles had to be available for middle managers and they needed encouragement in inventing new roles for themselves that would be different from their traditional supervisory duties.

In a second organization, TQM efforts had been proceeding as "sheltered experiments" with the support of an agency executive who wanted to transform the agency culture to encourage risk taking and innovation. However, this executive was replaced by a new appointee whose agenda was very different and who had little patience for the slow pace of TQM interventions and the difficulty in producing quick and concrete results in service outcomes. The position and status of the initial TQM experiments suddenly became very tenuous.

By identifying the obstacles to using quality management techniques in public human service organizations, I don't mean to suggest that all attempts will lead to failure or that such efforts should not be undertaken at all. Given the right set of conditions, some TQM efforts can make a difference. The point is that the techniques themselves won't lead to significant improvements in the quality of work life. The particular techniques matter much less than the total commitment of human service managers to taking the time to manage the processes of change. This implies questioning the existing reality, learning through experience, and having the courage and patience to empower everyone in the organization to participate in its redesign.

REFERENCES

Arches, J. (1991). Social structure, burnout, and job satisfaction. *Social Work, (36)*3, 202–206.

Camman, C. (1984). Productivity of management through QWL programs. In Fombrun, C. (Ed.), *Strategic human resource management.* New York: Wiley.

Cohen, B. (1992). Quality of working life in a public child welfare agency. *Journal of Health and Human Resource Administration (15)*2, 129–152.

Ewalt, P. (1991). Trends affecting the recruitment and retention of social work staff in human service agencies. *Social Work, (36)*3, 214–217.

Lynn, L. (1981). *Managing the public's business.* New York: Basic Books.

Walton, M. (1986). *The Deming management method.* New York: Putnam Publishing Group.

Rejoinder to Professor Cohen

KENNETH L. ROBEY AND
STEVEN E. RAMSLAND

Obviously, we agree with Dr. Cohen's contention that a management approach is effective only to the extent that it is embraced by the managers who use it. Regardless of the specifics of any given management approach, it is the managers who must embody that approach who ultimately allow it to live or die.

What we don't comprehend, however, is Dr. Cohen's readiness to dismiss an approach because not all managers will be interested in or capable of properly implementing it. Does a lack of readiness on the part of some negate the benefits of the approach for those agencies that do properly implement it? Would he similarly suggest that office automation in human service agencies has little value because managers in some agencies won't fully embrace it?

Dr. Cohen paints a picture of human services executives, *en toto,* as being unwilling, inflexible, lacking patience, and quick to lay blame. In short, they are bad managers. We agree that some are. The view should not, however, be "all or none." The fact is that some human service managers are not inflexible and short-sighted. They are embracing quality management and successfully adopting its principles. It is these managers whose organizations will survive (and even thrive) in the years ahead.

It is now widely recognized that human service agencies, more than ever before, need to be effective and efficient providers of service. Many agencies that fail to adopt a data-driven outcomes orientation and an ability to demonstrate and maintain a high level of quality will probably cease to exist. It will be imperative to an organization's survival to begin to adopt some of TQM's most basic principles.

Dr. Cohen also cites poor experience with PPBS, ZBB, and other management strategies as evidence that human services managers will not adequately commit themselves to any emerging management techniques. Unlike those previous movements, quality management fosters many of the values and principles held dear by human services professionals. After all, quality management techniques are geared toward producing positive change and toward encouraging slow, methodical, and measurable transformation in a system. This is far more compatible with the typical human services manager's value system than are the more budget-driven, defect-oriented approaches Dr. Cohen cites.

Beyond issues of acceptance and implementation, we do believe that management philosophies have qualities that make some inherently more effective than others. TQM's concentration on data and emphasis on process rather than on the individual make it uniquely capable of moving human service agencies toward more effective and efficient operation and toward a higher quality of work life for employees. Employees of those organizations that accept and meet the challenge of adopting quality management techniques will indeed benefit.

Would It Be a Disaster if Most Human Services Organizations Were Administered by Managers Who Were Not Educated as Social Workers?

EDITOR'S NOTE: The debate about whether human service organizations should be administered only by people trained as social workers has increased in intensity over the past decade as the environment in which services are delivered has undergone dramatic change. For example, the continuing shift in service delivery from the public to private sector has resulted in increasing attention being given to costs, profitability, and effectiveness, often at the expense of client needs. As a result, many argue that social service managers must possess a set of skills that incorporate the profession's values and beliefs as well as "business" technologies. Because the environment in which human services are delivered will continue to change and evolve, the critical questions underlying this debate are: Does academic grounding in content area of the organization increase administrative effectiveness? What changes must be made in social work education to meet the challenge of preparing social workers as administrators? Finally, the time has come to openly debate the issue of whether there is a generic set of skills, knowledge, and values that transcend professional boundaries required for managing human service organizations.

Jerome L. Blakemore, Ph.D., says YES. He is an assistant professor in the School of Social Welfare at the University of Wisconsin–Milwaukee. Dr. Blakemore coordinates the school's mental health concentration and teaches courses in mental health and health policy, cultural diversity, and research. He is the former executive director of the Mental Health Association in Illinois and currently serves as president of a newly developed mental health rehabilitation program in Milwaukee modeled after the Fountain House in New York City.

William E. Berg, Ph.D., and Deborah L. Padgett, Ph.D., argue NO. Dr. Berg is an associate professor in the School of Social Welfare at the University of Wisconsin–Milwaukee. He has had substantial experience in public welfare settings and in mental health clinics. Dr. Berg currently teaches courses in human growth and development and in advanced research methods. His current research involves patterns of adjustment among urban and suburban aged populations and elements of leadership style in social work agencies.

Deborah L. Padgett is an assistant professor in the School of Social Welfare at the University of Wisconsin–Milwaukee. Her primary teaching interests are in the areas of administration, management, and group work, and her research interests include leadership and management, the balancing of family and work responsibilities, and feminist scholarship. Dr. Padgett has clinical experience in both inpatient and outpatient settings and management experience in community mental health.

YES

JEROME L. BLAKEMORE

Will it be a disaster if most human service organizations in the year 2000 are administered by managers who are not educated as social workers? The answer is a clear and resounding yes, for several reasons.

The privatization of many governmental human services functions provides a glimpse of the potential disaster of having non–social-work-trained and profit-oriented managers running human service organizations in the next decade. The privatization of governmental services was used extensively beginning in the 1960s to help reduce the census of the country's state and county psychiatric hospitals. In many states the profit motive resulted in the building and operating of nursing homes whose living conditions were so poor that they have been referred to as the new asylums (Levine, 1981). In many states, nursing homes did not replace the mental health hospital but allowed states to trans-institutionalize its mentally ill population. Some states still have large numbers of persons affected with mental illness residing in nursing homes. Illinois, for instance, houses approximately 3,500 in its state-operated facilities but has, based on current estimates, nearly 25,000 mentally ill persons living in nursing homes, facilities that do not begin to address their most basic emotional, physical, or social needs. This has reduced the state's obligation but made large profits for proprietary organizations. The services in these institutions were so limited that they help to encourage the Omnibus Budget Reconciliation Act of 1987. The act was designed to remove mentally ill patients from facilities that were not meeting the need for active treatment. The for-profit managers were, in essence, warehousing individuals but not addressing their immediate needs.

The for-profit mind-set also compromises the quality of care that human service agency (HSA) clients receive. The number of private psychiatric hospitals has been increasing across the country. The increase has been heralded as a way to improve the quality of care received by persons suffering from mental illness. The argument has been that the private sector could provide better care because the profit motive would increase competition and thus increase service quality. What has actually happened is the development of a system generally referred to as *dumping*. Dumping is the practice of transferring patients from a private facility to a state- or county-operated facility not on the basis of clinical need but because the client's ability to pay for service has eroded. If the best measure for clinical success is continuity of the treatment, what benefit does transferring a client have other than ensuring adherence to the bottom line?

The typical position posited for supporting non–social-work-trained managers to run human service organizations is that HSAs are in need of more accountability because of a shrinking tax base and limited confidence in the ability of social agencies to be effective and efficient. The cost-benefit methods used by business compares net costs to net benefits. Because success is defined in financial terms, the assessment of costs often focuses on economic ones, neglecting social costs (Frederick, Davis, & Post, 1988). The business literature is full of examples of decisions that were made on the basis of the bottom line that were in fact harmful to people (e.g., Nestlé Corporation, Manville Corporation). This rationale has also been used to support a number of plant closures and relocation decisions that have had major adverse effects on families and communities. Business, both in its teaching and in practice, is concerned with health of the bottom line but not necessarily the health of the people. While social-work-trained administrators also need to assess costs and benefits, their training has emphasized human factors and client services.

In addition to preoccupation with the bottom line, other disasters await if HSAs are to be managed by persons trained with a for-profit orientation. Weinbach (1990) cites a number of areas of comparisons between non-profit and for-profit agencies. The most significant areas cited are the differences related to consumer dependency and consumer interaction with the organization. Regarding consumer dependency, social workers have as a primary goal the fostering of independence. People, the product of HSAs, must be treated in such a way that they eventually will no longer need the services provided by the agency. Substance abusers, for instance, are taught and encouraged to gain skills that allow them to lessen their dependence on substance without the continued involvement of a professional support network. Businesses, suggests Weinbach, actively court the dependency of its customers. The development of a dependent relationship between the corporation and its consumers is important, perhaps critical, to the continued life of the for-profit organization. Keeping a cadre of loyal consumers is beneficial to the for-profit organization seeking to manage inventories and promote sales which are necessary for maintaining solvency and the health of the bottom line. Promoting dependency is inconsistent with the values of social work.

Consumer interaction with the organization provides another example of a major difference between the for-profit and the not-for-profit organization. In for-profit organizations little if any interaction takes place between the organization and its consumers. The contact is limited to purchasing, and even this contact is with an owner whose only connection to the producer of the product is an agreement to sell a particular product. Consumers rarely have contact with the corporation. When there is contact with the corporation it takes the form of correcting the corporation's decisions through actions such as boycotting or picketing a particular organization, usually because of some questionable decision made by the company that has major negative consequences on individuals or communities. Human service agencies, however, have ongoing contact with consumers which is vital to the agency's mission. Issues of meeting the needs of consumers are more complex and demand more attention and energy than what is necessary in the for-profit realm. While measuring success using the bottom line is easy for the for-profit organization, evaluation is also much more complex for the not-for-profit agency. It is not so easy to measure when people may have varying notions about whether or not a problem exists and if it does exist how the problem is defined. What constitutes both an appropriate solution and a process for reaching the desired goal or solution is a complex issue that confront the human service administrator. Unless the administrator is armed with appropriate tools and technologies that are focused by value-guided insight, evaluating how well the organization is doing can be a difficult task (Patti, 1985).

Social workers, of necessity, develop an ongoing concern for urban areas and special populations based on their professional social work education and their agency-based careers. In contrast, other disciplines that might prepare managers and administrators do little in the way of teaching about or preparing students to deal with cultural diversity. During the next decade and throughout the next century the ethnic makeup of the country will undergo major changes. These changes will require that human service administrators are able to develop services that are conceptualized in ways that are both sensitive and appropriate to the people they serve.

A typical career path for social workers is: paraprofessional, direct service, supervisor, and finally administrator (Patti, 1983). That path, coupled with academic training, places students in environments and situations that promote an understanding of people processing and people changing organizations (Hasenfeld & English, 1977). Businesses, and perhaps the current mode of the country, do little to prepare administrators to have an understanding of the needs of people beyond that understanding motivated by profit. Businesses and the for-profit sector are removed from one of the major groups served by social workers:

those who live in the inner city. Even when there is a connection between the for-profit sector and the inner city, the connection is in many ways one-sided. The case of high-potency beer provides a classic example of how the profit mind-set controls a company's decision making despite the known negative effects of the product. Alcoholism and substance abuse are major problems that plague many groups in the nation's inner cities. Heileman's brewery introduced a high-potency beer called Power Master and directed its advertising to inner-city residents. Despite clear evidence that substances play a major role in crime, domestic violence, and the incidence of death from alcohol-related ailments, the company continued, despite protest, to promote its product. After yielding to pressure, the company ceased to sell the product only to reintroduce it a year later with a different name—a high-potency product marketed toward the same low-income inner-city group. Clearly health of the bottom line was of more concern to the beverage industry than health of residents in the inner city.

Yes, having the majority of human service organizations managed by non–social-work-trained persons would be a disaster. The increased need for accountability coupled with the need to manage with more limited resources requires making tough decisions. Making these tough decisions requires more, not less, sensitivity to the needs of people, sensitivity that is inherent in the values and training of social workers and that is not the emphasis of the curricula of business schools or of corporate life. Management tools and technology are teachable. While tools and technologies are important, it is the mind-set and the value system that guide how these tools and technologies are used that are most important.

Many people argue that we can sensitize administrators from other professions to social work values. Those who accept this argument are being short-sighted for two reasons: (1) they fail to fully appreciate the role that values play in the development and initiation of human service programs and (2) they are not benefiting from the lessons of the past. In addition to tools and technologies, people bring to the work environment a set of beliefs, values, and biases that have been developed over time. Despite decades of discussion about civil rights and equality, people of color and women still hit a glass ceiling when it comes to promotion and tenure in corporate America and are still not viewed as equals in a number of fields. Workshops and seminars cannot replace a strong orientation to the value of people and to their needs. This can best be developed through the experiences and commitment so basic to social work training and through the value system that guides it.

REFERENCES

Frederick, W. C., Davis, K., & Post, J. E. (1988). *Business and society: Corporate strategy, public policy, ethics* (6th ed.). New York: McGraw-Hill.

Hasenfeld, Y., & English, R. A. (1977). Human service organizations: A conceptual overview. In Y. Hasenfeld and R. A. English (Eds.), *Human service organizations* (pp. 1–24). Ann Arbor, MI: The University of Michigan Press.

Levine, M. (1981). *The history and politics of community health.* New York: Oxford University Press.

Patti, R. J. (1983). *Social welfare administration: Managing social programs in a developmental context.* Englewood Cliffs, NJ: Prentice-Hall.

Patti, R. J. (1985). In search of a purpose for social welfare administration. *Administration in Social Work, 9,* 1–14.

Weinbach, R. W. (1990). *The social worker as manager: Theory and practice.* New York: Longman.

Rejoinder to Dr. Blakemore

Deborah L. Padgett and William E. Berg

Dr. Blakemore has provided a cogent argument for that tradition which specifies that social agencies should be managed and administered by professional social workers. His position is based, in other words, on a value-based argument, one that asserts that, unlike the industrial or business manager, the trained social worker has been socialized within a value system that emphasizes "sensitivity to the needs of people" rather than those associated with profitability. Thus unlike his or her business or industrial counterpart, the social work administrator is more likely to develop, implement, and manage programs whose goals and objectives are consistent with this value system; that is, programs that seek to address these human needs in a humane and informed manner.

In support of this position, Dr. Blakemore provides a number of arguments, each of which appears to suggest that the goals, beliefs, and values of private industry are inimical to those of professional social work. He notes, for example, that the privatization of mental health services had the effect of encouraging the development of facilities that ignore the "most basic emotional, physical, or social needs" of the patient, or that engage in "dumping," or that "warehouse." This occurs, according to Dr. Blakemore, because these facilities are primarily concerned with profitability and, as a result, are more likely to foster dependency in their relationships with clients, are less likely to maintain contact with their clients, are held accountable to 'valueless' standards of success, and so forth.

While the cumulative effect of these arguments has a certain rhetorical appeal, they clearly lack any relevance or validity. Dr. Blakemore is certainly aware of the fact that the privatization of mental health services occurred, in part, precisely because patients had been "warehoused" in public facilities where they were subject to conditions that ignored their basic needs; facilities that were, in most instances, managed and administered by professionally trained social workers. Indeed, the private facilities that he offers as examples of the harmful effects of privatization are likely to be managed by professional social workers.

Dr. Blakemore's position implies a sense of moral superiority that verges on elitism. It rests on the claim that trained social workers are more likely to make moral decisions than are comparably trained business or industrial managers. This claim makes it impossible, in effect, to hold social work leadership accountable to critical, scientific standards of performance. It is this sense of moral and intellectual rigidity that serves to perpetuate the traditional agency system, a system that, as we have seen in recent years, has proven to be incapable of adapting to the needs and requirements of a changing environment. Such an environment requires not a commitment to the status quo, but a recognition of the need to deal with administrative concerns in a more reflective, scientific manner than has been the case. Indeed, one might suggest that what is required is a more "businesslike" approach to administrative practice in social agencies.

NO

DEBORAH L. PADGETT AND WILLIAM E. BERG

While the question of who should administer social agencies may not qualify as a "disaster" in the true sense of that term, it does have important implications for our understanding of those changes in agency structures and processes that have occurred during the past decade. The assumption that social agencies should be administered by professional social workers is based on a historical image of the agency, one which has, in many respects, been overtaken by those realities that increasingly define both the nature and the scope of professional practice.

Social work has traditionally assumed that the social agency possesses certain unique elements, structures, and processes that reflect the peculiar circumstances and demands associated with professional practice. This perception of the agency has been perpetuated by an educational curriculum that tends to emphasize the exclusivity of social work management and administration and by a body of literature and research that reinforces the notion that the agency system differs in certain vital respects from other organizations. In this respect at least, social work has tended to follow the model provided by education or nursing, where professional credentials are viewed as prerequisites for administrative or managerial positions, rather than, for example, that of medical practice where hospital or clinic administrators generally lack medical degrees.

To the extent that this image of the agency has some validity, its validity rests, not on the peculiar circumstances or demands of professional social work practice, but on those features or characteristics of the agency that contribute to what March and Olsen (1987) have defined as organizational ambiguity (p. 12). Those elements of agency structure and process that appear unique may be attributed to, in other words, the agency's general inability to identify clear, measurable goals and objectives, the lack of clarity in relationship to agency technologies and environments, the problems associated with the interpretation of agency history, and those patterns of shifting or dual allegiances that tend to characterize professionals who practice within an organizational environment that is often perceived as overly restrictive or demanding.

This sense of ambiguity which has characterized the social agency can be understood in historical terms as a transitional stage or as a phenomenon arising from the shift from an environment that was generally perceived as essentially benign and predictable to one that became, particularly during the past decade, defined by rapid, unpredictable change. This shift has, in effect, resolved many of the problems or circumstances that contributed to ambiguity within the social agency. There currently exists, in other words, an emerging consensus concerning the nature of the environment within which social agencies will operate during the coming decade and about the implications of this environment for agency structures and processes.

This environment has been associated, for better or worse, with the concept of privatization (Kamerman & Kahn, 1989). When applied to the social agency, the concept of privatization implies a shift from an environment that was essentially public in nature to one that is increasingly private in its orientation. Agencies have, in effect, moved from an environment in which they relied primarily on public resources—including those associated with funding, legitimacy, clientele, and so forth—to one defined by the expectations and demands of the private sector. While this shift began during the early years of the Reagan administration, it has continued during the current administration and has, in many respects, been institutionalized within those structures that determine how social services resources are allocated (e.g., private insurers, third-party payers).

Even among the traditional public agencies, the emergence of a privatized environment has critical implications for agency management and administration. This occurs, in part, because the impulse toward privatization represents a political response to what is generally perceived as a social and economic crisis; that is, a response to deficit spending at all levels of government, and a response to certain emergent and intractable social problems that have, for all intents and purposes, defied solution through the traditional public-sector agency system. This situation has been complicated, moreover, by the growth of a political climate that is essentially conservative in nature, one dominated by an ideology characterized by those values and beliefs that foster a private rather than public approach to social problems.

These developments have had the cumulative effect of producing an agency culture that differs significantly from that found in the traditional agency system. Social agencies have historically operated under the assumption that they differ in certain important respects from the business firm. Thus a recent text on social work administration indicates that social agencies generally place less emphasis on the goal of efficiency, are less concerned with maintaining customer dependency, are less competitive, are less involved in marketing activities, and so forth (Weinbach, 1990, pp. 31–45). Although this image of the agency as something other than a business has a certain evocative appeal, the degree to which it is applicable to the realities of the agency environment is open to question.

The role that the environment plays in defining agency culture reflects the impact of both the general culture of the society and the more focused values and beliefs found within its environment (Ott, 1989, pp. 74–98). The shift from a public to a private agency environment originated, in other words, from the emergence of certain cultural values and beliefs associated with an ideology that, for a variety of reasons, subscribes to a private rather than public approach to social problems.

The more specified role that the task environment plays in this process has been explored in the literature, a literature which suggests that agency culture is a product of those organizations with which the agency interacts in the pursuit of its goals and objectives and of the values and beliefs held by those persons who dominate these organizations (e.g., Schein, 1985). Thus to the extent that social agencies find themselves involved in an environment that is dominated by private business firms rather than public institutions, and to the extent that the leadership of these firms—and, indeed, of public institutions themselves—possess those values and beliefs associated with the pursuit of profits, cost containment, cost efficiency, and other fiscal concerns, it may be assumed that agency culture will increasingly be defined by these same values and beliefs.

The focus on cost issues provides what is perhaps the most relevant and useful example of the impact of the task environment on agency culture. The attempt to apply cost standards to agency services has the effect of producing an accountability system that differs in certain important respects from those employed within a public agency model. As Weinbach (1990) has indicated, accountability has been a problematic issue among public agencies, one that they have attempted to resolve through the use of evaluative "criteria that are much 'softer' than those available in business or industry" (p. 38). One of the effects of the shift to a privatized agency system has been that it has forced agencies to adopt "harder" accountability criteria, or criteria that are, in fact, consistent with those employed in business and industry. Thus, success in the privatization of services has been defined, in most cases, in relationship to cost savings, cost efficiency, and so forth, regardless of whether the services involved refuse collection or child care services (Kamerman & Kahn, 1989, pp. 235–260). Although a number of problems are associated with the attempt to apply these standards to the provision of social services, their use has a certain inherent appeal to private insurers and, more importantly perhaps, to public policy makers.

The values associated with the use of these cost standards have, in any case, been internalized within the cultures of the private social agency and, in many cases, of public agencies. These values, in common with other characteristics of the task environment, have the effect of producing certain changes in agency structures and processes. They require, for example, a greater emphasis on management information systems and other routine record-keeping procedures than may have been the case within a public agency system. They are frequently associated, moreover, with the emergence of what may appear to be more cost-efficient technologies; that is, technologies that involve short-term treatment, crisis intervention, case management, and so forth.

The emphasis on cost factors represents one part of a larger cultural shift, one that includes such things as the use of languages that are consistent with a more "businesslike" approach to services, the development of normative systems that reflect the emphasis on efficiency, and so forth. The cumulative effect of these developments has been to create a situation in which the ability of the agency to adapt and adjust to the demands of its environment is contingent on the development of those management skills and capacities that will enable it to respond to these demands. To the extent that these demands are couched within the expectations of what is essentially a business culture, it would appear that these skills and capacities are most likely to exist in those arenas where management has been socialized within this culture; that is, the formal training and education that provides both the requisite skills and the legitimacy to effectively manage within this environment.

While it may appear, therefore, that managers in social agencies should possess degrees in business administration, this issue is ultimately less important than the larger issues involved in agency adjustment and adaptation. It may very well be that schools of social work will respond to the demands of the current agency environment by developing curricula that provide social workers with the skills and training necessary to this environment. It is clear that agencies will have a difficult time surviving during the coming decade without properly trained and educated administrative leadership.

REFERENCES

Kamerman, S., & Kahn, A. (Eds.). (1989). *Privatization and the welfare state.* Princeton, NJ: Princeton University Press.

Kamerman, S., & Kahn, A. (1989). Child care and privatization under Reagan. In S. Kamerman & A. Kahn (Eds.), *Privatization and the welfare state.* Princeton, NJ: Princeton University Press.

March, J., & Olsen, J. (1987). *Ambiguity and choice in organizations.* Oslo, Norway: Universitetsforlaget.

Ott, J. S. (1989). *The organizational culture perspective.* Pacific Grove, CA: Brooks-Cole.

Schein, E. (1985). *Organizational culture and leadership.* San Francisco: Jossey-Bass.
Weinbach, R. (1990). *The social worker as manager.* New York: Longman.

Rejoinder to Drs. Padgett and Berg

JEROME L. BLAKEMORE

The position forwarded by Drs. Padgett and Berg serves to emphasize that the importance of the changes in the environmental context and the implications for agency administration are relevant ones. We have seen dramatic shifts in the political and ideological context in which social agencies have been functioning—shifts that have indeed modified the external and internal cultures of agencies. To posit this time, then, as a transitional one for human service agencies, as the authors have suggested, is warranted and makes this longstanding debate about the management of human service agencies in an era of change a debate worthy of continuing.

The essay by Drs. Padgett and Berg supporting the position that it will not be a disaster if the majority of HSAs are managed by individuals other than social workers does, however, raise a number of important questions and concerns. My initial concern is a need for being clear about two realities: (1) major differences exist between the human service agency and other profit-motivated organizations and (2) these differences are not merely a function of an evolving state of ambiguity. Ambiguity is a constant state when the work of an agency is measured not by profit or the means needed to ensure a profit, but by the changing state of peoples' needs, concerns, and demands. The ambiguity described should not be heralded as a call for replacing nonprofit managers but for keeping them in place with an expanded set of skills, tools, and technologies that will help them make the difficult decisions related to retrenchment and limited resources. The challenge for human service administrators lies in managing effectively within the dual context of professional values and the changing environment. Suggesting that management is valueless and merely a function of ''skills and capacities'' is a myth that business ethicists have long been struggling to expose.

The authors' view of privatization is also of concern. The view that privatization moves the agency from a reliance on public resources with regard to funding, legitimacy, and clientele to one defined by the expectations and demands of the private sector is incorrect and sounds like an argument for ending this grand experiment called privatization. These agencies, despite the link or connection to the term *privatization,* should not and cannot function in a vacuum. The social programs of the colonial and progressive eras were primarily private. Not only did they address the need of the clients of the day, but the programs of those eras also served to shape the human service system as we know it today. Social agencies, private or otherwise, should still address the needs of their clientele and should remain accountable to the unit of government that gives it legitimacy. Public dollars still fund privatized programs. The very demands that necessitate the development and continuation of any human service program are true for those deemed private as well as public, and clients whose needs do not allow for packaged responses still need to be served. These realities have not changed because a cost-saving mechanism called privatization has been introduced to the world of human services.

There is some level of agreement between both positions. The agreement centers around a recognition that HSAs need to be more efficiently managed. This efficiency, however, given the nature of the social work practice can be accomplished only by providing new methods and skills to administrators who are armed with a belief and value system that is critical for the development of structures that recognize and maximize each individual's potential for growth and development.

Should Social Work Administrators Function as Managers as Well as Client-Oriented Social Workers?

EDITOR'S NOTE: Most social work administrators would agree that their agencies exist to provide services to clients. The nature and type of services depends on the mission and resources of the agency. However, when agencies are examined closely, there often appears a separation between the administrators and the staff and between the administrators and the clients. This has tremendous implications for staff morale and productivity, for service delivery, and for client outcomes. Too often staff are overwhelmed by rules, policies, and procedures that interfere with their ability to deliver services to clients. Too often the process of seeking help is dehumanizing, and services provided are ineffective. Thus, the critical issue for administrators is how to manage their agencies so that staff are empowered to provide services that meet the needs of clients. This debate centers on one question underlying this issue: Should administrators carry both management and direct-service functions?

Eli Teram says YES. Eli Teram is an associate professor of Social Work at Wilfrid Laurier University. He is interested in the relations between social service organizations and their clients. With Prue Rains, he is the author of *Normal Bad Boys: Public Policies, Institutions and the Politics of Client Recruitment* (McGill-Queen's University Press, 1992).

Judith A. Peterson, M.S.W., A.C.S.W., L.C.S.W., and Jaye R. Nichols, M.S.W., A.C.S.W., L.C.S.W., argue NO. Judith A. Peterson is the Deputy Director of Crusaders Central Clinic Association, a federally funded Community Health Center in Rockford, Illinois. She has nineteen years of experience as a social worker and over ten years of experience as a social services and health care administrator. She has written and presented papers in the areas of case management and research.

Jaye R. Nichols is a clinical social worker also at Crusaders Central Clinic Association. She has six years of mental health practice experience.

YES

ELI TERAM

The wonder-rabbi of Helm once saw, in a vision, the destruction by fire of the study house in Lublin, fifty miles away. This remarkable event greatly enhanced his fame as a wonder-worker. Several days later a traveller from Lublin, arriving in Helm, was greeted with expressions of sorrow and concern, not unmixed with a certain pride by the disciples of the wonder-rabbi. "What are you talking about?" asked the traveller. "I left Lublin three days ago and the study house was standing as it always has. What kind of a wonder-rabbi is that?" "Well, well," one of the rabbi's disciples answered, "burned or not burned, it's only a detail. The wonder is he could see so far."[1]

Social service organizations are replete with wonder-administrators who can see very far. Many of them are so farsighted that they are blind to the daily mundane realities encountered by their subordinates and clients. The fact that the organizations they manage implement policies developed by policymakers who are often further removed from these realities only reinforces the gap between administrators and workers. These gaps are not evident in the common graphically sophisticated charts that proudly present neatly coordinated organizational worlds, with elaborate vertical and horizontal communication channels. They can be found, however, in the tales of frustrated workers, and poorly served clients, who wonder why managers can't get down to earth.

In response to this malaise, I argue, administrators should perform some client-oriented functions.[2] This argument is associated with other propositions made in this book, in particular, Zeke Hasenfeld's claim that clients should have control over the policies of social service agencies and Jerome Blakemore's conviction that it would be a disaster if the majority of human service organizations were administered by managers who were not educated in social work. Although they may disagree with my argument, our respective positions share a concern for, and an attempt to address, the increasing distance between the world as seen by administrators and the one experienced by street-level workers and their clients.

The structuralist approach helps us understand the vertical division of labor in human service organizations.[3] Particularly relevant to our debate is the "work-levels approach," developed by a group of researchers associated with the Brunel Institute of Organization and Social Studies.[4] The essence of their argument is that the work done in organizations is naturally stratified. An understanding of this stratification, and the nature of work within each level, is a key for determining both the optimum number of strata in a given organization and the appropriate relations between them. For example, Jacques (1976) distinguishes varying "time span[s] of discretion" in each organizational level and associates them with the "level of abstraction" required to perform in each level. In a framework based on research in social welfare organizations, Rowbottom and Billis (1987) suggest that all organized work falls into a hierarchy "in which the range of objectives to be achieved, on the one hand, and the range of environmental circumstances to be taken into account, on the other, broaden and change in quality at successive steps" (p. 23).

Although one may question whether the above stratification of work is "natural" or necessary, it is difficult to deny its existence. Equally indisputable is the collateral observation that the world view of organizational members is determined by their position; to expect otherwise is to ignore human nature. Kouzes and Mico (1979) capture the behavioral consequences of this organizational stratification in their "Domain Theory." They propose that human service organizations comprise three domains—the Policy Domain, the Management Domain, and the Service Domain—each of which functions with a separate set of governing principles, success measures, structural arrangements, and work modes (p. 456). They go on to propose that the sets developed by each domain are incongruent and that they are accompanied by legitimating norms that contrast with the norms of the other domains. Not surprisingly, the interactions between these domains lead to what they describe as an "internally disjunctive and discordant" organization.

There are many examples of the disparities between the world of managers and that of workers. For example, time sheets and other standardized forms, which workers must complete in many human service organizations, could not have been developed by managers who understand the nature of professional work. More seriously, some managers attempt to use data from these reports to "correct" workers' behavior (e.g., "you spend too much time on home visits") or decisions (e.g., "you place too many [or too few] children in custody"). Still others arbitrarily limit the quantity (e.g., maximum number of sessions per client in a counseling agency) or quality of intervention (e.g., group work for one category of clients, individual work for another), ignoring the uniqueness of each client.

Where the above examples may reflect gaps between bureaucratic and professional thinking, more progressive managers can equally misunderstand, or ignore, the realities faced by their subordinates. A doctoral student I supervise is currently interviewing managers and workers about their experience with inter-disciplinary teams. What he hears from managers is the ideology of inter-disciplinary teams: why we need them, how professional schools fail to prepare workers for interdisciplinary work, what makes a worker a good team member. These people feel very strongly about interdisciplinary teams and believe that the success of their organizations depends on interprofessional cooperation. Workers who are members of interdisciplinary teams, however, seriously doubt the value of this mode of cooperation. They talk about unresolved conflicts, lack of respect for the knowledge of each other's profession, and dynamics that do not serve the needs of clients.

The vision of managers who believe in interdisciplinary work is only one example of thinking at a relatively high level of abstraction that is not translated into constructive action at the lower levels. The failure of this and other good managerial ideas often relates to ignorance of the context in which they are being implemented. As an example, let us consider one conflict I observed in an institutional team comprised of child-care workers and social workers. The issue concerned whether to allow adolescents a weekend pass despite their not having earned the points to ''purchase'' the privilege. Social workers, who were work-ing to reunite these adolescents with their families, argued for a relaxation of the rules to allow trips home despite the lack of points.[5] The social workers expected child-care workers to tolerate the deteriorating behavior that accompanies pro-cesses of family reunification because of its contribution to the ultimate mutual goal. Because management had no clear policy regarding this issue, social workers and child-care workers became embroiled in case-by-case negotiations, which sometimes resulted in what social workers considered inappropriate ar-rangements. The conflict was known to managers; however, without familiarity with context or consequences, they had little reason to establish non-negotiable priorities. On the contrary, the abstract vision of interdisciplinary teams would make these negotiations seem a mutual adjustment, an appropriate coordination mechanism for such situations.

Although the context of street-level work can be communicated to man-agers in different ways, direct experience with the realities of workers and clients is probably the most powerful means of comprehending and responding to this world. Rowbottom and Billis (1977) refer to this practice as ''zooming.'' They suggest that managers who are involved in activities of lower work levels approach these tasks in a way that characterizes their own level of functioning. In other words, managers should consider the implications of this experience and assess the congruence of the contingencies faced by lower-level workers and the arrangements designed to facilitate, coordinate, and control their work.

If we reconsider the examples cited earlier, a manager who works directly with clients will realize that reporting activities in five-minute increments is not only frustrating but meaningless. Knowing the reasoning behind the request for information, a perceptive manager can develop a more appropriate method for collecting data. Such a manager will also discover that relying on organizational statistics to "correct" the behavior of "deviant" workers, or their decisions, may well result in manipulations with consequences worse than those "corrected." Direct experience with lower-level work will allow an insightful manager to envision the options for workers who are requested to "regress towards the average."

Similarly, managers attempting to diffuse interdisciplinary work in their organizations will find direct involvement with these teams most enlightening. Their participation will highlight not only the hypothetical positioning of different occupational groups but also their ability to exert influence within the unique context of the organization. In our earlier example, the manager will recognize that child-care workers control access to adolescents. Thus, the dynamics of discussions regarding weekend passes include the unstated understanding that if child-care workers are pushed too far they can retaliate by limiting access to clients. This understanding provides a different perspective on what was framed as mutual adjustment.

Such perceptions cannot be communicated through traditional channels. Workers and managers live in distant worlds, and their modes of thinking are very different. Therefore, the impact of "zooming" to lower-level work activities is beyond what can be accomplished in any report. Two personal examples illustrate the point.

As a director of the social work department in an organization working with the mentally handicapped, I was called on to deal with the arrest of one of our clients. It was an important experience as I learned how the police and the prosecutor were implementing new policies. Although the policies had been in place for some time, and although workers had some experience with the system, it was only after this "zooming" that I spent time on developing relations with the police and the justice system to ensure proper implementation of the policy.

Another zooming occurred when I was program manager of vocational services in the same field. I was asked to meet with a client who had decided to "resign" from his "position" in the sheltered workshop. He had cerebral palsy, with a severe speech impediment. He told me he had had enough of the workshop because he was treated as though he were stupid. He went on to say that the pretense that the sheltered workshop was a "real" workplace[6] did not fool anyone because they knew that real employees get paid much more, don't live in group homes, and have a good life. The encounter forced me to change my thinking not only about the programs I was directing at the time, but also about management. Many years later, his broken words and intense emotions stay with me, mainly because I was shocked to discover my own ignorance.

One may argue that these experiences reflect poor management rather than demonstrate the power of zooming. However, this argument may well serve the need of managers who are afraid to discover and react to the real worlds of their subordinates and clients.

ENDNOTES

1. As recited by Lewontin (1992).

2. The specific arrangements and the extent of crossing role boundaries should be determined in the context of each organization.

3. For a synthesis of the contingency literature and a typology, which includes professional bureaucracies, see Mintzberg (1979).

4. Some of the prominent members of this group are Elliott Jacques, Ralph Rowbottom, and David Billis.

5. For a discussion of the control of clients and interdisciplinary teams see Teram (1991).

6. Following the principle of normalization, an attempt was made to create the image of a real workplace; clients were called "employees," received "pay cheques," and were treated in other ways as workers rather than clients.

REFERENCES

Jaques, E. (1976). *A general theory of bureaucracy.* London: Heinemann.

Kouzes, J. M., & Mico, P. R. (1979). Domain theory: An introduction to organizational behavior in human service organizations. *Journal of Applied Behavioral Science, 15,* 449–469.

Lewontin, R. C. (1992). The dream of the human genome. *New York Review of Books, 39*(10), 34.

Mintzberg, H. (1979). *The structuring of organizations: A synthesis of the research.* Englewood Cliffs, NJ: Prentice-Hall.

Rowbottom, R., & Billis, D. (1987). *Organizational design: The work-levels approach.* Brookfield, Vt.: Gower.

Rowbottom, R., & Billis, D. (1977). The stratification of work and organizational design. *Human Relations, 30,* 53–76.

Teram, E. (1991). Interdisciplinary teams and the control of clients: A socio-technical perspective. *Human Relations, 44,* 343–356.

Rejoinder to Dr. Teram

JUDITH PETERSON AND
JAYE R. NICHOLS

Dr. Teram makes a good case for social work administrators to remain client-oriented. Certainly, all social service administrators would concur that serving the clients' best interests is central to agency existence. The administrator has multiple responsibilities: developing services for clients, involving the community, managing staff and information, raising resources, communicating with the media, working with the board of directors, and so forth. We disagree with Dr. Teram's suggestion that the administrator should assume responsibility for working at the "street level" of service delivery. The additional responsibility of providing actual client services creates role confusion, unclear role expectations, and diffused boundaries for the social work administrator. The more feasible scenario is for the administrator to accompany the direct service worker as he or she interacts with the client. This provides the administrator with an understanding of street-level interventions.

We suggest that a more appropriate approach to the issues of client-oriented administration is the use of participatory management. The same information gained through "zooming" can be collected through employee action groups, where staff set the principles and objectives as well as determine the evaluation process and data collection systems. Further, communication between the administration and workers can be improved when workers are able to determine the means for such contact. Another advantage of participatory management is that it is ongoing, a part of the organizational structure; "zooming" is episodic and short-term.

We support client and staff involvement in the policy domain. This is best achieved by having a consumer-based board of directors. The use of staff and the consumer board can set the future of the organization through their active involvement in the strategic planning process as well as in providing feedback on service delivery.

Finally, the administrator has to manage competing and often conflicting demands. His or her success will be predicated on the ability to optimize both the services provided to clients and the agency's functioning.

NO

JUDITH A. PETERSON AND JAYE R. NICHOLS

The manager of a social service agency has multiple leadership roles to perform and essentially serves as the "parent" of the organization. When a social work administrator functions as a manager as well as a client-oriented social worker, the administrator replicates a dysfunctional family system. In a dysfunctional family, the identified patient is the focus of the parent instead of the whole intrafamiliar problems. Similarly, an administrator who focuses on only the client neglects the whole system's problems.

In family systems theory, boundaries and power are central to the analysis of the system. The system boundaries include communication, ethics and values, conflict resolution, and teamwork. Power issues for the system include norms and rules, management style, and administrator/employee relations. The social work administrator must balance three separate and occasionally conflicting identities: corporate, institutional, and professional (Keney, 1990). As in the family system, power and boundaries affect the administrator's relationship to the system which includes staff, community, board of directors, funding sources, clients, and the media. Conflict for the director arises when he or she chooses a client-oriented social work approach to direct the organization rather than a systems approach that promotes growth of the organization. The successful manager is able to reach an equilibrium between meeting clients' needs and wants and maintaining the well-being of the organization.

Boundaries

In a dysfunctional system, communication is constricted and messages are mixed. The communication patterns of dysfunctional families are constricted between parents or between parents and children when rules and consequences are not explicitly discussed. An administrator can replicate this problem when he or she restricts communication between subsystems and does not facilitate information exchange between the board and staff. Like the functional family, the functional organization is characterized by *open communication.* Clear boundaries are permeable between defined subsystems where subordinates are able to identify client needs to the executive. The role of the administrator is to communicate the mission of the organization to the staff. The effective leader uses a variety of communications to further the ideology, such as employee newsletters, staff meetings, management retreats, employee action groups, and the community newspaper. The potent manager is responsive, easily understood, approachable, and open to dialogue with staff.

The astute executive *resolves conflicts* with open communication and negotiation. He or she is able to achieve consensus by bringing staff together to problem solve difficult situations. The clear administrator finds implementing change to be relatively easy since he or she involves personnel from the beginning in planning for the change.

When ethics and values are forced into members of a dysfunctional family, members become rebellious as in the acting-out teenager. In contrast, the organization is characterized by a set of *ethics* and *values* which are usually accepted by the employees who participate in the decision-making process. This philosophy encourages the staff to manage themselves.

In a dysfunctional family, roles are ambiguous and relationships fluctuate between enmeshment and disengagement. In contrast, a major focus of the effective administrator is to identify clear roles and foster team building. *Good teamwork* is an essential component of effective social work delivery and an integral ingredient of many aspects of social work practice (Illes & Auluck, 1990). Team-building interventions are probably the single most important group of interventions in organization development (French & Bell, 1990). Forty-five percent of team building studies reported by Porras and Berg (1978) showed significant positive changes on "process" variables, such as trust, communications, support, involvement, and problem solving.

A variety of team-building techniques have been devised, in addition to standard techniques such as brainstorming and force field analysis. In most such interventions, the classic action research model of problem identification, data gathering, data feedback, diagnosis, action planning, action taking, and evaluation is followed. Actions taken might focus on goal setting, mission identification, or prioritizing. Other actions might focus on role analysis and role clarification to resolve issues of role conflict or role ambiguity (Iles & Auluck, 1990).

A central task of a leader is to *influence* subordinates, peers, and at times superiors. This includes influencing people to follow orders and suggestions, to listen to and be persuaded by ideas and opinions, to do tasks or do them differently, to put forth more effort, and to act or not act in a certain manner. A leader must be able to exert influence to be effective as a manager (Seltzer, 1986).

A major role of the leader in *motivating* employees is to reduce barriers to goal attainment by providing the coaching, guidance, and support (as well as the rewards) necessary to assist subordinates in performing effectively (Seltzer, 1986).

Power

Norms and rules in a dysfunctional family are coerced by punitive parents. The functional system encourages employees to participate in determining the rules and policies and to abide by them because of a shared agreement and not because the administrator is "looking over their shoulders."

Parents in a dysfunctional family seek to control the child. The parent has excessive expectations of the child's abilities and responsibilities, and the roles become reversed where the child becomes responsible for nurturing the parent. Understanding that motivations come from within the individual and are unique to each person (Sargent, 1986), the discerning leader can display a nurturing *management style*. Employees are recognized on a personal as well as professional level (e.g., outstanding employee awards, individual notes of congratulations, social gatherings, recognition of birthdays). A participative leadership style can assist individual managers in achieving improvement in motivational levels throughout an organization. Staff who participate on policy-setting committees related to safety, ethics, confidentiality, and personnel policies are able to expand their understanding of the organization and enhance their skills so that they may assume greater responsibility within the organization.

The exemplary leader utilizes a strategic planning process to determine long-range goals for the organization. This process involves extensive input from all areas of the system including the board of directors, staff, and community. The most effective strategic plan is completed with an outside consultant working with a staff team. Administrators also provide consultation throughout the process, but generally are not directly involved with data gathering and assessment. Evaluation of the organization is based on the strategic plan.

The fiscally responsible manager devotes time and effort to marketing the services of the organization as well as developing the management information system. Middle managers are responsible for evaluation of their own areas and report to the executive. The leader is characterized by an ability to build coalitions. These coalitions may be interagency or intra-agency as in a homeless program where mental health, substance abuse, housing, and entitlement agencies work with the primary health care team to provide comprehensive services to the client. Rather than advocating for individual clients, the executive advocates for the organization within the larger system. This will most certainly involve government lobbying activities as well as local fund raising.

Effective administrator-employee relations are characterized by widespread involvement in decision making at all levels. Middle managers are delegated greater discretionary power to resolve problems and make judgments that impact their program areas without always consulting with the executive. In the past, administrators focused on enhancing the managerial skills of middle managers, but today they spend more time identifying and rewarding individuals who are risk takers, who seek to innovate and develop visions of the future rather than become institutional caretakers. Reasonable and appropriate risk taking is encouraged. Feelings of ownership among middle managers are prevalent because the leader promotes employee responsibility and at the same time provides staff with the power to achieve goals. Boundaries are well established as is the chain of command. The administrator, of course, reports directly to the board of directors. In a functional organization, program managers have ample opportunity to interact with the board through board subcommittees and reporting at board of directors meetings.

A study by Reisch (1990), comparing effective and noneffective organizations, indicated several key characteristics of effective organizations. Effective organizations were more likely to concentrate their decision-making responsibilities in a board of directors and were more than twice as likely to use staff in key decision-making roles. Efficient organizations also were much more likely to use formal documents such as policy manuals and organizational bylaws. These organizations were more likely to have women as leaders and to have a leadership corps that encompassed a range of ages. Impressive organizations were more likely to have leaders from a balance of geographic locations and were more likely to have leaders who were considered to be strong leaders. Effective organizations were more likely to have established a structured goal-setting process and to have maintained consistent goals over the previous five years. Efficient organizations were more than twice as likely to use a variety of means of intraorganizational communication.

In summary, the following question emerges: Is the administrator first responsibility to the client, organization, personnel, or the board of directors? In theory, the administrator is responsible for ensuring that services are provided according to the mission statements that has been set through the strategic planning process and approved by the board of directors. Since the mission statement will be related to client services, it would seem, then, that the client is the administrator's first point of responsibility. However, if the administrator fails to ensure that the system is functioning in terms of employees, facility, community relations, and financial management, there will be no client services because there will be no viable organization.

REFERENCES

French, W. L., & Bell, P. H. (1984). *Organization Development,* Englewood Cliffs, N.J.: Prentice Hall.

Iles, P., & Auluck, R. (1990, April). Team building, inter-agency development and social work practice. *British Journal of Social Work, 20*(2), 151–164.

Keney, J. J. (1990, February). Social work management in emerging health care systems. *Health and social work, 15,* 22–31.

Porras, J. I., and Berg, P. O. (1978). Impact of organization development. *Academy of Management Review, 3,* 349–366.

Reisch, M. (1990, January). Organizational structure and client advocacy: Lessons from the 1980s. *Social Work, 35,* 73–74.

Sargent, K., & Sargent, A. (1986). Effective motivation. *The effective health care executive: A guide to a winning management style* (pp. 44, 50). Rockville, MD: Aspen Publishers.

Seltzer, J. (1986). Developing an effective leadership style. *The effective health care executive: A guide to a winning management style* (p. 41). Rockville, MD: Aspen Publishers.

Hirschhorn, L. (1978). The stalemated agency: A theoretical perspective and a practical proposal. *Administration in Social Work, 2,* 425–438.

Hirschhorn, L., & Gilmore, T. (1980). The application of family therapy concepts to influencing organizational behavior. *Administrative Science Quarterly, 25,* 18–37.

Minuchin, S. (1974). *Families and family therapy.* Cambridge, MA: Harvard University Press.

Rejoinder to Ms. Nichols and Ms. Peterson
ELI TERAM

For proper family functioning, the boundaries of subsystems must be clear. They must be defined well enough to allow subsystem members to carry out their functions without undue interference, but they must allow contact between the members of the subsystem and others. The composition of subsystems organized around family functions is not nearly as significant as the clarity of subsystem boundaries. (Minuchin, 1974, p. 54)

The application of family systems theory to organizations is useful[1] and can provide insight into both families and organizations. Unfortunately, Ms. Nichols and Ms. Peterson have chosen to ignore some of the theory in favor of an analogy between "dysfunctional families" and organizations with administrators who focus "on only the client." Furthermore, although they begin with this promising analogy, what follows does not address the possibility that managers' direct involvement with some client-oriented activities does not always result in an exclusive focus on clients, nor in the neglect of managerial responsibilities. In Minuchin's terms, Ms. Nichols and Ms. Peterson present a good argument for maintaining clear boundaries between the managerial and street-level sub-systems. They fail to explain, however, why these boundaries do not remain clear when crossed by managers, especially while they support the crossing of boundaries by workers to participate in management-oriented activities.

We do seem to agree that well-functioning organizations must have clear boundaries between their subsystems. (Indeed, much of the work I quote argues for designing organizations based on clear divisions between the work performed and the contingencies faced by those functioning in different levels.) However, while I consider the ability to maintain clear boundaries a prerequisite for usefully involving managers in client-oriented activities, Ms. Nichols and Ms. Peterson seem to believe the reverse: lack of managerial involvement is a prerequisite for maintaining clear boundaries. Thus, they tend to reject managers' involvement in street-level tasks under all circumstances.

In doing so, they exclude from practice one of the most powerful means of intraorganizational communication. Notwithstanding the advantages of the communication methods outlined by Ms. Nichols and Ms. Peterson, the worlds of street-level workers and clients cannot be more effectively understood by managers except by entering them more directly. These managers must remember that the purpose of "zooming" is to sensitize them to the needs of workers and clients; the response to this reality, however, must be managerial; that is, broader and more abstract. Just as a parent would gain in understanding if he or she could briefly experience life again as a child, so too will managers who take time to experience the life of workers and clients not stop being managers—they will become better for it.

ENDNOTES

1. In particular, when the differences between families and organizations are taken into consideration. For application and discussion of some of the

differences between families and organizations see Hirschhorn (1978) and Hirschhorn and Gilmore (1980).

REFERENCES

Hirschhorn, L. (1978). The stalemated agency: A theoretical perspective and a practical proposal. *Administration in Social Work, 2,* 425–438.

Hirschhorn, L., & Gilmore, T. (1980). The application of family therapy concepts to influencing organizational behavior. *Administrative Science Quarterly, 25,* 18–37.

Minuchin, S. (1974). *Families and family therapy.* Cambridge, MA: Harvard University Press.

Should Marketing Techniques Replace Traditional Planning and Coordinating Methods in the Design and Development of Programs?

EDITOR'S NOTE: Human service organizations increasingly are using marketing concepts and tools to improve and expand services. Yet there exists within the profession a discomfort with the language and techniques of marketing. Some argue that the language of marketing distorts the mission and goals of human service organizations by replacing social work principles and values with business principles and values. Referring to clients as consumers or customers and to agency services as product lines suggests transformation and empowerment, but in reality does not ensure that the organization is more sensitive to or aware of client needs. Others argue for a strategic social marketing approach that recognizes the many stakeholders in agency programs, and as a result programs are designed to meet a range of interests. This debate is timely and relevant as more human service organizations find themselves being pushed by both internal and external forces to adopt marketing strategies. The following questions are central to this debate: Are marketing concepts new or are they well-established principles of planning and administration? Does the application of marketing techniques to the delivery of human services ensure more effective service delivery? Will the combination of strategic management and marketing orientation lead to greater success and survival among human service organizations?

Armand Lauffer, Ph.D., says YES. He is author of *Strategic Marketing for Not-for-Profit Organizations, Grantsmanship, Working in Social Work,* and more than a dozen other texts dealing with planning, resource development, and community organization. Dr. Lauffer is Professor of Social Work at the University of Michigan where he directs Project STaR (Service, Training, and Research in Jewish Communal Development).

E. Allan Brawley, D.S.W., argues NO. He is Professor of Social Work at Arizona State University West. The author of four books and over forty book chapters and articles in his various areas of professional interest, he is currently working on a new book on the use of the mass media to promote human well-being.

YES

Armand Lauffer

The Problem Is the Problem

A problem with traditional approaches to social planning and services coordination is that they tend to assume that if a problem can be well-defined, alternative interventions can be explored and the efforts and resources of those in agreement can then be concerted towards goal attainment. So what's the problem? Focusing on problems diverts attention from the interests of consumers and other stakeholders in the enterprise and reduces the likelihood of innovation.

The Marketing Imagination

About fifteen years ago, the executive staff of Black and Decker, finding itself with a shrinking share of the market for low-cost power tools, did some stock taking. Once it defined the corporation's primary business as making "household tools," the staff was free to explore creating a whole new line of tools for a market Black and Decker was not yet identified with, the kitchen tool user. To find out what might make Black and Decker products more attractive than those distributed by GE, Phillips, Hamilton-Beach, Oster, and Braun, they asked potential consumers a simple question: "What do you need more of in the kitchen?" The answer was equally simple: "More counter space."

Black and Decker accommodated by building toaster ovens, coffee makers, can openers, and other tools that could be hung from the upper cabinets rather than placed on the counter tops. Now, for $30 a consumer could buy $300 worth of counter space and have a new appliance as a bonus. A more traditional planning approach might have focused on problems consumers were facing in the workshop. At best, some of Black and Decker's current tools might have been redesigned and a line of higher priced semiprofessional power tools might have been added. The kitchen tools opportunity would have been missed.

Are there parallels in the nonprofit world, in social agencies, and other settings? Certainly. Homebuilders, an agency that provides intensive and comprehensive services to families for concentrated periods, demonstrated how services could be redesigned to articulate with consumer needs and interests while reducing the demand for service from other providers. JEFF (Jewish Experiences for Families), a sectarian agency in Detroit, recognized that when wives and husbands both work, few hours are left over for quality "family time." By developing camp weekends and holiday workshops in collaboration with synagogues and social agencies, JEFF responded both to consumer interests and to the needs of other organizations to serve their members better. In each example, planners began by examining the interests and capacities of consumers and other "publics."

The Strategic Social Marketing Approach

"Publics" make up one of the "Five Ps of strategic social marketing." There are four others: products, price, place, and promotions. By publics, I mean all those individuals, groups, and organizations on which an agency is dependent or with which it is interdependent. Some, like the paid and volunteer staff, are internal to the organization; others are external. These include: resource suppliers; legitimators (e.g., boards of directors and government licensing bureaus); and other service providers with whom they share consumers, board members, facilities, service programs, staff, and even budgets.

An agency's products are generally defined as tangible services and other activities conducted by staff and volunteers and offered to a consuming public. Frequently, they are grouped into departments by age (from preschoolers to seniors) or function (such as child placement, mental health, culture). These groupings comprise the agency's service programs, or *product lines* (in marketing terms). A Black and Decker electric drill is a product, its total array of low-cost power tools for the workshop makes up a product line. But products can also be defined more intangibly. If the toaster or coffee maker make up part of Black and Decker's product line, why is it that the firm sold consumers on a reasonable way of getting more counter space? Is service delivery what a neighborhood center is all about, or is it raising the quality community of life?

The term place most often refers to the geographic location of a service agency or the area from which clients and other resources are drawn. For example, mental health centers are mandated to provide services to residents of designated catchment areas, but some may seek clients from other locales to maintain programs that could otherwise not be justified on the basis of local demand and funding from agencies even further removed. In some cases, such as meals-on-wheels for the elderly and infirm, an agency's services are located outside the building as a matter of design.

Alternatively, it may decide to offer a hot lunch program in a central facility to dispel the loneliness that accompanies isolation. Should this be promoted as a nutrition program, or as an opportunity to participate in community? The answer may depend on whom one is trying to reach: the elderly themselves, volunteers to provide transportation, or funders to subsidize costs.

Promotion refers to the persuasive communication that takes place between producers and distributors and their various publics. It could include advertising new services, consciousness raising about community needs, or generating support for the agency itself. Some organizations, like a city bus line that serves a broad public with similar interests (in getting to where they want to go conveniently, cheaply, and safely), may employ a relatively undifferentiated promotional approach. Often, however, it may be necessary to reach different segments of the public for specific services. For example, a family planning clinic would use one approach to reach pregnant teens and another to attract infertile married couples. This requires a process of targeting specific market segments.

Segmenting the Market

Market segmentation generally refers to a process of partitioning the consumer and supplier markets according to some criteria that are useful in determining levels of demand for specific products. By catering to different markets, each with somewhat unique characteristics, it becomes possible to design more effective programs and to adjust demand on the basis of price and place, cost and distribution. Agencies do this all the time, when they design some programs for the aged and others for children, some for all the residents of the community and others for those who live in specific neighborhoods, or those for consumers with different tastes and social backgrounds.

Markets can be segmented geographically, demographically, and psychographically. For example, although a neighborhood center may wish to attract members from a limited geographic area, it may recruit participants more broadly for its cultural or sports programs and expand beyond the city limits when seeking competent staff and volunteers. Programs and services are often designed for populations with different demographic characteristics (e.g., age, levels of education, family status, numbers of children, income, ethnic identity, years in the community).

Psychographic characteristics include life-styles, patterns of social behavior and "user status" (i.e., some participants are regulars, some are seasonal, and others one-time users). By creating descriptions of "target markets" composed of individuals who have interests and capacities in common, it is then possible to target both programs and promotions more realistically.

Managing Demand

I use the terms *interests* and *capacities* purposefully. Together they make up what market analysts call *demand*. Demand is an interest in something backed up by a capacity to act on that interest. The marketing challenge is to increase or decrease either interest or capacity or to redefine interest in terms of the products or product lines the firm or agency produces. For example, when Black and Decker found that consumers were interested in counter space but did not have the capacity to act on that interest (at least not at the cost of $300/foot), it created a new product line that reduced the cost (increasing consumer capacity to act on their interests) while creating demand for the products that Black and Decker was able to produce. It was not necessary for the firm to redefine its mission in terms of carpentry and home remodeling. Service agencies can work much the same way, if they have a well-developed marketing imagination.

To be successful, however, voluntary agencies and nonprofit entities must make the appropriate linkages between the demands expressed by its various publics. For example, it does not make sense to encourage demand for a home handyman service if the family service agency is unable to secure external sources of financial support to subsidize the program, if it cannot recruit volunteers to provide the necessary service, or if staff find the new program threatening or otherwise unattractive.

Demand, however, is rarely static. To understand this, it might be helpful to use some ''qualifiers.'' For example, we can speak of actual or potential demand and of full, faltering, excessive, or insufficient demand. Actual demand is reflected in what consumers, funders, auspice providers, and staff want in relation to participating in or supporting a program. Potential demand reflects an assessment of what they would do if they were interested or had the capacity to do it. When there is capacity but no interest (say on the part of potential concert goers or funders), the marketing challenge is to increase interest in the agency's programs.

When the interest exists but consumers do not have the capacity to act on it in terms of time, money, or other resources, then the marketing challenge is to reduce the cost in time and dollars, to increase program benefits, or to redesign a program to make it more accessible. For example, if there is no way for clients to come to a program at the agency because of the unavailability of bus service, the marketing challenge might be met by offering private transportation, subsidizing cab fares, or relocating the program. When the capacity exists (say, for occupational aptitude) but interest is low, the marketing challenge may to increase awareness of a program's benefits or to redesign it so as to increase interest (for example, by adding job placement services to a job training program).

This is an important point. It shifts the emphasis away from the agency or its programs and to the interests and capacities of the consumer and other key publics. This is totally consistent with social work values and community organizing principles.

What Distinguishes Strategic Social Marketing?

The recognition that many publics may have stakes in an agency's programs and services and the development of programs that directly address those interests is what distinguishes strategic social marketing from other approaches to social planning and program development. There is a tendency on the part of some human service workers to complain that they can't do their jobs because funders are too stingy, the board is unimaginative, or clients are unaware of what they really need. That, of course, is just one perception of reality. Those with the marketing imagination see things differently.

It is just because each of these publics expects something different that we can find new opportunities for program development and resources for program coordination. If we can effectively address the issue of interest and capacity (demand) among staff, consumers, funders, legitimators, and others with whom our organizations are interdependent, we can begin to free up the marketing imagination to create new products and to find the resources needed to support their development and delivery. Traditional social planning, by focusing on problems and their amelioration may be inadequate to uncover the interests and capacities of the stakeholders in the enterprise.

REFERENCES

Fine, S. H. (Ed.). (1990). *Social marketing: Promoting the causes of public and nonprofit agencies.* Boston: Allyn and Bacon.

Kotler, P., & Andreason, A. (1991). *Strategic marketing for nonprofit organizations,* 4th edition. Englewood Cliffs, NJ: Prentice-Hall.

Lauffer, A. (1984). *Strategic marketing for not-for-profit organizations: Program and resource development.* New York: The Free Press.

Rejoinder to Professor Lauffer
E. ALLEN BRAWLEY

Professor Lauffer presents a strong argument for the advantages of adopting a marketing approach in place of established social planning methods. Based on the arguments and examples that he presents (and elaborated in the substantial literature on this topic, to which he is a significant contributor, and some of which we have both cited), a case can probably be made that macro social workers should become familiar with the ways in which marketing concepts and techniques might contribute to their practice. What advocates of marketing usually fail to do, however, is articulate its limitations and pitfalls. The individual or organization engaged in social service delivery who is considering the adoption of a marketing approach needs to be aware not only of its potential but also its problems. Therefore, the following remarks constitute a cautionary commentary on Professor Lauffer's presentation.

First of all, despite what Professor Lauffer suggests, there is no reason why social planners, community organizers, or social agency administrators should be more preoccupied with problems than the marketer. On the contrary, all available evidence suggests that the marketer, in hot pursuit of profitable opportunities for action is more apt to be single-minded or tunnel-visioned. The social planner who does not engage in environmental scanning or needs assessment activities is simply not a competent practitioner, and the one who does not constantly look for and regularly come up with innovative and proactive approaches to client/ community/public needs is simply not being very creative.

Designating an agency's services or programs as products or product lines, referring to clients as consumers or customers (as some social marketers do), and reconceptualizing (or more accurately renaming) certain social agency system elements and functions to conform to the language of marketing is an interesting conceptual exercise, but it does not necessarily lead to a transformation of those elements into something else nor does it automatically lead to better agency performance. However, what the change of terminology does is to risk obscuring the essential differences between the market-driven profit-oriented business enterprise and the social service organization which, by necessity, operates outside that arena. After all, if the market were absolutely efficient in distributing goods and services, there would be no need for social welfare programs and services. Over the last decade or so, a concerted and largely successful effort has been made by conservatives in this country and elsewhere to reassert the supremacy of the market, at great cost to the social services and their clients. Buying into that ethos, even if only linguistically, not only distorts reality, but also affirms the appropriateness of market mechanisms in the social welfare arena and does a disservice to clients, communities, and publics that have not been well-served by the unfettered market.

In the world of human services marketing, clients become consumers and sometimes customers. The impression given is that they are somehow empowered by this transformation. This seems to have something to do with the idea that in the marketplace the customer reigns supreme and may be linked to the consumer movement. However, this is a cruel joke on the frail elderly consumer of nursing home care whose care is being purchased by the state under its Medicaid program. Even less empowered by being called a consumer is the person or family who uses the local food bank or homeless shelter. That most social service organizations should and can be more client-oriented than they are there can be no argument. That a social service organization that adopts marketing concepts and language will be more sensitive to clients (the most valuable and the least profitable, in particular) than one that does not is doubtful.

Marketers are consumption-oriented rather then consumer-oriented; that is, they are more interested in promoting consumption of their products than in responding to the actual needs of the public, including the consumers of their products. In the best case, the two goals coincide but it is important to remember which has primacy. Why else would the business world devote such time, expense, and effort to convince us to consume what we patently do not need?

Lauffer blithely talks about "market segmentation" and "managing demand" and gives hypothetical examples of how these concepts might apply in the human services. However, it is important to note that it is also possible to cite more pernicious examples of these strategies. Hospitals, specialized rehabilitation facilities, and other health care providers have been among the earliest and most sophisticated exponents of marketing in the human services. For example, some hospitals have pioneered such market segmentation strategies as targeting affluent health care consumers by offering deluxe accommodations, gourmet meals, and other customer inducements, and a substantial portion of the nursing home industry is well-versed in managing demand by not accepting Medicaid patients, setting a quota on the number of such patients, or only accommodating them when the demand by higher-paying target consumers is insufficient.

To suggest that competent social planners, community organizers, and social service administrators ignore or are insensitive to the interests of such stakeholders as staff, consumers, funding sources, and legitimating bodies unless they are prodded into a higher consciousness of their environment by the tools of marketing simply does not square with reality. Those who might manifest the type of tunnel vision suggested by Lauffer are clearly not familiar with or skilled in sound macro social work practice principles. Unfortunately, it is these self-same people who, in turning to marketing to bail them out of the predicament that has resulted from their myopia, are most likely to be unaware or careless of the pitfalls of this approach.

NO

E. ALLAN BRAWLEY

Two decades ago, human service organizations responded to political attack and reductions in funding for social programs and services by adopting the tools and techniques of the economist and accountant. Social work administrators, social planners, and policy analysts jumped on the efficiency bandwagon and set about trying to "do more with less" without much awareness of the limitations of the technology involved (Patti, 1975) or the consequences of allowing themselves to be driven by the efficiency ethos (Hasenfeld, 1984; Gruber, 1991). Now, primarily in response to the same resource constraints, we are being urged to adopt the tools of marketing without much consideration of the limitations of that technology or the consequences of adopting it. The fact that the marketing arm of the commercial world is largely responsible for our being as consumption-obsessed, wasteful, and debt-ridden a society as we are should give us pause.

Strictly speaking, marketing theory is derived from economics rather than management science (Kerr & Littlefield, 1974) and, as such, it can be useful in illuminating the exchanges that take place between the funders and producers of human services and the consumers of these services. Attempts to apply these basic economic exchange principles to the human services are linked to recent moves to privatize a wide range of public services (Pritchard, 1976). The idea is that rewarding organizations for results rather than simply funding services will improve organizational performance. Philip Kotler (1975), the leading proponent of this approach in the not-for-profit sector, and his disciples have convinced many universities, hospitals, and human service organizations to view marketing as an essential management tool. A burgeoning marketing literature has appeared in social work and related human service fields in recent years (e.g., Lauffer, 1984; Winston, 1984) and this seems likely to continue to grow. However, before embracing it wholeheartedly, and certainly before discarding established social planning, administrative, and organizational practices, we need to take a hard look at the limitations of marketing and the ethical baggage it brings with it.

In the first place, how comfortable can we be with a technology that has a history and public perception of being exploitative and manipulative? How much confidence can be placed in a technology whose practitioners are urged, without tongue in check, to test their aptitude for a career in that field by taking the Mach (Machiavelli) Test, which gives high ratings to people who believe strongly that "the best way to handle people is to tell them what they want to hear," "it is hard to get ahead without cutting corners here and there," and "never tell anyone the real reason you did something unless it is useful to do so." Other questions in this vein require strong positive agreement if one is to be judged suitable for a career in marketing. On the other hand, persons agreeing that "honesty is the best policy," that "you should take action only when you are sure it is morally right," "there is no excuse for lying to someone else," or that "all in all, it is better to be humble and honest than important and dishonest" are urged to consider a different career from marketing—in the clergy perhaps (McIver, 1987, pp. 27–40). While this may be an example of the marketing mentality at its worst, it is by no means exceptional, as the following sampling of recent marketing publication titles reveals: *Marketing Warfare* (Ries & Trout, 1986), *Pursuing Customers* (Prus, 1989), *Street Smart Marketing* (Slutsky, 1989), *How to Create Your Own Fad and Make a Million Dollars* (Hakuta, 1988), *Market Smarts: Proven Strategies to Outfox and Outflank Your Competition* (McGrath, 1988), *Marketing Immunity: Breaking through Customer Resistance* (Lazarus & Wexler, 1988). These examples are not gleaned from the supermarket book section, the airport bookstore, or the pages of the sleazier mail-order book catalogs. These are textbooks and practitioner guides gracing the shelves of the library of a major university with a nationally ranked business school. Furthermore, the content of these publications does not diverge greatly from the content of marketing textbooks with more sedate titles. The only obvious difference is that the authors of these luridly titled books are simply practicing what many of the others are preaching.

In spite of abundant evidence to the contrary, we are urged to regard the tools of marketing as value-free. Proponents of marketing in the human services claim that it can be used for socially useful as well as socially corrosive purposes. However, twenty-five years ago, a repentant marketing executive lamented that, among the end results of the exercise of the techniques of his profession, "We spend more on packaging than on schools, more on advertising than on education, more on sales promotion than on health services" (Fisher, 1968, p. 108). What evidence is there that this situation has changed for the better in the last two decades, and can we really afford to disregard these kinds of issues?

If marketing is simply calling well-established social planning and administrative functions by new names derived from the business administration literature, the central question is why this is necessary. Do we simply desire to appear more businesslike? For example, does renaming the intake unit of an agency "customer service," as has occurred in some British Social Services Departments in recent years (Cumbria, 1988), result in improved intake services for clients or give clients a different image of the organization? There is no evidence to suggest that it does. If, on the other hand, the intent is to bring about significant changes in organizational practices by substituting those more common in the commercial world than in the social services, then one needs to be cautious at the very least. "If all a nonprofit organization accomplishes by the application of marketing is to become more market driven, as opposed to becoming more effective in helping the society or the community with needed services or ideas, then that nonprofit organization is not meeting its obligation to serve the public good" (Bates, 1991, p. 110).

Marketing has come to the fore in the human services in an era of severe fiscal constraint and fierce competition for available funds, and it has been promoted as a particularly valuable tool for helping financially stressed organizations survive in this type of environment. However, it is precisely under these conditions that the negative characteristics of marketing are most likely to be in evidence. Health and social welfare organizations that turn to marketing as a survival strategy are the ones most likely to be driven by the same profit motives characteristic of the commercial sector and are least likely to resist opportunism, goal displacement, and competitive behavior that is detrimental to existing community networks of care.

The proponents of marketing in the human services generally use the term to mean a comprehensive planning strategy that often encompasses a range of established social planning, community organization, and social service administration concepts such as needs assessment, resource generation, client participation, public relations, program development, and the like but that packages them in a new way, using the language of the business administration specialty of marketing (Lauffer, 1984; Stoner, 1986). At its most innocuous, this may serve to freshen up some old and perhaps tired social planning concepts. However, to the degree that it successfully promotes the replacement of social work principles and practices with business principles and practices there are dangers for the unwary. It both promises more than it can deliver and pushes macro social work practice in a direction that may not be compatible with its central mission and core values.

On the one hand, the language we use is significant. It colors our own views of what we are about and also sends signals to others—supporters, community, and clients—about our values and goals. While the adoption of the jargon of marketing might communicate a more businesslike approach to administering programs and meeting customer/consumer/client needs, it can just as easily be read as signifying a more self-serving, slick, and profit-oriented organization.

On the other hand, going beyond simple linguistic tinkering is fraught with even greater danger because it involves the adoption of new technology which may or may not be appropriate or useful. As already noted, technology is not value-neutral since it is imbued with the values that motivated its development and, as Hasenfeld (1983) has cautioned, the technology used in human service organizations "must be morally justified because every activity related to clients has significant moral consequences" (p. 9).

Proponents of marketing in the health and social welfare field frequently equate it with social planning and the way the topic of this chapter is framed reflects this thinking. However, strictly speaking, market mechanisms and social planning procedures are in principle antithetical or at least contain inherent contradictions. While it is possible to mask or mute these contradictions, they keep cropping up. Reisch and Wenocur (1986) have observed that "The current crisis in the unfinished welfare state results, in part, from the need of the socioeconomic system to reproduce the relations of production in all phases of social life (e.g., the emphasis on competition as opposed to cooperation and the treatment of all goods and services as if they were commodities)" (p. 74). Using the tools of the market in the social planning/community organization/agency administration arena might be rationalized as an attempt to fight fire with fire, but a more likely explanation is that it represents yet another indicator of how far we have gone in ceding the battle for comprehensive social welfare services to the unfettered forces of market capitalism.

Several years ago, Reichert (1982) observed that we were approaching the final stages of a relatively long-term process that has resulted in "the ascendancy of market capitalism over the cushioning influence of a partly realized welfare state" (p. 173). This has been accompanied by "the direct intrusion of the market system and its ideology into the human services" (p. 173). He noted that the provision of a wide range of personal social services on a fee-for-services basis has grown into a veritable cottage industry that increasingly resembles traditional fee-for-service medical care. Contemporaneously with this trend, private not-for-profit health and welfare organizations have begun to use business marketing practices in such a way that they mimic the behavior of the commercial sector "in the way that they piece together services with no other purpose than getting a piece of the action" (p. 174). These developments are taking place without regard to their negative impact on comprehensive service planning efforts, not to mention what Reichert sees as the inevitable "distortion of humanistic values under market conditions" (p. 175). Using marketing techniques to plan services, develop resources, and target consumers is fraught with pitfalls and consequences for human service organizations and client groups that are sometimes overlooked or, at least, are only beginning to be understood.

For example, the pursuit of entrepreneurial marketing strategies has led many health and welfare organizations to target market segments or niches that do not include social work's primary client groups. This has happened most obviously in the medical field (Kronenfeld, Baker, & Amidon, 1989) but is certainly not limited to this sector (Hasenfeld, 1984, p. 525). In the health care field, "there is . . . evidence that 'product lines' and 'markets' are altered in response to the fiscal constraints of DRG's. Hospitals appear to increase the services that are more profitable (surgical services) and, simultaneously, they attempt to move into the unregulated market" (Gruber, 1991, p. 185). Within that unregulated market, some hospitals target well-heeled private-pay patients or those consumers with "cadillac" medical insurance coverage (Super, 1986).

This type of goal displacement occurs when the resource-development and consumer-targeting aspects of marketing replace or distort the core service mission or goals of the organization. The agency becomes a straw in the winds generated by funding sources and sectional or profitable consumer demand.

In the current fiscal environment, when there are almost irresistible incentives for human service organizations to go after the most lucrative markets or compete with each other for any potential source of funds, an operating principal of "beggar thy neighbor" is likely to apply, in that some organizations are left to make do with less and at the same time are expected to serve the least attractive and least remunerative but perhaps most needy sectors of the market. This is a situation in which the most skilled exponents of marketing are likely to prosper but, unfortunately, "successful marketing of social work programs does not automatically advance health or well-being or promote the equitable and wise use of public dollars" (Kane, 1982, p. 171). A critical issue, then, is how we can be assured that the adoption of marketing strategies will be used to help us more adequately address pressing individual, family, group, and community needs rather than simply directing us to where the money is and where the markets for specific services are.

We have no solid evidence to believe that marketing technology is more effective in achieving macro social work goals than existing social planning, organizing, and administrative methods. Other than the fact that it is yet another technology emanating from the business world, with its aura of rationality, effectiveness, and efficiency, there is limited justification for its present strong appeal. Especially in light of the ethical and other questions that surround marketing practices in the commercial sector and the undesirable consequences of the use of marketing techniques already evident in segments of the health and human service fields, we need more convincing evidence of its usefulness and appropriateness as an alternative to the more established planning, administrative, and coordinating mechanisms in the social welfare field.

REFERENCES

Bates, D. (1991, January). Review of *Social marketing: Strategies for changing public behavior* by P. Kotler and E. L. Roberto (New York: Free Press, 1989) and *Social marketing: Promoting the causes of public and nonprofit agencies* by Seymour H. Fine (Needham, MA: Allyn and Bacon, 1990). *Journal of Marketing, 55*(1), pp. 108–110.

Cumbria Social Services Department (1988). *Care in Cumbria: Developing social services for the 1990s.* Carlisle, England: Cumbria County Council, Social Services Department.

Fisher, J. (1968). *The plot to make you buy.* New York: McGraw-Hill.

Gruber, M. L. (1991, Spring-Summer). In and out of the rabbit hole with Alice: Assessing the consequences of efficiency prescriptions. *Administration in Social Work, 15*(1 & 2), pp. 175–192.

Hakuta, K. (1988). *How to create your own fad and make a million dollars.* New York: Morrow.

Hasenfeld, Y. (1983). *Human service organizations.* Englewood Cliffs, NJ: Prentice-Hall.

Hasenfeld, Y. (1984, November–December). The changing context of human services administration. *Social Work, 29*(6), pp. 522–529.

Kane, R. A. (1982, August). Editorial-entrepreneurs. *Health and Social Work, 7*(3), pp. 170–171.

Kerr, J. R., & Littlefield, J. E. (1974). *Marketing: An environmental approach.* Englewood Cliffs, NJ: Prentice-Hall.

Kotler, P. (1975). *Marketing for non-profit organizations.* Englewood Cliffs, NJ: Prentice-Hall.

Kronenfeld, J. J., Baker, S. L., & Amidon, R. L. (1989, March). An appraisal of organizational response to fiscally constraining regulation: The case of hospitals and DRGs. *Journal of Health and Social Behavior, 30*(1), pp. 41–55.

Lauffer, A. (1984). *Strategic marketing for not-for-profit organizations: Program and resource development.* New York: Free Press.

Lazarus, G., & Wexler, B. (1988). *Marketing immunity: Breaking through customer resistance.* Homewood, IL: Dow Jones-Irwin.

McGrath, A. J. (1988). *Market smarts: Proven strategies to outfox and outflank your competition.* New York: Wiley.

McIver, C. (1987). *The marketing mirage: How to make it a reality.* New York: Nichols Publishing.

Patti, R. J. (1975, Spring). The new scientific management: Systems management for social welfare. *Public Welfare, 33*(2), pp. 23–31.

Pritchard, A. (1976). *Alternatives to public service.* Washington, DC: National League of Cities.

Prus, R. C. (1989). *Pursuing customers: An ethnography of marketing activities.* Newbury Park, CA: Sage Publications.

Reichert, K. (1982, August). Human services and the market system. *Health and Social Work, 7*(3), pp. 173–182.

Reisch, M., & Wenocur, S. (1986, March). The future of community organization in social work: Social activism and the politics of professional building. *Social Service Review, 60*(1), pp. 70–93.

Ries, A., & Trout, J. (1986). *Marketing warfare.* New York: McGraw-Hill.

Slutsky, J. (1989). *Street smart marketing.* New York: Wiley.

Stoner, M. R. (1986, Winter). Marketing of social services gains prominence in practice. *Administration in Social Work, 10*(4), pp. 41–52.

Super, K. E. (1986). Tampa General changes image to attract private-pay patients. *Modern Healthcare, 16*(6), pp. 52–56.

Winston, W. S. (Ed.) (1984). *Marketing for mental health services.* New York: Haworth Press.

Rejoinder to Professor Brawley   ARMAND LAUFFER

In 1969, at the height of the "People's Park" confrontations, I taught a course on the "tools of planning" at Berkeley. Among the tools taught were, PERT, Delphi, and Functional Job Analysis. I was expecting a challenge, and I got it. "How could you, a social worker, push tools developed by and for the military industrial complex?" I was asked. PERT, as you may know, was used to coordinate efforts that led to launching the first nuclear submarine. Delphi was pioneered by the Rand Corporation to anticipate defense needs. FJA was first used to redefine job descriptions when the old Army Air Corps was converted to the United States Air Force during WWII.

Fortunately, I was prepared for the question. Without saying anything, I took a hammer and picture frame out of my brief case and smashed the frame to pieces. I then reached down, took out a few nails and a fresh piece of glass and proceeded to put it all back together again. "Interesting about hammers," I observed. "The first one ever used was probably a club or tomahawk. A cousin of mine uses a more precise tool for gem cutting." The message was clear. Misuse or abuse is no reason to abandon a useful tool; nor should a tool's origin obscure its social utility. These are precisely the points that Professor Brawley misses in both his concept paper and rejoinder to mine.

By focusing on what he perceives to be a consumption-oriented profit motive in business marketing, Brawley obscures their meaning in social marketing. Substitute dictionary synonyms like "use" for the term "consumption" or "benefit" for the word "profit" and you'll understand how meanings can be twisted by negative association. Incidentally, I used neither of these terms in my paper, although I did refer to the "nonprofit" world. But I have no difficulty with them. In business terms, the profit motive is defined as "enlightened self-interest" and often begins and ends with consideration of the entrepreneur's or business firm's interests.

But in social marketing, self-interest, while always present, is not central to program or product development. Public or social interest are. And when we think of profit as a benefit that exceeds the cost of production and distribution, we are also forced to address the question of whose interests. These, I suggest, include the many publics whose interests are at stake: consumers or users, funders and other resource suppliers, auspice providers, producers (staff and volunteers), partners (in program development and delivery), and the general public. No program is likely to be successful or long-standing if it does not articulate with the interests and capacities of each of these stakeholders. Citing abuse and misuse or focusing on the narrow self-interests of abusers denies the utility of a powerful complex of tools.

Brawley's paper is scholarly and extensively referenced. Interestingly, it includes virtually no references to social planning. Had he chosen to draw on the planning literature, the chances are he might have referred to articles by people like Richard Bolan, James March, Charles Lindblom, John Friedmann, Barclay Hudson, and others whose work derives from the fields of urban and economic planning. We have, over the years, integrated this literature into social work and social planning, just as we have made effective use of the tools created, as my students pointed out, by and for the military industrial complex. What makes it so difficult for us to adapt and integrate the most powerful tools of the business world?

Can Administrative Controls and Pressure for Efficiency and Effectiveness Be Balanced with the Staff's Demand for Decentralization and Participation?

EDITOR'S NOTE: Social service organizations often seek to maintain the existing service delivery system by use of centralized administrative control. By centralizing decision-making authority, it can be argued that administrators are better able to hold staff accountable and can control the variations in service delivery that affect efficiency and effectiveness. However, system maintenance is challenged by the demand for system change. These demands can result from external changes in the social, economic, or political environments or from internal changes in how staff view the workplace. The demand for change in social service agencies is increasing as these organizations are asked to do more with fewer resources, manage more complicated social problems brought by clients, and respond to outside pressures to demonstrate the effectiveness of services quickly. The tensions felt by staff and administrators who confront the demand for organizational change have led some to use a centralized management model and others to acknowledge the need for a participatory management model. Thus, the two questions that frame this debate center on whether conflicts of interest are inherent in the relations between staff and agency administrators and on which management approach is most functional for ensuring accountability and service effectiveness on the part of staff.

Dr. Jean Kantambu Latting says YES. She is an associate professor at the Graduate School of Social Work, University of Houston. She received an M.S. from the Columbia University School of Social Work and a Dr. P.H. from the

Department of Health Administration, School of Public Health, University of North Carolina. Her area of specialization is organizational behavior and change with a subspecialty in cultural diversity in the workplace. She conducts research and provides training and consultation services to human service organizations on participatory management and managing change. From 1989 through 1992, she was the principal investigator of a National Science Foundation grant on intrinsic and extrinsic work motivation.

Burton Gummer, Ph.D., argues NO. Dr. Gummer is a professor in the School of Social Welfare, Nelson A. Rockefeller College of Public Affairs and Policy, The University at Albany, State University of New York. He is the author of *The Politics of Social Administration* and a number of articles on social welfare administration and planning. His "Notes from the Management Literature" is a regular feature of *Administration in Social Work.*

YES

JEAN KANTAMBU LATTING

The debate question juxtaposes two management philosophies. On the one hand, some people view centralized management as a mechanism to ensure accountability and thereby increase efficiency and effectiveness. Others believe that decentralized, participatory management may increase staff creativity and provide a more humane quality of work life. Advocates also insist that decentralization and participation will increase, not decrease, organizational effectiveness.

I support participatory management as a method for increasing the quality of worklife *and* organizational effectiveness for three reasons: (1) participatory management enables organizations to use more fully their staffs' knowledge about rapidly changing environmental conditions and emergent client needs; (2) it discourages burnout and encourages greater intrinsic motivation toward improved job performance; and (3) it promotes peer support for accountability, increased service coordination, and effective services delivery.

Before explaining these three reasons, I will clarify some terms and provide a case example of participatory management. Levels of *participation* may vary from input by employees with managers retaining final decision making authority, through shared decision making between managers and employees, to transfer of decision-making authority to employees. Managers may transfer decisions to lower-level employees by either *decentralization* (lowering the hierarchical level for specific decisions) or *delegation* (giving employees the authority to make decisions). Although mere input is technically a form of participation, most employees feel that their input does not constitute true participation if their advice is ignored repeatedly. Consequently, throughout this essay, I refer to participation as shared or transferred decision making at either the individual job level or in broader organizational decision making.

A Case Example

Inspired by one of my management classes and Peter Block's book, *The Empowered Manager,* a former student who is a unit supervisor in a large public human services organization decided to reconstitute her unit as a self-managing work team. After overcoming initial opposition from her supervisor, she formulated a plan and introduced it to her unit. Her innovations included inverting the organizational pyramid and reframing her role from manager of the unit to its consultant; promoting feedback from subordinates about her performance as a manager, peer review of each other, and team review of all applicants to the unit; developing a unit mission statement that included guidelines on how they would operate in her absence, valuing the primacy of client service; and scheduling regular unit meetings and review of all procedures for their relevance to their work.

After she overcame staff's initial skepticism and convinced them that she indeed was sincere, the unit began problem solving with a gusto. The results have been dramatic. Based on the criteria that they developed to measure their internal effectiveness as well as the organization's productivity measures, the unit is now one of the top performers in the region. The manager has been invited to present to other units and other regions on how she accomplished it. Her greatest disappointment is the resistance voiced by other supervisors who insisted that she would "lose too much control" if she persisted in her efforts.

Her story is not unique. I know others including a regional manager in a nonprofit legal services organization who have instituted reforms with similar results. Why did her approach work?

• *Participatory management enables organizations to use more fully their staff's knowledge about rapidly changing environmental conditions and emergent client needs.* Centralized, hierarchical management was formulated as a system of management in this country during the early twentieth century when environmental conditions were relatively stable and job tasks were routine. To maximize production in the nation's factories, classical management theorists (as they are now called) formulated such principles as division of labor and specialization of tasks, hierarchy of authority and unity of command ("one man, one boss"), clearly delineated rules and procedures, and impartial performance appraisal. The underlying assumptions of these principles were that people are economically, not intrinsically, motivated; rules and regulations are needed to control employee behavior; and "higher-ups" have greater knowledge than their employees and may anticipate problems in advance.

Seven decades later, the conditions under which those principles were salient no longer exist. Much of the work performed in today's human service organizations (HSOs) is far from routine and requires professional staff capable of exercising independent judgment. Further, HSOs operate in political and socioeconomic environments that are notoriously turbulent (Hasenfeld, 1983). HSOs that rely solely on top managers and their boards to act as sensors on emergent needs and opportunities are likely to deprive themselves of valuable resources within their own employees. Staffs at all levels are likely to have access to information about the changing needs of the community, changing foci of related organizations, areas for potential cost savings or income, and possible political minefields.

• *Participatory management discourages burnout and encourages greater intrinsic motivation towards improved job performance.* American businesses today are responding to the challenge of declining national productivity, increased international competition, and an educated work force by cutting hierarchical levels and implementing participatory management. Ironically, while the private sector is eagerly seeking information on how to employ their staffs' skills and knowledge more fully, HSOs are responding to recent demands for greater accountability by increased centralization, expanded reporting requirements for employees, and additional rules and regulations.

In organizations that try to tighten controls over staff, employees resist and may bypass regulations so that a client may qualify for services, display disenchantment with senior management, and engage in internal conflicts between service-providing units and those responsible for managerial controls. The result is burnout, which in turn leads to withdrawal and insensitivity to client needs. This tug of war occurs partially because the nature of professional social work practice is antithetical to top-down controls. The competent macro or micro social worker provides a caring mix of seasoned experience, theoretical knowledge, intuition, personal warmth, and positive regard as tools of the trade. It is illogical to expect social workers to use their professional judgment and emotions in their work with clients, and then to ignore their own judgment and feelings by responding unquestioningly to dictates from a centralized management.[1]

Burnout stems from feelings of powerlessness or inability to make a meaningful change (Toch & Grant, 1982). Conversely, feelings of autonomy or self-determination help stimulate intrinsic motivation. As illustrated in the case example, the manager witnessed a remarkable change in her staff's intrinsic motivation to do their jobs well after they had gained feelings of ownership and control over their work.

Research has supported the benefits of participation on intrinsic motivation and job performance. Participation in job-related goal setting has been shown to increase performance because workers who participate in setting their work goals are likely to set more difficult goals and to accept the agreed-on goals (Locke &

Schweiger, 1979; Miller & Monge, 1986). Also, employees who participate in deciding what is to be done and how it is to be done have reduced role ambiguity and have a better understanding of how decisions are to be implemented (Schuler, 1980).

• *Participatory management promotes peer support for accountability, increased service coordination, and effective services delivery.* During the 1920s, the Hawthorne studies uncovered the "informal organization," the network of interpersonal relations, informal leadership, and "grapevine" communications that characterize employee relationships beyond the formal organizational chart. Modern-day investigators have expanded those early studies into a fuller understanding of cultural, structural, and social-psychological factors affecting job performance. One interesting discovery relates to the social influence of peer groups. Under conditions of ambiguity, researchers have shown that people are more likely to emulate others similar to themselves rather than distant authority figures (Salancik & Pfeffer, 1978).

Centralized managers attempt to regulate employees' behavior through directives, while ignoring the potency of the informal organization's social influence. Yet, as organizational researchers have noted, in centralized organizations, the flow of information among work units is often impeded, informal coordination among staff in different work units is inhibited, and suggestions from employees on how to improve the organization are usually discouraged. In contrast, when work groups have true decision-making authority, they hold each other accountable for enforcing work standards, correcting problems as they occur, and coordinating their work. Their mutual support and reinforcement provides greater incentive for accountability than the threat of sanctions from an external authority. For example, before my former student revised her management style, she would arrange for her unit to be assigned to a substitute supervisor whenever she took vacations. During a recent vacation, however, they requested and were granted permission to manage themselves. As she boasted, "They did just fine! And when I came back, they were so proud that they had done it!"

Making It Work

Implementing participatory management while maintaining accountability is more than possible but is not an easy task. Because of space restrictions, I can provide only a few brief guidelines. Interested readers are advised to check the appended references for additional information.

1. *Redefine leadership as articulating a vision, providing inspiration, and modeling desired behavior.* Centralized managers erroneously assume that leadership comes from controlling undesirable behavior. As Kanter (1979) notes, such actions reflect managers' powerlessness—their inability to produce meaningful change:

> What grows with organizational position in hierarchical levels is not necessarily the power to accomplish—productive power—but the power to punish, to prevent, to sell off, to reduce, to fire, all without appropriate concern for consequences (p. 72).

Participatory managers understand that real leadership occurs by inspiring desirable behavior. In the participatory organization, the executive and key managers recognize that excessive, unexplained, top-down rules and regulations reflect powerlessness—inability to produce meaningful change, not the power to actually lead. Consequently, they lead by inspiration and example, recognizing that employees monitor the executive's behavior with keen interest (Peters, 1988). Their proactive leadership activities include articulating a clear vision of the organization's direction, publicizing positive efforts and staff accomplishments, networking and soliciting new resources, asking questions, modeling desired behavior, and ensuring that their own calendars reflect their priorities.

2. *Implement process monitoring for programmable tasks and outcome monitoring for nonprogrammable tasks.* Several theorists recommend that managers maintain accountability by specifying the *process* by which programmable tasks are performed and the desired outcome of nonprogrammable tasks (see, for example, Morse & Lorsch, 1970). Programmable tasks require little or no independent judgment in their execution. For example, a programmable task may be routinely locking a community center at night. To ensure the building's safety, a supervisor might develop with staff a checklist to ensure that certain lights are left on, all windows are locked, the extra latch at the back door is thrown, the security system is turned on, and so on. Such a procedure is necessary to ensure that all the staff adhere to the procedure correctly.

Nonprogrammable tasks are those that require the exercise of judgment. Most social work tasks fall into this category, although even lower-level jobs may also be nonprogrammable. For example, I recall facilitating a problem-solving meeting between a supervisor and a custodian. With visible emotion in his voice, the custodian expressed his appreciation that the manager told him what he wanted done and "then just let me do my job." The supervisor, in turn, expressed appreciation that he could count on the employee to "keep the building real clean." The supervisor maintained accountability and earned the employee's respect by gaining agreement with the employee on the desired outcome—a clean building, delegating the work to the employee and permitting him as much autonomy as possible in doing his job, periodically monitoring that the job was indeed being achieved, and providing the employee with feedback on his job performance.

3. *Establish participatory systems to review and reward efficiency and effectiveness.* Several characteristics of HSOs make it difficult to establish meaningful performance evaluation and pay systems. First, no clear criteria exist for choosing an intervention (Hasenfeld, 1983). Second, much of social work falls beyond the purview of supervisors. Workers may see their clients in the street, in a client's home, in a private office, or even within an auditorium. Third, few clear measures of effectiveness exist.

Despite these obstacles, performance evaluations are often performed by an untrained supervisor based on highly subjective and ambiguous criteria. Usually no effort is made to solicit the input of others who are in an equal if not better position to comment on the employee's work. As Lawler (1990) has noted, managers often seek to promote team spirit and coordination and among their employees and then undo these efforts by evaluating and rewarding people individually and competitively. A better approach is to train and then involve employees in hiring decisions of new staff and regular peer evaluations of each other and to establish group rewards for effective performance. Often both managers and staff initially resist the idea of peer evaluations fearing that it may generate conflict among staff. However, if mutual support and improvement of the entire work group are emphasized rather than punishment of errant individuals, research and my own experience have shown that such evaluations do indeed improve job performance as well as enhance the credibility of the evaluation process.

4. *Provide training in conflict resolution, negotiation, and group problem solving.* Instituting participatory management requires patience, tolerance for dissident views, and, above all, the will to make the system work. Ironically, while good communication and problem-solving skills are the tools of the trade for social work practice, managers and staff often fail to practice these skills with one another. Organizations in the private sector that are instituting self-managing teams recognize the importance of training their employees to reconcile differences. My own observations show that such training is equally essential for managers and staff in our field.

5. *Avoid attempting participation under some conditions.* Quite obviously, not every decision can be subjected to group review and decision making. Participation may be counterproductive, if not a sham, if participants have inadequate knowledge to make a decision, insufficient time is available for discussion before a decision must be made, or the participating individuals truly prefer to problem solve alone rather than in a group.

A Concluding Note

Weatherly (1985) has cited several difficulties in implementing a participatory management strategy in public welfare organizations. Among them is the inability of many top management to command resources as needed, which affects their ability to make and keep commitments to staff. Another obstacle is conflicting interests between managers who stress accountability and staff who are more concerned with client service. In my consultant work, I have noted that other impediments are norms of secrecy about budgetary information, the belief of some managers that workers "cannot handle" knowledge of the constraints they face, unfavorable opinions of workers' cognitive abilities and organizational commitment, and a reluctance to share power.

Participatory management can work. I believe it may work, though, only if those at the top of the organization are passionately committed to making it work. Without such a commitment, the will and patience to respect others' opinions and to work through conflicts may be lacking, and participatory management may become a meaningless slogan. With true commitment, the organization has the best chance of fully utilizing its most valuable resource—its people.

ENDNOTES

1. The impact of asking professionally trained staff to suspend their own good judgment was humorously made to me by a friend who recounted a dispute she once had with her manager. He had ordered her to do something to which she strenuously objected. Her indignant response was, "Don't hire me for my intelligence and then expect me not to use it! If you want someone to blindly follow your orders, get yourself a dog!"

REFERENCES

Block, P. (1987). *The empowered manager: Positive political skills at work.* San Francisco: Jossey-Bass.

Hasenfeld, Y. (1983). *Human service organizations.* Englewood Cliffs, NJ: Prentice-Hall.

Kanter, R. M. (1979). Power failure in management circuits. *Harvard Business Review, 57*(4) 65–75.

Lawler, E. E. III (1990). *Strategic pay: Aligning organizational strategies and pay systems.* San Francisco: Jossey-Bass Publishers.

Locke, E. A., & Schweiger, D. M. (1979). Participation in decision-making: One more look. In B. M. Staw (Ed.), *Research in organizational behavior: An annual series of analytical essays and critical reviews,* 1, 365–339.

Miller, K. I., & Monge, P. R. (1986). Participation, satisfaction, and productivity: A meta-analytic review. *Academy of Management Journal 29*(4), 727–753.

Morse, J. J., & Lorsch, J. W. (1970, May–June). Beyond theory Y. *Harvard Business Review, 48.*

Peters, T. J. (1988). *Thriving on chaos: Handbook for management revolution.* New York: Alfred Knopf.

Salancik, G. R., & Pfeffer, J. (1978). A social information processing approach to job attitudes and task design. *Administrative Science Quarterly, 23,* 224–253.

Schuler, R. S. (1980). A role and expectancy model of participation in decision making. *Academy of Management Journal, 23,* 231–340.

Toch, H., & Grant, J. D. (1982). *Reforming human services: Change through participation.* Sage Library of Social Research 142. Beverly Hills: Sage Publications.

Weatherly, R. A. (1985). Participatory management in public welfare: What are the prospects? *Administration in Social Work, 7* (1), 39–49.

Rejoinder to Professor Latting   BURTON GUMMER

Professor Latting presents a strong and sound case for the many advantages that can be gained from introducing participatory management techniques to social agencies. The point of contention between our papers, however, stems not from the *desirability* of participatory management in social agencies, but the *possibility* of this occurring in a substantive way. This difference, moreover, reflects two very different approaches to thinking about social agencies as organizations.

Ever since organizational scholars broadened their attention from their traditional concern with the functioning of economic organizations, there has been a debate about whether other organizations—notably not-for-profit and public sector organizations—are best thought of as similar to the economic organization or uniquely different. Those taking the first position argue that all organizations are more alike than unlike, and the management tools that have been found to be effective in business organizations can be successfully transferred to other kinds of organizations. Those taking the position that social agencies and other non-economic organizations are qualitatively different from economic organizations argue that the likelihood that technology transfers will work is low.

People who argue that social agencies are distinctly different from economic organizations point to a number of important differences between these organizational types, such as the lack of a "market test" for not-for-profit organizations, the comparative vagueness of goals of social agencies, and the comparatively underdeveloped and indeterminate nature of the technologies used in social agencies. Another point of difference, and the one that I stress in my paper, is that social agencies are, first and foremost, instruments for the implementation of public policies.

For any organization that is part of the public policy process, the ultimate test of organizational success is not program effectiveness (which rarely can be measured to anyone's satisfaction) or up-to-date management practices such as quality circles or participatory decision making. The crucial determinant of a social agency's success is its ability to *establish a constituency* that will support its continued funding and operations. This places social agencies right in the middle of political arenas at the local, state, and national levels.

As part of the policy process, social agencies are confronted with the dilemma that I outline in my argument. Namely, the managers and workers are likely to operate in different arenas, with different goals, norms, and values. Professor Latting argues that powerlessness was one of the reasons why managers were loathe to involve subordinates in decision making. Another perspective, and one that I subscribe to, is that social agency managers, rather than being powerless, are powerful, but most significant is the power characteristic of the political arena, namely, *the power to do what you're told to do.* The political superiors to whom agency administrators are accountable, moreover, are increasingly telling them to do things that run counter to the goals of professional social workers.

NO

Burton Gummer

Social workers have long been partial to theories of participatory management when it comes to thinking about how social service agencies should be organized. The belief that all members of an organization should have a say in setting agency policy and deciding how programs should be run fits in with core social work values such as self-determination and a preference for democratic forms of governance, whether at the societal, organizational, or group level. A participatory approach to management also reflects social workers' inclination to think about organizations along a harmony of interests theme that assumes a unity of purpose for the organization as a whole. This orientation emphasizes broad-based acceptance of organizational goals and views organizations as essentially cooperative systems, highlighting what Kenneth Boulding called organization's "friendly face." From this perspective, the proposition that administrators can balance their need for centralized control with the staff's desire for increased decentralization appears to be one that can be supported because both administrators and workers are pursuing the same goals.

Another perspective on organizational behavior is one that views organizations less as cooperative systems and more as arenas of conflicting interests and values. This perspective rejects the notion that organizations have a unitary goal that unites all members within a common cause, concentrating instead on the multiple and conflicting goals that are present in most organizations, including social agencies, and the political processes that develop as different interests compete with each other in vying to establish *their* goals as *the* goals for the organization as a whole. Within this framework, the idea that the needs of administrators for centralized control can be reconciled with staff demands for increased decentralization is insupportable. This is the position that I argue in this paper.

Before looking at the substantive differences between the interests of administrators and staff, we need to define what we mean by *centralization* and *decentralization.* I approach these terms from the perspective of organizational decision making: a centralized organization is one in which key decisions are made by a few top-ranking administrators, and a decentralized organization is one in which staff at all levels, including line workers, have a say in organizational decisions. Participation in decision making, moreover, is a variable that proceeds along an "influence power-sharing" continuum. Dachler and Wilpert (1978) suggested that the points along this continuum could be described as follows: (1) No advance information is given to employees about a decision to be taken. (2) Employees are informed in advance of the decision to be made. (3) Employees can give their opinion about the decision to be made. (4) Employees' opinions are taken into account in the decision process. (5) Employees have a veto, either negatively by blocking a decision that has been made or positively by having to concur in advance.

A second consideration in defining centralized and decentralized organizations is the *nature* of lower-level staff's involvement in the decision process, regardless of the degree of that involvement. Scholl (cited in Dachler & Wilpert, 1978) argued that participation refers to the process of exchanging information, where information exists in various combinations of fact and value premises. Values are evaluated against facts of reality and against other value standards, and facts are interpreted according to held values:

> Therefore, one can classify participatory social arrangements into a two-fold matrix, with one dimension indicating whether or not special consideration is given to the value orientation of participants, and the second dimension reflecting whether or not the factual knowledge of participants becomes an integral part of the participatory system. (Dachler & Wilpert, 1978, p. 19)

These dimensions of participation in decision making suggest that *substantive participation* occurs when lower-level employees enter the decision process at least at point three along the influence power-sharing continuum, and their participation involves issues of values as well as facts. Participation that occurs at lower levels of the continuum, or that is confined to questions of fact only, will be viewed here as *operational participation.* That is, while the latter form of participation allows lower-level employees some say in organizational decision making, they are not involved in the big decisions that set agency policy.

The central argument of this paper is that administrators of social agencies cannot decentralize their decision-making processes in a substantive way, that is, in a way that involves major agency policies, because the value premises on which agency executives make decisions are very likely to be qualitatively different from those of other members of the organization. Members of social agencies differ from each other not only in the kind of work they do, but also in how they are held accountable for their work. One of the defining characteristics of social service organizations is that

> ... they are highly dependent on resources controlled by other organizations and are often subject to extensive regulations by various legislative and administrative bodies. . . . [I]n many instances, human service organizations become captives of external units and thus come to serve their interests rather than the interests of the population they were established to serve. (Sarri & Hasenfeld, 1978, p. 4)

The fact that social agencies are highly dependent on external funding and regulating bodies was not a major problem in the 1960s and early 1970s, when these bodies were staffed by people who essentially agreed with the program and policy goals of social agency administrators. Since the late 1970s, however, our social policies have become steadily more conservative under the leadership of the Reagan and Bush administrations. Even with the Democrats' triumph in the 1992 presidential election, the prospects for liberal changes in the domestic policy agenda are not very good. This means that agency administrators must be responsive to political and administrative superiors whose social policy goals often are very different from those of the social work community.

The social policy agenda is driven by two major issues: the federal budget deficit (and the state and local budget deficits that this has created) and the middle-class backlash against the welfare system. The budget deficits have meant that cost containment in all spheres of governmental activities has become a priority item for all elected officials. This has been especially true in the social welfare area because of the lack of a strong political constituency that can lobby in opposition to cuts in social welfare spending. Agency administrators, consequently, are under considerable pressure to cut costs at the same time that caseloads are rising due to the poor economy. This invariably leads to reductions in the quality (as well as the quantity) of services. Providing quality social services, moreover, is a primary concern of direct service providers; fiscal constraints on doing this are a major source of conflict between administration and staff in social agencies (Whetten, 1977).

The middle-class backlash against the welfare system stems, in part, from the growing resentment toward the "blaming the victim" ideology that has dominated social policy thinking since the mid-1960s. This perspective has stressed the importance of environmental deficits ("blocked opportunities") as the primary, if not sole, cause of social problems. Conservative critics of the welfare system have argued that this approach, rather than solving problems, has exacerbated them by preventing official representatives of mainstream society (such as social workers and teachers) from insisting that the recipients of social services take responsibility for their behavior and conform to traditional (that is, middle-class) social norms. These critics increasingly use the term "underclass," as Jencks (1992) observed:

> . . . to describe people who seem indifferent to these values. Three middle-class values (or as I would prefer to say, ideals) are especially salient in discussions of this kind: Working men should have a steady job. . . . Women should postpone childbearing until they are married. . . . Everyone should refrain from violence. (Jencks, 1992, p. 144)

As politicians from both parties recognize the growing importance of the "middle-class vote" in determining electoral outcomes, the policies that they advocate more and more reflect the conservative critique of the welfare state. Thus, legalized abortion is under siege, welfare "reform" is confined to efforts to get AFDC mothers off the roles through "workfare" programs, and prison sentences become longer and more compulsory.

I do not mean to imply that, as a rule, professional social workers reject mainstream American values; some do, but most do not. However, to understand why line social workers often have a difficult time implementing programs based on these values, we have to look at two pieces of conventional wisdom subscribed to by policy planners and social service providers. Service providers frequently say that "complicated problems require complicated programs." This reflects their in-depth knowledge of the intricate complications of peoples' lives and the difficulty in trying to reduce the problems they face to a simple formula. Policy planners, on the other hand, are often heard saying that "you can't fine-tune social policy." In fact, one of their favorite slogans is K.I.S.S., or "keep it short and simple" (or, less generously, "keep it simple, stupid").

Thus, for policy makers who want to be responsive to the concerns of a middle-class constituency, preserving mainstream values translates into relatively uncomplicated injunctions that female heads of poor families enter the work force, at whatever cost, and that out-of-wedlock births be punished by reductions in public assistance payments. Line workers familiar with the actual life situations of these clients find themselves in a bind. While they agree with the broad, long-term policy goals underlying these programs, they are reluctant to implement them in the ways set forth by program planners because of what they believe to be the immediate harm they are likely to cause.

The upshot of these divergent forces is to prevent administrators and line workers from sharing major decision-making responsibility in social service agencies. They do not share a common policy framework because of the different constituencies that they are primarily responsible to (funders versus clients). This often takes a heavy toll on social agency administrators who come from social work backgrounds because of their sympathy with what their workers are facing, and many make valiant efforts to reconcile the differences. Unfortunately, however, the conflict between the interests of administrators and staff is probably also one of the reasons that political executives have been turning to non–social workers to head up social programs, particularly large public service institutions.

REFERENCES

Dachler, H. P., & Wilpert, B. (1978). Conceptual dimensions and boundaries of participation in organizations: A critical evaluation. *Administrative Science Quarterly, 23*(1), 1–39.
Jencks, C. (1992). *Rethinking social policy: Race, poverty, and the underclass.* Cambridge, MA: Harvard University Press.
Krupp, S. *Pattern in organizational analysis: A critical analysis.* New York: Holt, Reinhart and Winston.
Sarri, R. C., & Hasenfeld, Y. (1978). The management of human services—A challenging opportunity. In R. C. Sarri & Y. Hasenfeld (eds.), *The management of human services.* New York: Columbia University Press.
Whetten, D. A. (1977). Coping with incompatible expectations: Role conflict among directors of manpower agencies. *Administration in Social Work, 1*(4), 379–393.

Rejoinder to Professor Gummer   JEAN KANTAMBU LATTING

Professor Gummer proposes that social workers support participatory management because it is consistent with our core beliefs in self-determination and democratic governance. I agree. He also states that managers and staff are likely to have differing values that would make it difficult to implement participatory management. I also agree. I disagree, however, that advocates of participatory management adhere to a "harmony of interests theme that assumes a unity of purpose for the organization as a whole." To the contrary, if there were no competing interests, there would be no need for participatory management because the administrator's views would reflect the sentiments of his or her staff. Participatory management becomes an imperative because the consequences of not facing these conflicting interests are severe.

Professor Gummer proposes that managers are caught in a conflict of values between funders who are demanding punitive policies to curtail social welfare costs and staff who advocate more humanistic approaches to serving clients. In such a scenario, he believes that managers have no choice but to choose to side with the funders. As he concludes, "the conflict between the interests of administrators and staff is probably also one of the reason that political executives have been turning to non–social workers to head up social programs. . . ."

I partially agree with the dilemma that he poses, but not with his proposed solution. Conservative *public* policy makers indeed are voicing exasperation at current social welfare programs that they believe foster dependency or indulgence. I personally have not witnessed a similar tendency about voluntary foundations. *Private* foundations appear to want support programs that work, and many do recognize that complex problems cannot be solved with simple solutions.

I disagree that the resolution to the demands from public funders is to knock the line social worker out of the decision-making loop. This sets up a win-lose scenario that can only backfire—indeed, is backfiring—at the operational level. As I indicated in my initial statement, the technology of social work practice involves the use of professional judgment and emotional involvement. Further, supervisors cannot easily monitor social workers on a day-to-day basis. Asking professional social workers to work under agency directives with which they disagree can only create an agency at war with itself. Indeed, I have witnessed this happening several times. Usually, lower-level staff were incredibly creative in figuring out ways to circumvent injunctions issued by their autocratic managers.

Professor Gummer implies that the differences between managers and staff are irreconcilable. Again, I disagree. Granted, however, that many differences are exceedingly difficult to resolve. For this reason, I recommend that agency staff and managers receive training in conflict resolution, negotiation, and group problem-solving skills. Notably, these are included in the repertoire of skills in our profession. I continue to find it remarkable that social work managers and practitioners consider these skills useful when working with clients, but fail to recognize that the same skills are equally applicable to addressing conflicts within the workplace.

Professor Gummer's and my definitions of participation reflect our different perspectives. He provides a five-point continuum of influence ranging from employees not even knowing about an impending decision to "employees have a veto." I defined participation as ranging from input through shared decision making to transfer of decisional authority. Note that his model did not consider shared decision making—managers and employees hashing it out, or more positively, working it out—let alone transfer of decision-making authority to employees. On the other hand, I did not consider his first *three* levels because they represented unilateral decision making by the manager. Professor Gummer considers "substantive participation" to begin at the third point in his model. The opportunity to give opinions that are not heeded may constitute voice—the opportunity to speak, but not input—the opportunity to be heard.

In distinguishing between the importance of fact or value disputes in organizations, Professor Gummer states:

Participation that occurs at lower levels of the continuum, or that is confined to questions of fact only, will be viewed here as operational participation. That is, while the latter form of participation allows lower-level employees some say in organization decision making, they are not involved in the big decisions that set agency policy.

I am frankly puzzled by the implication that operational participation at the lower levels involves questions of fact rather than values. Human nature is such that people will dispute alleged facts as well as values. Further, such disputes may occur within organizations about operational as well as policy decisions. Consequently, the facts versus values distinction employed by Professor Gummer may not be salient to two contentious individuals who view the same phenomenon differently.

The solution to disputes about either values *or* facts is not to attempt to impose a win-lose scenario on a work force that can blithely and creatively circumvent those injunctions. Rather, top administrators must be creative themselves in figuring out how to involve their staff in the decision-making process while making sure that staff clearly understand the constraints under which they operate.

In summary, Professor Gummer warns agency administrators to expect value conflicts if they attempt to involve staff in "big decisions." To his warning, I add my own: expect value, operational, *and* policy conflicts if you do not.

Is State Licensing an Obstacle to Social Work Students' Selection of Macro Practice as a Specialization?

EDITOR'S NOTE: A license to practice a profession signifies that the individual practitioner possesses special expertise. Licensing also protects the public and holds professionals accountable for their actions. Over the past decade, social workers have lobbied hard to achieve state licensing in all fifty states. Support for licensing has been driven by the shift toward private clinical practice, by third-party reimbursement for mental health services, and by the profession's desire to establish a set of specific qualifications that must be met for someone to be called a social worker. The licensing requirements of the states vary, but all are generally designed to certify direct, but not macro practice, competence. Within the field of social work, there has been much discussion about the impact of licensing on the selection of practice modalities. Does licensing imply that the only acceptable form of social work practice is direct/clinical? Do social work students avoid macro practice because they cannot be licensed in this area? Should the profession develop a generic license for social work practice?

Barbara A. Pine, M.S.W., Ph.D., and Lynne M. Healy, M.S.W., Ph.D., answer YES. Dr. Pine is Associate Professor at the University of Connecticut School of Social Work, where she currently chairs the administration concentration. In addition to social work administration, she teaches and writes on child welfare practice and policy.

Dr. Healy is Professor at the University of Connecticut School of Social Work. She teaches program management, supervision and leadership, and women and management in the administration concentration, as well as courses in ethics and the profession and international social work. Dr. Healy is a member of the editorial board of *Administration in Social Work.* Among her publications on management is a recent book coedited with Barbara Pine, *Managers' Choices,* the inaugural publication of the National Network for Social Work Managers.

Leila Whiting, A.C.S.W., argues NO. She is the Director of the division of Professional Affairs in the national office of the National Association of Social Workers (NASW), where she has served in a variety of capacities since 1976. One of her current responsibilities is to provide technical assistance to NASW chapters in their efforts to achieve legal regulation of social workers.

YES

BARBARA A. PINE AND LYNNE M. HEALY

We contend that professional preoccupation with licensing and vendorship and the thirty-seven–year drive that has now accomplished licensing in all fifty states (Landers, 1992) have been detrimental to the logical growth and development of macro practice in social work, especially administrative practice. Thus, this period of great legislative success for the clinical side of the profession may ultimately diminish professional control over social services and negatively affect the quality of services provided to the public. The historic dual mission of social work, which emphasizes changing people *and* systems, may also be damaged by the misguided elevation of one form of practice over all others.

Much recent attention has focused on the survival of macro social work practice methods including policy/planning, community organization, and administration (Schwartz & Dattalo, 1990; Gummer, 1987; Neugeboren, 1986, 1987). Nowhere is this more evident than in the decreasing number of students electing macro methods, which dropped from 16 percent of enrollees in United States graduate social work programs in 1977 to 10 percent in 1986 (Neugeboren, 1986). At the same time, student enrollment in micro methods nationally has increased from 66 percent to 78 percent. These trends reflect the increasing homogenization of the field as direct service provision, particularly clinical mental health services (Gummer, 1987). State regulation through the licensing, registration, or certification of social work practice, has been a key influence in this development.[1]

Mark Battle, former head of the National Association of Social Workers (NASW), has said that certification is essential for professional recognition, advancement, influence, and remuneration (Battle, 1991). By most accounts, the number of states passing licensing laws is a measure of the remarkable success of NASW and its local chapters during the past fifteen years in gaining recognition for the profession. However notable these gains, we believe that the goals of recognition, and in particular remuneration, have been achieved at the expense of macro practice principally because the success of licensing activities has further perpetuated the notion of social work practice as synonymous with direct, mostly clinical, practice. This is evidenced by the fact that in over half of the states, certification for clinical practice represents the highest level of regulation (Whiting, 1991). While licensing is only one factor accounting for these trends, we argue here that the profession's attention to, and success in achieving, regulation of social work is inextricably linked to the forces that have marginalized macro practice within the profession and that licensing has had both direct and indirect negative effects on student selection of macro specializations, particularly social work administration.

The Downside of Success: Specialty Licensing

The drive for the licensing of social work coincided with the expansion of specialized education in administration. Licensing was a top priority of NASW during the 1970s when many of the licensing laws were passed. The decade of the 1970s was also marked by a heightened emphasis on accountability and the efficient management of human service programs, concerns that led to a dramatic expansion of administration specializations in schools of social work. By 1977, thirty-five schools had developed administration concentrations (Jansson, 1987).

Thus, during the time that the profession was preoccupied with licensing and vendorship, administration, as a relatively newly defined specialty in social work, was at a disadvantage in defining criteria for specialty licensing. Why, then, did practicing social work managers remain relatively silent while hierarchical systems favoring clinical social work were passed into state law? Several guesses may be advanced. First, administrators are relatively fewer in number than direct practice social workers. Second, the attentions of social agency administrators may have been more focused on securing funds (through vendorship extensions) for their agencies than in protecting and advancing social work administration/management as a specialty training in administration. Finally, many social work administrators who were active at the time had been trained as casework practitioners and were promoted into administration on the basis of longevity and casework competence. Thus, as a group, these administrators were probably less identified with social work management as a specialty area. Also, by virtue of their own training and prior experience, such administrators were eligible for a clinical license and thus faced no personal prospect of holding a "lesser license." However, concern about future career opportunities strongly influences the choices of new entrants into the profession, including those with potential for assuming leadership roles in social work agencies.

Students Want the "Best" Credential

Regardless of their current job responsibilities, most students selecting a graduate social work program are preparing for future career opportunities; their decisions are based on options offering the greatest job flexibility. Some applicants believe that a concentration in direct practice will aid in acquiring clinical state licensure; others think it is a requirement for licensure. In states licensing clinical practice as the highest level, agencies may even require that applicants for management positions be licensed to ensure that the agency meets requirements for receiving third-party payments. Schwartz and Dattalo (1990) surveyed fifty-four students who enrolled in micro courses but who had a strong interest in macro specialization. A total of 61 percent reported that their desire to attain a license was a major factor in their decision to select a micro, not a macro, concentration. Of eight factors these researchers considered, this was one of only two that significantly affected student choice.

The authors recently surveyed seventy-eight faculty members in macro concentrations from schools of social work in thirty-eight states regarding structures that facilitate or impede macro specialization (Pine, Healy, Havens, & Weiner, 1991). Asked if the licensing process impeded macro practice in any way, over one-third indicated that it did through heavy (or exclusive) focus on clinical content in the licensing exam; the need for macro-trained students to take special preparatory courses; and the feeling that the entire process had a clinical emphasis, embodying standards that bore no relation to the expertise of social workers trained in macro practice methods. In addition 66 percent reported that macro students were ineligible for the highest level of licensing. In short, whether the obstacles to student selection of macro methods are real or perceived, when a hierarchy of practice specialties is created that sets clinical practice at the top, it is human nature for students to aspire to, and prepare for, what they perceive to be the most prestigious work of the profession.

Direct Practice Is the Foundation of the Profession

In addition to perpetuating the myth that clinical practice is the pinnacle of the profession, licensing is related to the view that direct practice is also its foundation. This professional ideology of micro before macro has been cited as a key factor in both student selection of direct, instead of indirect, practice concentrations (Schwartz & Dattalo, 1990) and the lack of legitimation for administration as a field of professional social work practice (Neugeboren, 1987).

The view that direct practice is a prerequisite for management practice has been likened to the notion that ''you have to know how to build the car in order to run the factory'' (Neugeboren, 1987, p. 59), and it is a view that pervades the profession and its educational standards. Despite the well-known fact that M.S.W.-trained staff are hired into or promoted to supervisory positions soon after completion of the degree, many agencies support education only in direct practice (Neugeboren, 1986).

Persuasive evidence of the pervasiveness of the micro before macro ideology can be found in professional education. For example, Neugeboren (1986) surveyed seventy-nine deans of graduate schools of social work and found that 63 percent agreed that "direct service skills is a necessary foundation for effective performance of administrative roles and functions" (Neugeboren, 1986, p. 5). Moreover, there was a direct relationship between the deans' views and the number of macro-educated students graduating from their programs. Deans who believed direct practice was the professional foundation headed schools that educated fewer social work administrators (Neugeboren, 1986).

This "long-held belief in social work that learning about administration is simply a matter of superimposing a layer of management knowledge and skill on an intact foundation of clinical competence" (Patti & Austin, 1977, p. 269) will, in the long run, undermine the quality of social work services and ultimately the integrity of the profession. The face of management today has changed. As Keys (1992) has noted, more is now demanded of the social work manager, especially the CEO (chief executive officer). The call for leadership, the increased technology in the workplace, the complexity of laws governing personnel, the austerity and increased emphasis on fund development, and the rapidly changing socioeconomic and demographic environment all have made the clinician-administrator obsolete. It is crucial, therefore, to adopt an approach to legal regulation that retains its benefits while removing disincentives for specialization in administration.

Where Do We Go From Here?

What, then, do we recommend? We do not advocate that social workers mount campaigns to repeal licensing laws. Clearly, licensing benefits the profession in a number of ways. It also protects the public by establishing minimum criteria for social work and sanctioning procedures. There are two more moderate options for resolving the dilemmas discussed above. The first is the development of a specialty license in social work administration at the same level as the clinical specialty licenses established in some states. The other is to move to a generic independent practice level license.

Specialty Licensing for All

Proposals have been advanced to develop a specialty license in social work administration (Battle, 1991). As with the special clinical licenses, only those social workers who had received M.S.W. training in administration, with experience in administration, would be eligible. As with the current range of regulatory laws, states might protect the title of social work administrator-manager, certify and list all those specially qualified, or restrict the practice of social work administration to those holding the special license. Imagine—no more promotion through the ranks! Actually, this position is consistent with arguments made by those who favor restrictive clinical licensing. Why should practice be open to those who do not have specialty training? The best and most administratively elegant way of ensuring competence is to require a sequence of formal education and a narrowly defined practice requirement. Thus, specialty licensing for all could be defended, but the approach is problematic.

First, the practice options of clinical social workers would be severely restricted. Agency management would no longer be a career option. Long debates would ensue to determine whether supervisors are managers (Austin, 1981) or direct practitioners. Second, the domain of social work administration would have to be defined and defended from the competing claims of public administrators, public health administrators, and generically trained managers (Faherty, 1987; Rimer, 1987). Finally, conflict and opposition would arise from the other macro disciplines within social work. As Jansson (1987) concluded, "it is doubtful that a truly unified or single model of macro practice can be developed" (p. 13). Efforts to create a specialty license in social work administration/management could stifle the field by cutting off practice opportunities; prematurely impose limits on the field of social work; and set off conflict among planners, organizers, and administrators.

Generic Social Work Licensing

The preferred alternative is to limit state authority over the profession to the generic licensing of social work at appropriate levels, leaving regulation of specializations to the professional organizations. Thus, as was originally proposed in the model statute suggested by NASW in the 1970s, states would license B.S.W. graduates, new M.S.W. graduates, and those social workers with an M.S.W. plus two years of supervised professional social work experience, broadly defined. The top license would be given a broadly applicable label. *Independent practitioner* would be acceptable, so long as the concept is understood to apply not only to private practice but also to readiness for autonomous practice within agencies and as administrator, consultant, organizer, or planner as well as clinician.

This approach would preserve the true benefits of licensing. Clients and the public would be able to seek redress of grievances against members of a regulated profession. Social workers would be identified as trained individuals, distinguishable from those merely adopting the name. And, in those states with true licensing laws, the practice of social work would be restricted to licensed social workers. Missing would be the competitive efforts to set one branch of the field apart from all others, establishing in the minds of students and all too many social workers that some are more equal than others.

ENDNOTES

1. We have used the term *licensing* throughout to mean all forms of state regulation of social work practice.

REFERENCES

Austin, M. (1981). *Supervisory management for the human services.* Englewood Cliffs, NJ: Prentice-Hall.

Battle, M. (1991, April). Management certification crucial, overdue. *NASW News, 36*(4), 7.

Faherty, V. (1987). The battle of the Ms: MBA, MPA, MPH, and MSW. *Administration in Social Work, 11*(2), 33–43.

Gummer, B. (1987). Are administrators social workers? The politics of intra professional rivalry. *Administration in Social Work, 11*(2), 19–31.

Jansson, B. (1987). From sibling rivalry to pooled knowledge and shared curriculum: Relations among community organization, administration, planning and policy. *Administration in Social Work, 11*(2), 5–18.

Kahn, A. (1969). *Theory and practice of social planning.* New York: Russell Sage.

Keys, P. R. (1992). Foreword. In L. M. Healy and B. A. Pine (Eds.), *Managers' choices: Compelling issues in the new decision environment.* Boca Raton, FL: National Network for Social Work Managers.

Landers, S. (1992, June). Social work now regulated across nation. *NASW News, 37*(6), 1.

Neugeboren, B. (1987). Enhancing legitimacy of social work administration. *Administration in Social Work* 11 (2): 57–66.

Neugeboren, B. (1986). Systemic barriers to education in social work administration. *Administration in Social Work, 10*(2), 1–14.

Patti, R., & Austin, M. (1977). Socializing the direct service practitioner in the ways of supervisory management. *Administration in Social Work, 1,* 267–280.

Pine, B., Healy, L., Havens, C., & Weiner, M. (1991). Social work trained leaders: Issues of supply and demand. An unpublished paper presented at the Council on Social Work Education Annual Program Meeting, New Orleans, Louisiana, March 1991.

Rimer, E. (1987). Social administration education: Reconceptualizing the conflict with MPA, MBA, and MPH programs. *Administration in Social Work, 11*(2), 45–55.

Schwartz, S., & Dattalo, P. (1990). Factors affecting student selection of macro specializations. *Administration in Social Work, 14*(3), 83–96.

Whiting, L. (1991). *State comparison of laws regulating social work.* Silver Spring, MD: National Association of Social Workers.

Rejoinder to Drs. Pine and Healy Leila Whiting

Drs. Pine and Healy present interesting and persuasive arguments about social work licensing and what they believe are its effects on recruiting macro students into the profession of social work. I believe, however, that they put the cart before the horse. As early as 1982, ten years before universal legal regulation was achieved, a study by Rubin and Johnson (1984) found that the vast majority of entering graduate social work students were interested in and intended to pursue a career in direct service (or even psychotherapy). Furthermore, Drs. Pine and Healy quote a study of deans of graduate social work schools, where 63 percent of the seventy-nine deans surveyed agreed that "direct service skills is a necessary foundation for effective performance of administrative roles and functions." Perhaps this is true.

Thus, the decline of macro students cannot be laid at the door of licensing: in fact, the licensing efforts of the professional association were in response to the expressed needs and wishes of the majority of the membership. Drs. Pine and Healy make a lukewarm appeal for specialty licensing, and I support their dislike of that. It is the function of the state to protect the public, not to define professional practice. It would be more appropriate for the state to regulate some basic level of social workers and leave the identification and recognition of those with specialized skills or knowledge to the profession. We are clearly not in disagreement on this issue. We are also not in disagreement that an advanced license should be inclusive and not limited to "clinical," and, as a matter of fact, the NASW model statute advocates for just that. The development of a clinical license was a result of the pressures delivered by clinical practitioners who saw that as a road to insurance reimbursement. Bread-and-butter issues always carry the most passion and persuasion.

Historically tension has existed in the profession between what is now called "macro" and "micro," but was once called "cause" and "function." The tension was between those who believed that alleviation of social problems and misery could be achieved only through altering the environment—policy, systems, service delivery—and those who believed that individuals needed help to adjust to their situations. Historically, also, society has swung between focusing on these two approaches. The 1950s and 1960s saw an upsurge of social action advocates while the 1970s and 1980s moved to an individual adjustment emphasis. Licensing was part of this latter movement and both the movement to achieve licensing and away from macro to micro practice are part of this swing. Neither part should be assigned blame for the occurrence of the other.

Reference

Rubin, A., & Johnson, P. J. (1984, Spring). Direct practice interests of entering MSW students. *Journal of Education for Social Work, 20*(2), 5–14.

NO

LEILA WHITING

Legal regulation of any occupation or profession is the exercise of the police power of the state to protect the health and welfare of the public. Legal regulation of social workers takes one of the following three forms:

- registration—qualified individuals' names are entered in a state register;
- certification, or title protection—the title, such as "certified social worker," is restricted to those who are so certified; and
- licensure—the scope of practice is defined and all those practicing within this scope must be licensed.

All forms of legal regulation share the objective of holding the person regulated to a set standard of behavior. Social workers who are legally regulated are accountable to the public for their performance. Should a social worker's behavior violate set standards, charges can be brought to and investigated by the appropriate state agency. Each state determines the range of sanctions for violations, including removal of the certification or license.

Although the safety of the public is the only defensible reason for a state to enact a licensing law, social workers have, for the past quarter of a century, struggled to become legally regulated in every state jurisdiction. This objective has finally been reached: as of June 1972, all states, as well as the District of Columbia, Puerto Rico, and the Virgin Islands, have enacted some form of legal regulation.

Could it be that social workers are so altruistic that they have spent untold hundreds of thousands of dollars to achieve this end? Do social workers really believe that the public is so threatened by social work misbehavior that state protection is needed? It would appear that there are other reasons in addition to the need for accountability and public protection for groups to push for such legal recognition. These reasons are not hard to find: social work early on recognized that legal regulation was legal recognition. Social workers struggled to identify themselves as members of a profession that included qualified mental health practitioners. As health insurance expanded to include mental health coverage, psychologists moved quickly to enact state laws recognizing them, along with psychiatrists, as reimbursable providers of mental health services.

As social workers increasingly moved into clinical practice, they realized that, because the health insurance industry was established to ensure payment for physicians and hospitals, reimbursement for health services provided by non-physicians could be accomplished only through legislation. Thus, it became apparent that acceptance of social work as a legally recognized profession, and reimbursement for social work services, were closely related goals most effectively achieved through state legislation. At the same time, legal regulation would provide protection from unscrupulous or incompetent practitioners.

Some argue that social work teachers, administrators, community organizers, policy analysts, and others engaged in non–direct practice with clients should be exempted from licensure. (For ease of reading, all forms of legal regulation will be called *licensing*.) The argument usually raised is that because these social workers do not deal directly with clients, no clients are at risk of their unethical practice. Since the health and welfare of the public is not threatened, licensing of these social workers is not only unnecessary, it is burdensome both to them and to the state. But are clients receiving social work services the only "public" at risk? What of administrators or teachers who sexually harass or otherwise misuse their positions of authority and power with social work staff members or students? What of the community organizer who behaves unethically and does not, perhaps, damage an individual client but behaves in a reprehensible manner, for example, influencing decisions that will result in personal financial gain?

Legal regulation of a profession creates a regulatory board responsible for developing administrative means to issue and renew licenses and, even more importantly, for developing and enforcing a code of behavior. This is similar in many ways to the NASW code of ethics, which can be interpreted so that specific violations can be adjudicated. Thus, if licensing is mandatory for all social workers, a charge of misconduct can be filed both with an employer or policy-making body, such as a board of directors, and with the established regulatory board. An additional advantage of adjudication of public complaints is that a state regulatory board can be objective in its search for facts where its only interest in the outcome is the public good and not, for example, protection of an organization. Moreover, an administrator found by the agency to have misused a position of power can, indeed, be fired but may also find another position in the same or another state. If that social worker had been licensed and the state regulatory board removes the license because of a proven and serious violation of the statute, then permission to practice is removed, preventing that social worker from further practice. With the advent of state regulatory boards routinely checking with a central system to identify those social workers whose licenses have been removed for cause, such a social worker would also be unable to obtain a license in another state.

As we are well aware, social workers who are involved in questionable practice, misconduct, fraud, or in some cases criminal activity are not limited to clinical practitioners and adversely affect the total profession and its image. Thus, both the public and the profession are well served by removing incompetent and unethical social workers from the professional ranks. By narrowly defining "the public" as only those clients served by the social worker in direct practice, an argument can be made for licensing only those in direct practice. But if the "public" is conceived as both clients and staff, as well as agencies themselves, then all social workers should be licensed regardless of their practice field. Social work values and ethics apply to all social workers in all areas of practice. If this keeps students from moving into macro practice arenas, it is a sad commentary on their commitment to ethical practice.

Social workers in direct practice will have to be licensed. This protects the public and enhances their visibility as members of a sanctioned profession. Would macro social workers have it any other way?

REFERENCES

Hardcastle, D. (1990). Legal regulation of social work. In A. Minahan, (Ed.), *Encyclopedia of Social Work,* 18th ed., 1990 Supplement. Silver Spring, MD: NASW Press.

Thyer, B. A., & Biggerstaff, M. A. (1989). *Professional social work credentialing and legal regulation,* Springfield, IL: Charles C. Thomas.

Whiting, L. (1992). *State comparison of laws regulating social work.* Washington, DC: National Association of Social Workers.

Rejoinder to Dr. Whiting

BARBARA A. PINE AND
LYNNE M. HEALY

Ms. Whiting suggests that macro practice social workers may attempt to evade licensing. The scant research available shows just the opposite: those entering the profession are so concerned about qualifying for licenses that they will modify their career aspirations, divert their talents, and select an aspect of the profession in which they have less interest and perhaps less aptitude to ensure that they remain eligible for licensing. Thus, licensing begins to rule and regulate the profession in unintended ways.

We believe it is important for a majority of social service agencies to be managed by social workers—competent, specially trained social work administrators. The social work profession needs to assert its leadership in the domains of the planning and management of social services. This, even more than licensing, gives real substance to professional responsibility for the quality of services to the public. If social work actively or passively abdicates service leadership, the public will suffer, as will agency practitioners and the profession as a whole.

The ethics and values of social work need to be present not only in the clinician's private office, but also in the planning meetings and board rooms when services are designed and prioritized, resources allocated, and agency structures and processes determined. The complexity of management and the public concerns with accountability make the manager trained in direct practice only an artifact of the past. The planners and managers of social services will be specialty trained either in schools of social work or in MPA, MBA, or other programs. Thus, licensing laws that discourage social workers from selecting macro practice or diminish the importance of macro practice by setting up a professional hierarchy with clinical practice at the pinnacle will ultimately lead to the takeover of service leadership by other professions.

In our main argument, therefore, we do not advocate throwing out the "baby" of public recognition and access achieved through legal regulation, but only the "bath water" of overregulation and narrow specialty self-interest.